THE SECRET CONSTITUTION

An Analysis of the Political Establishment

By the same author:

The How and Why of Socialism
Mr Secretary of State (fiction)

THE SECRET CONSTITUTION

An Analysis of the Political Establishment

Brian Sedgemore

HODDER AND STOUGHTON
LONDON SYDNEY AUCKLAND TORONTO

British Library Cataloguing in Publication Data

Sedgemore, Brian
The secret constitution.
1. Great Britain – Politics and government – 1964–
2. Civil service – Great Britain
I. Title
354′.41 JN309

ISBN 0 340 24649 9

 Printed in Great Britain for Hodder and Stoughton Limited, Mill Road, Dunton Green, Sevenoaks, Kent by St Edmundsbury Press, Bury St Edmunds, Suffolk. Photoset by Rowland Phototypesetting Limited, Bury St Edmunds, Suffolk. Hodder and Stoughton Editorial Office: 47 Bedford Square, London WC1B 3DP.

To Audrey

Acknowledgements

I am most grateful to HMSO for permission to quote from various government documents, including Hansard, Command Papers and Reports of Select Committee Proceedings in Parliament. I am also indebted to the following authors and publishers for permission to quote from their works.

Politics in Industrial Society, Keith Middlemas (André Deutsch); *Taking Rights Seriously*, Ronald Dworkin (Gerald Duckworth); *The Dilemma of Democracy*, Lord Hailsham (Collins); *Final Term*, Harold Wilson (Weidenfeld); *A Growing Concern*, Nigel Broackes (Weidenfeld); *The Cecil King Diaries*, Cecil King (Jonathan Cape); *The Politics of Power*, Joe Haines (Jonathan Cape); *The Diaries of a Cabinet Minister*, Richard Crossman (Hamish Hamilton and Jonathan Cape); *What Went Wrong?*, Ken Coates (Spokesman Books); *The Political Constitution*, Prof. J. A. G. Griffith (The Modern Law Review, Vol. 42, January 1979); *Rita Hinden Memorial Lecture*, Sir Peter Parker (10 February 1979); *The Powers that Be*, David Halberstam (Chatto and Windus); *Statements to Annual Conference 1978 – The Civil Service*, The Labour Party.

Contents

List of Tables

Preface

The purpose of this book is to describe what happens in government as opposed to what some people think happens or ought to happen; to seek to substantiate and illuminate its analysis with evidence, including and in particular my diaries and papers; and to name names, including those of civil servants who are at present working in government, in order to avoid the charge of lack of specificity. Some of the conclusions concerning the nature of Parliamentary democracy and the relationships between Parliament and the executive, ministers and civil servants, and all of them and the outside world challenge much of the conventional wisdom on these issues.

The initial idea behind the book upon which I seized eagerly was that of the publisher. It was to tell people something of the way in which we are governed by investigating some of the nooks and crannies of Whitehall and Westminster using my experience as a civil servant and politician. I was in the administrative class of the civil service from 1962 to 1967. From 1964 to 1966 I was Private Secretary to the Rt. Hon. Robert Mellish, then a junior minister at the Ministry of Housing and Local Government. From February 1974 to May 1979 I was privileged to represent Luton West in Parliament on behalf of the Labour Party. During that time I worked for two years (January 1977 to December 1978) as Parliamentary Private Secretary to the Rt. Hon. Tony Benn when he was Secretary of State for Energy.

Although the book is neither a constitutional text-book nor a book on political theory I would hope that constitutionalists and those interested in political theory as well as practice will find something of interest in it, whether or not they agree or disagree with all or any of the points in it. My one regret is that I lacked the time and facilities to make a detailed study of the workings of the E.E.C. bureaucracy and its political institutions.

I should perhaps make one point about quotations from my diaries in the book. The quotations are given as they appear in the original save that on occasions I have omitted phrases such as 'X said' and 'Y confirmed' in order to protect a source or keep a confidence.

It goes without saying that I would not have written the book had I not had the pleasure of working for Tony Benn for two years and the enjoyment of the company of his two distinguished political advisers, Frances Morrell and Francis Cripps. They are however in no way responsible for any of the contents of the book.

I must also acknowledge the inspiration of the many meetings of the Labour Party Machinery of Government Committee which tóok place under the admirable chairmanship of Eric Heffer M.P. My thanks are also due to the Speaker of the House of Commons, H.M. Stationery Office, the General Secretary of the Labour Party, my former colleagues in Parliament, the Library of the House of Commons, David Butler and Ann Sloman, Sir Peter Parker, David Halberstam, Keith Middlemas, Professor Griffith, Harold Wilson and Joe Haines for their help in providing new material or for their permission to use or quote from existing material.

My special thanks and appreciation are due to Anthony Sampson who read the first draft of the book and made a number of invaluable suggestions and to Elizabeth Thomas who not only edited the book with great skill but forced me to clarify my thinking on many important issues.

BRIAN SEDGEMORE
October 1979

1 The Secret Constitution

Two things only can be said with certainty about Parliamentary democracy in Britain today. First, effective power does not reside in Parliament. Secondly, there is little that is democratic about the exercise of that power.

In a democracy it is the people who govern. Democracy entails too the notion that ideas should be allowed to compete for acceptance in society. Unless these two characteristics are present then terms such as freedom, liberty and pluralism, which are those most often used by people who claim to support democracy, cease to inspire and maybe lose their meaning. The democratic principle extends beyond the concept of periodic elections, representative government and doctrines of ministerial responsibility and Parliamentary control, important though these are. Democracy in this sense requires the involvement of citizens in all the processes of government and is founded on trust by governments in the people rather than on reliance on the people's trust in the governing élites. The exception rather than the rule in the modern world, democracy has rightly been described as 'a radical and revolutionary concept, feared by those who would wield illegitimate power and unacceptable to oligarchs and authoritarians alike'. (Professor John Griffith – Introduction, Freedom of Information Bill, Statements to Annual Conference, The Labour Party, October 1978.)

Democracy is certainly a principle that is unacceptable to the establishment in our society. That establishment, by which I mean leading men in the City, captains of industry, press barons, those at the top of the Church hierarchy and the professions, is determined that government in Britain should remain élitist, oligarchic, bureaucratic and secretive.

Indeed government in Britain today is so secretive that even the true nature of our constitution is hidden from the people. Our constitution is hidden not in the sense that it is unwritten but in the sense that its structure and working are an official secret and in the sense that those few people who are privy to the way in which, by whom, and in whose interests power is exercised are unwilling to tell what they know. In consequence half-truths, myths and outright lies abound.

If the language should seem too strong I would remind readers that I was dismissed by the Prime Minister, James Callaghan, from my post as Parliamentary Private Secretary to Tony Benn, Secretary of State for Energy, because I caught Denis Healey, the Chancellor of the Exchequer, seriously misleading a Select Committee of Parliament (First Report from the Expenditure Committee, Session 1978–79 page 68, The European Monetary System) over the contents of a confidential Cabinet document which set out the disadvantages to Britain of joining the European Monetary System. The interesting point was not that I was sacked. That was a trivial issue. It was that if a member of the Cabinet can seriously mislead Parliament at a hearing of one of its most important committees then democracy is seriously at risk. For it is part of the essence of our democracy that the elected representatives of the people should exercise control over what the executive is doing in such a way as to prevent ministers from acting in an arbitrary fashion.

The authors of the section on the Labour party pamphlet referred to above on the need for a Freedom of Information Bill argued that involvement in the processes of government by the citizen is impossible without the release by governments of adequate information. At the very least people must be given sufficient information to know who is governing and in whose interest. They must be told how and where their views can be expressed and procedures, formal and informal, must be established to help them. At the very least public authorities must be made to disclose to the citizen not only what their policies are and how they can be analysed, assessed and interpreted but what are the intentions, motives and values behind them. At the very least any individual who wants to engage in the democratic debate should have access to some factual information that is available to the most informed person in government. The sharing of such information in this way is an essential bulwark against tyranny.

We have no such bulwark in our society: on the contrary we have a closed society that has enshrined secrecy in law. In open societies such as America and Sweden the citizen has a right to know what the government is doing. In these societies the right to know is enshrined in law. In our society everything that the Government and public officials do is an official secret under Section 2 of the Official Secrets Act 1911 unless the release of the relevant information is specifically authorised by a minister. The Protection of Official Information Bill, introduced in Parliament in October 1979 was designed in theory to narrow the area of government information protected by criminal sanctions. In practice it was thought to be such as might suppress legitimate public disclosure of information by making criminal prosecutions more likely in certain spheres and it was withdrawn in November of the same year as a result of concern expressed about its provisions following on disclosures of the spying activities of Mr Anthony Blunt. Some of the implications of this case are discussed in the next Chapter.

On the whole ministers advised by civil servants are very chary of releasing all but the most innocent information.

The Hierarchy of Secrecy

The problem in Britain goes much deeper than that. It is not just that top people distrust the rest of us and so withhold information from us because they are scared that *vox populi* might become *vox diaboli*, as Bagehot once put it. Top people do not trust each other. So they have developed a hierarchy of secrecy in government. Indeed our society can be likened to a pyramid in which the further away people are from the apex of the pyramid the less information they are allowed to have – officially. The Prime Minister withholds information from Cabinet colleagues: indeed the Prime Minister can and does withhold Cabinet papers from Cabinet colleagues. That is surprising because it is difficult to see how collective Cabinet responsibility can have any meaning if Cabinet ministers do not know what is going on because they cannot see Cabinet papers.

I give two examples. Tony Benn, when Secretary of State for Energy and a Cabinet minister, three times asked the Prime Minister if he could see a copy of the Cabinet paper on the European Monetary System the publication of whose details led to my own dismissal. Once he asked in writing and was refused. Twice he asked at Cabinet meetings. So here we had the odd situation of the contents of a Cabinet paper which dealt with one of the biggest issues that the Cabinet had to deal with in five years denied to almost all the members of the Cabinet but mysteriously available to a Parliamentary Private Secretary.

The other example is equally important and bizarre. Most decisions taken by the Government are taken not by the full Cabinet but by Cabinet sub-committees of which the most important are the Economic Strategy Committee, the Home Affairs Committee, the Defence and Overseas Policy Committee and the Legislation Committee. In his booklet, *The Case for a Constitutional Premiership*, based on a lecture given on 14th July 1979 Tony Benn records that there were 23 standing committees of the Cabinet and that 'probably' 150 ad hoc committees had been set up over the previous five years. The very existence of these Cabinet sub-committees is an official secret. The public is not supposed to know that they exist. Very few people outside the Cabinet and top civil servants know who sits on them, when they meet or what they discuss. It is impossible for a rational man to understand why such basic information about the nature of our constitution should be withheld from the public. One explanation given to me by a Cabinet minister in the Labour Government 1974–79 was that if Members of Parliament knew when these Cabinet sub-committees were meeting and who was on them and what they were going to discuss then they might buttonhole the ministers concerned and ask them awkward questions. Unless Members of Parliament are meant to be zombies it is difficult to see what is wrong with their asking awkward questions.

However my point goes even deeper than that. There are some Cabinet sub-committees whose meetings are kept secret from all but those ministers who sit on them. There are meetings at which very important decisions affecting all our lives are taken about which nothing is known by some members of the Cabinet. One such meeting concerned with economic policy took place late in 1977. I first heard about it from a former minister on 9th January 1978 just before a minister's lunch at the Department of Energy. I subsequently confirmed that the meeting had taken place and what had been discussed with one of those who had been present. The decision taken at the meeting was so important that I could hardly believe my ears when Tony Benn said he had not known about it, had not subsequently been told about it and that the Cabinet had not been informed of the decision that had been taken. In fact no members of the Cabinet other than those present were ever officially told that the meeting was taking place or afterwards that it had taken place.

Present at this little corporatist cabal were the Prime Minister (James Callaghan), the Chancellor of the Exchequer (Denis Healey), the Chancellor of the Duchy of Lancaster (Harold Lever), the Head of the Treasury (Sir Douglas Wass) and the Governor of the Bank of England (Gordon Richardson). The decision they took was that the devaluation strategy of earlier years was over and that in future economic policies should be aimed at allowing the pound to appreciate. The meeting in effect confirmed, unknown to the Cabinet, a complete U-turn in economic policy. It decided – and I make no comment on the rightness or wrongness of the decision – that the Government would henceforward pursue a monetarist policy. By any standards this was an awesome decision. For a Labour government it was mind-boggling in its consequences. For example letting the pound appreciate makes imports cheaper and exports dearer. It imposes a potential burden on British industry and has implications for jobs. In that case one might have expected even the most supine Secretary of

State for Industry to have had a view and to have been consulted. But no.

The truth is, of course, that this was a decision which the Cabinet should have taken collectively. It was not one for a cabal. But convention in British politics has it that policy on the value of the pound and the operation of the exchange markets is *never* discussed in Cabinet.

This is but one example of secrecy in economic decision taking – secrecy dictated by the Prime Minister – a subject which I discuss in more detail in Chapter 2.

Secrecy is not just a question of the Prime Minister withholding information from his Cabinet colleagues. Civil servants are every bit as addicted to secrecy as Prime Ministers. The reason for that is not accidental. Prime Ministerial power and civil service power constitute two of the most important influences on the way in which we are governed. This book contains many documented examples of the way in which secrecy dominates civil servant thinking and leads top civil servants, acting as politicians writ large, to withhold information deliberately from ministers. Civil servants, to take just one example, act as a filter for information which reaches a minister. And there is no way in which even the most zealous minister can, given the existing institutional arrangements, keep a check on that filter. The result is that civil servants can refuse to filter some information at all, can filter other information away from the minister, can filter it so slowly that the minister only gets it when it is too late or can filter it in such a way that it actually misleads the minister. In this case secrecy and the illegitimate use of civil service power come together; clearly civil servants could not do these things if the information they were dealing with was widely available to the public and subject to public scrutiny. Civil servants realise only too well that information is power.

One startling example of the use of the civil service filter of information came to light in July of 1978 at the Department of Energy. It concerned the desire of the Atomic Energy Authority to move large quantities of plutonium nitrate, the stuff from which nuclear bombs can be made, from the Windscale nuclear plant to the prototype Fast Breeder Reactor plant at Dounreay in Scotland. I discuss the issue in some detail in Chapter 4.

The ordinary backbench Member of Parliament finds himself in an even more difficult situation. He finds that the machinery of Parliament, though technically geared to enable him to extract information about what is going on, in practice presents him with subtle and insurmountable barriers. Both ministers and civil servants deny him information. So the backbench Member of Parliament goes around trying to make sensible judgments on big issues almost wholly lacking the information he needs to perform that task. Neither Question Time nor the Select Committee system or the legislative process itself enable him to get the information he wants. Although he is an elected representative of the people he simply has no right to information. Whether a minister or civil servant will give him a piece of information is entirely at their discretion and therefore an arbitrary matter. The subject is so important that I shall return to it later but for the moment one example will suffice.

The House of Commons Expenditure Committee is one of the most powerful Parliamentary committees. Ministers and civil servants are wary of insulting it. Yet they have no hesitation in refusing to answer even simple questions put to them by members of the committee.

In 1976–1977 the committee produced a report on the civil service which was passed to the Cabinet and the Government response was prepared by a Cabinet sub-committee. In April 1978 Lord Peart, the Cabinet minister in charge of the civil service, appeared before the Expenditure Committee to answer questions about the Government response. He was accompanied by Sir Ian Bancroft, the head of the civil service, on whose advice he relied heavily.

Just how informative and helpful Lord Peart and Sir Ian were can be seen in the answers to some important questions which I put. The questions concerned both secrecy and the illegitimate use of power by civil servants. The Sir William Armstrong referred to in the questions was one of Sir Ian Bancroft's predecessors and a former head of the civil service. He is now Lord Armstrong, chairman of the Midland Bank. The questions and answers are taken from the Minutes of Evidence taken before the Select Committee on Expenditure on Tuesday, 18th April 1978. All the questions were asked by me. All the answers were given by Lord Peart.

> *Question*: Let us go back to late last year when the Government decided to let the pound appreciate – a major economic decision. I understand there was a meeting between the Prime Minister, the Chancellor of the Exchequer, Harold Lever, the Governor of the Bank of England and Sir Douglas Wass, but no member of the Cabinet was told of the meeting. It was at that meeting that the decision was taken to let the pound appreciate. I am not saying it is a good or a bad thing, but is that not an example of a cabal of which the Cabinet is not informed? Are you saying that that did not happen?
> *Answer*: I cannot comment on that. I am a member of the Cabinet.
> *Question*: Here we have Sir William Armstrong talking about secret meetings and about advice given to the Prime Minister. We know that Cabinet ministers are subject to a 15-year rule. Are civil servants subject to that rule, or can Sir William Armstrong break confidences and the Official Secrets Act?

Answer: I make no comment.

Question: You talked about the Government moving towards a system of open government. Is it not right that the Government have just taken the decision not to tell the public how the Cabinet sub-committee works, and how does that square with the Government's desire to move towards a more open system of government?

Answer: I cannot comment on that.

Question: Can you tell us something about the Cabinet sub-committee which considered this report?

Answer: No, I cannot, and you know I cannot. How can you expect me to answer that?

Question: I am asking the questions, Lord Peart, if you do not mind. I am here to help the public understand how we are governed. Do you not think it is right that the public should be told about the basic principles of the British constitution?

Answer: The basic principles of the British constitution are well known to many people outside Government circles. We are not arguing about that. You are asking me about matters which you say are secret and were discussed by Cabinet committees. I cannot reveal this. It would be very wrong of me to do so. There are some people who would like to have it open, but I think it would be crazy.

Question: Could the Prime Minister reveal it if he came along and gave us some answers?

Answer: I cannot comment on that.

Such answers speak volumes for the impotence of backbench Members of Parliament. They insult the ministers and civil servants who give them as much as they insult the Member of Parliament concerned. That in this case was apparent from the look of consternation on the faces of Lord Peart and Sir Ian Bancroft as the answers were being given. To say that they lost their cool and in the process discredited the democratic process would be to put it kindly.

Lord Peart said that he could not comment on the Cabinet sub-committee which considered the Report of the Expenditure Committee on the civil service. I can fill in some of the gaps. He, Lord Peart, chaired the Cabinet sub-committee which sat under the GEN series (ad hoc Cabinet sub-committees). The minister responsible for the civil service in the House of Commons was not even on the committee. The members of the committee were selected by the Prime Minister precisely because none of them were too concerned to extend democracy and accountability in public life. But the Government response prepared under the auspices of the Cabinet sub-committee, was largely the work of Sir Ian Bancroft and his civil servants. So in effect civil servants were reporting on themselves. After the Cabinet sub-committee had drawn up its report other cabinet ministers were invited by letter to send in written amendments. With the help of Francis Cripps I drafted some modest amendments which Tony Benn sent in. Lord Peart and his colleagues did indeed reject the amendments subsequently because they hinted at criticism of civil servants.

Right at the bottom of this hierarchy of secrecy is the public. They, the people for whose benefit society is allegedly organised, have less access to information than anyone else. Governments and public authorities keep files on them – security files, social security files, education files – and they do not even have the right to see these and check if the information on them is correct. If the public is bewildered by all the secrecy and its many strange and illogical manifestations and feels that nothing can be done to put an end to endemic secrecy in society it should at least pause and reflect on the sort of frightening consequences that could arise.

Secrecy in Action – Sanctions Busting

The secrecy that surrounded sanctions busting and the consequences that flowed from it present us with one of the shabbier stories in our history. It illustrates the way in which some ministers, Parliament and the public are misled by other ministers, civil servants and industrialists. My intention here is not to rehearse the whole story or even a fraction of it but simply to make available to the public and Parliament certain information that has been withheld from it.

Parliament never obtained all the information it needed to ascertain the truth of what happened over the busting of sanctions by British oil companies. It never got to the bottom of misleading statements which were made to the House of Commons by ministers on the advice of civil servants in a series of answers to Parliamentary Questions. It tried but failed to find out the truth. On 1st February 1979 it voted by 146 votes to 67 to set up a Special Committee agreeing to the following motion which was put to the House on behalf of the then Labour Attorney-General, Sam Silkin:

> That it is desirable that a joint committee of both Houses to be known as 'the Special Committee on Oil Sanctions' be appointed to consider, following the report of the Bingham Enquiry, the part played by those concerned in the development and application of the policy of oil sanctions against Rhodesia with a view to determining whether Parliament or Ministers were misled, intentionally or otherwise and to report.

The majority of the 67 Members of Parliament who voted against the motion were Conservatives. A few Conservative M.P.s like Hugh Fraser, Peter Rees, and Barney Hayhoe voted for an enquiry. Amongst those Conservatives who voted in effect for a cover-up were the Rt. Hon. Margaret Thatcher, then Leader of the Opposition now Prime Minister, and the Rt. Hon. Sir Michael Havers M.P., Q.C., then an opposition frontbench spokesman, now Attorney-General. Their vote against the setting up of an enquiry to discover whether Parliament or ministers were misled by civil servants or industrialists or ministers does not augur well for the future.

Conservative Members of Parliament in the debate spoke about the absolute integrity of all civil servants, which was silly. They also said that all there was to know had been established by the Bingham Enquiry. That argument will not stand a moment's analysis. Moreover there is a certain circularity – *petitio principii* – in it. How could they know whether there was any more information that would be of value to the House of Commons without the enquiry? Despite the House of Commons decision to set up the enquiry the proposal was voted down by the House of Lords who were encouraged to do so by Mrs Thatcher and her friends.

The crux of the conclusions of the Bingham Report (Report on the Supply of Petroleum and Petroleum Products to Rhodesia by Mr T. H. Bingham Q.C. and Mr S. M. Gray F.C.A.) were that Shell and B.P. subsidiaries in South Africa supplied oil to Rhodesia but their local management did not make the position plain to their head offices in Britain and there was so much confusion that Shell and B.P. directors and managers and civil servants and politicians were misled as to what was really going on. Consequently Bingham concluded in good faith, that there was no organised conspiracy by the oil companies or the government to break sanctions. Consequently Parliament was told in good faith by ministers that they had no reason to believe that British oil companies were breaking sanctions.

I believe that evidence not available to Bingham points in the other direction. It suggests that oil company industrialists in this country, civil servants and ministers did know or had good reason to suspect that oil was getting into Rhodesia through the subsidiaries of Shell and B.P. Only those who wanted to shut their eyes to what was going on did not know. One civil servant in the Department of Energy who was concerned with work on the Beira blockade organised by the Ministry of Defence at the time which was designed to stop tankers getting oil into Rhodesia said that he and *all* his colleagues knew that what they were doing was a farce and all knew that oil was getting through into Rhodesia via subsidiaries of Shell and B.P. Other evidence substantiates this.

The Ministry of Power files on sanctions which were not made available to Bingham suggest that civil servants and others not only must have known what was going on but that, able people that they were, they anticipated what would happen. And they told ministers. And some ministers unquestionably knew what was happening. The evidence in my view points to the fact that Whitehall's civil servants embarked on a save white Rhodesia campaign so far as oil sanctions were concerned.

The note in my diary for 21st September 1978 reads:

> The Ministry of Power files on oil sanctions which were not made available to Bingham show that the then Foreign Secretary, George Brown, anticipated sanctions busting by the subsidiary companies of B.P. and Shell and others. And so did his civil servants. So he proposed making the main companies criminally liable for breaches of sanctions busting by their subsidiaries.

Had this been done then, it is likely that the directors of Shell and B.P. in London would soon have seen to it that their subsidiaries played no part in sanctions busting. They would hardly have been prepared to put themselves at risk of criminal prosecutions.

The note for 21st September 1978 in my diary continues:

> In Cabinet George Brown's only support came from the Minister of Technology, Tony Benn. Callaghan, the Chancellor of the Exchequer, opposed Brown: when this was mentioned at this morning's Cabinet meeting Callaghan winced. So much for Callaghan's innocence. So Ministers decided in 1966 on a policy to stop oil getting into Rhodesia which they knew would not work. They were told it would not work by civil servants. Civil servants did not want it to work. Ministers were given options which could, if implemented, have stopped sanctions busting but refused to take them up.
>
> There is a remarkable minute on one of the files with a November date on it from the Assistant Secretary, Mr Powell, to the Under Secretary Mr Beckett. In it Mr Powell says in effect that the Foreign Secretary must be stopped before he gets to the Prime Minister. The Foreign Secretary's proposal, says Mr Powell, is his own and runs counter to the advice of the Foreign Office civil servants. Mr Powell recommends that the Ministry of Power should get to the Prime Minister first.
>
> The Foreign Secretary's proposal involved discussions with the French and Americans prior to calling in the oil companies. Mr Powell argued that the oil companies should be consulted first on it and they most likely, indeed said Mr Powell 'they should', reject the Foreign Secretary's proposal. Then argued Mr Powell, there will be no need to go to the French and Americans.

The minute went from Mr Powell to Mr Beckett thence to the Deputy Secretary Mr Marshall and thence to the Permanent Secretary all of whom agreed with Mr Powell. Finally the minute went to the Minister of Power, Richard Marsh, who also agreed with it. He wrote on the file that he never thought sanctions would work and felt that the whole exercise was a charade.

It is difficult to interpret the papers in any other way than to say that civil servants and ministers would not be taking steps to make sanctions legislation effective. X, a civil servant, tells me that he was working on the Beira blockade at the time of sanctions legislation with others. They *all* knew, he said, that it was a farce and that oil was getting through via the subsidiaries of British oil companies.

I pause here merely to ask if we are to believe that it is conceivable that whilst civil servants throughout Whitehall knew what was going on, the U.K. directors and managers of those oil companies did not know?

The note in my dairy continues:

There are a number of telegrams on the files which passed between Britain, South Africa and America about these matters. One telegram from Pretoria refers to distinguished personnel from Shell and B.P. having been welcomed by the South Africa government to 'the nicest dictatorship in the world'.

It is an extraordinary story.

A number of ministers including the Prime Minister were against any further enquiry at today's Cabinet meeting. The Home Secretary was concerned that if there was an enquiry then some Labour M.P.s might criticise civil servants and personnel who worked for the oil companies.

My diary note picks up the story on 12th October 1978:

The Cabinet have been discussing Bingham and sanctions. Callaghan is haunted by the whole thing. Perhaps that is why Mike Cocks [the Government Chief Whip] talked to me about accepting a job in government after the election at the Labour Party Conference last week.

Two major facts are now clear:

1. Ministers in 1966 consciously decided to adopt a form of sanctions that they were told would not work.
2. According to one Cabinet Minister, who has been checking the files, five ministers came to know that oil was getting through to Rhodesia and that sanctions were being busted. They were Rt. Hon. Harold Wilson, Rt. Hon. Richard Marsh, Rt. Hon. George Thomson, Rt. Hon. Michael Stewart and Rt. Hon. Tony Crosland.

Five men of conscience knew. Five noble men from the right wing of the Party. Five social democrats. All the ministers are checking their files.

Reference is made again to the telegram from Pretoria in which Shell and B.P. were welcomed to the 'nicest dictatorship in the world'. The Shell and B.P. personnel told the South African government that they could not concern themselves with the interest of countries. They were private and companies had to be flexible.

The Attorney-General is worried because it is not just small fry who are involved.

The Government now propose a White Paper and the Cabinet considered a draft which had three parts:

Part 1 – a summary of Bingham
Part 2 – a defence of what Labour did
Part 3 – options for various types of enquiry that might be held. A pros and cons argument with the emphasis on the cons for each possibility.

The Cabinet decided to scrap Part 2 as being too contentious and Part 3 because it offered no guidance and Part 1 because it contained only allegations. So no White Paper.

The Chancellor thinks that the Government should sweat it out.

The reader can make up his own mind as to whether he thinks that Bingham was able to tell the full story in the light of the foregoing.

One puzzling point of great interest to the constitutional theorist which I raised in the debate on sanctions in the House of Commons on 1st February 1979 (Hansard Vol. 961 No. 47 Col. 1746) remains obstinately unanswered.

The Bingham Enquiry was set up by the Foreign Secretary, Dr David Owen. The Foreign Secretary authorised Mr Bingham to see certain papers. What he could not authorise him to see and what he did not authorise him to see were Cabinet papers for the period concerned. There is a 30-year rule on the publication of Cabinet papers and to have given them to Mr Bingham would have been to publish them. Only the Prime Minister could authorise their publication and he did not do so. Yet Bingham did see some Cabinet papers from the time – all Labour Government Cabinet papers. These were mixed up with departmental Foreign Office papers and were handed over by Foreign Office civil servants.

This raises a number of issues about the conduct of Foreign Office civil servants. Firstly they broke the strict rule of government that all Cabinet papers on departmental files should be returned to the

Cabinet Office at the end of the period of office of a Government. These papers should therefore have been returned to the Cabinet Office with the calling of the General Election in 1970.

Secondly when Foreign Office civil servants handed these papers over to Bingham they broke the 30-year rule on publication of Cabinet documents.

Thirdly they handed the papers over without the consent of the Foreign Secretary.

Fourthly no Cabinet papers relating to actions of the Conservative Government from 1970 to 1974 were handed over to Mr Bingham.

One senior civil servant at the Department of Energy suggested to me that it was accidental that Cabinet papers were handed over and that the Foreign Secretary was not consulted. If that is so then the time has surely come to put civil servants who are less accident prone in charge of the Foreign Office. The Permanent Secretary of the Foreign Office at the time must take responsibility for this even though he may have known nothing about it.

More than one Labour Cabinet minister expressed concern at the passing over of these papers to Mr Bingham. I myself take no exception to what happened but I can appreciate their point when they said that it was a pity that the papers were handed over just when everyone – industrialists, civil servants and ministers involved at the time of sanctions – was seeking to pass the blame on to someone else.

The essential point to emerge from all this is that it was because of the strict maintenance of secrecy that doubt has been cast on everybody's motives and it may be that that secrecy cost lives in Rhodesia from 1965 to 1979. If all this information had been public knowledge then, Labour Members of Parliament from 1966 to 1970 would surely not have allowed the Government to continue turning a blind eye to sanctions busting.

To be fair, no one knows what the course of events in Rhodesia would have been if steps had then been taken (assuming that the Americans and others would have allowed them to be taken) to make sanctions effective. But it is possible, to put it no higher, that open government and the call for action that would have stemmed from it might have saved lives. Can it all really be summed up in the words of one former Permanent Secretary who said to me, 'It may have been that the problem was just too difficult to enable the right thing to be done'?

Anthony Sampson, in his introduction to Martin Bailey's book, *Oilgate*, clearly takes a different view when he writes:

> The title of this book, *Oilgate*, implies a resemblance to Watergate, and with good reason; for not only do the two stories have some

> important resemblances, including the network of lies, the political corruption, and the creeping cover-up and self-deception . . . it is about the whole character of government, the relations between politicians and civil servants, and between governments and multinational corporations.

This brings me almost to the end of this section on secrecy. What I have tried to show is that secrecy is all pervading in our constitution : it stretches into every nook and cranny in Whitehall and Westminster : it affects issues large and small : it shrouds policies of every kind : and it adversely affects the relationships between almost everybody, ministers, civil servants, Members of Parliament, and the public.

I have tried to show that it is absurd and conducive only to bad government that a hierarchy of secrecy should exist and that the general public should have less access to information than favoured academics to argue their case, who in turn have less access to information than junior ministers who in turn have less access to information than their Cabinet colleagues who in turn have less access to information than certain civil servants.

I cannot see what governments desirous of governing by consent have to gain by secrecy and the withholding of information. Secrecy about how we are governed, how power is exercised in our society and the way in which institutions and individuals that buttress it operate can only lead to cynicism about the democratic process. It can only cast doubt, maybe unnecessary and unjustified doubt, on the validity and integrity of decisions on matters of policy which governments take. Secrecy may be a weapon that suits weak ministers and strong bureaucrats but it is of no advantage to ministers and public servants dedicated to a powerful, vigorous democracy.

The Concentration of Power

I began this chapter by asserting that not only was government in Britain today characterised by secrecy but that it was also élitist, oligarchic and bureaucratic. It is to these latter assertions that I now turn.

There are at least five characteristics in government in Britain today that justify the use of the terms élitist, oligarchic and bureaucratic. They are:

1. the Prime Ministerial nature of our government;
2. the centralised nature of public and private institutions;
3. the development in the civil service in Britain and the E.E.C. of a political power and authority that lies outside the concept of minis-

terial responsibility unless that term is used in a strictly nominal and theoretical sense;
4. the acceptance by all modern Governments of the conventional establishment wisdom;
5. the corporatist nature of government.

There may be other characteristics and/or developments but these strike me as the most important.

1. Prime Ministerial Government

Because the media concentrate their coverage of politics on personalities everyone is aware that the Prime Minister is the most important political figure in our society. Few people really understand, and no Prime Minister would readily admit, just how powerful a figure the holder of that office is. Prime Ministers do not want to admit the full extent of their power not merely because to do so might destroy the illusion that they preside over a democratic government but because to do so would be to encourage challenges to the maintenance of the very power that they so much enjoy. The power of the Prime Minister derives from and is sustained by three things – secrecy, patronage and a unified system of Cabinet government, buttressed by parties controlled by the Whips in Parliament. These latter points make Britain a strongly governed country and a centrally governed country with a powerful executive over which the Prime Minister presides and predominates.

2. The Centralisation of Public and Private Institutions

The second of my five points is that the centralised nature of public and private institutions in Britain both allows and encourages power to be concentrated in the hands of a relatively small number of people. There are many aspects to this. Government itself, as I have said, is centralised. There is the size of London and its dominance in our cultural, economic and political life. The dissemination of information in Britain is highly concentrated. The national press consists of a small number of newspapers which are read by a large number of people. The B.B.C. provides a national television service which reaches a far higher proportion of the population than say any one American television network and the regional independent television companies have a common news service (I.T.N.) and buy each other's programmes. Industry and particularly manufacturing industry and commerce are both highly concentrated and centralised so far as major decisions are concerned. For example a hundred firms control half the output of manufacturing industry. Most top people in Britain gravitate to the south east of England and are thus able to reinforce each other in their views.

All these things may or may not be desirable in themselves, but they all make it easier for power to be concentrated in the hands of a relatively small number of people and accordingly those who administer and make policy are correspondingly that much more powerful.

3. The Development of Civil Service Power

The civil service in Britain today is an élite arrogating to itself political power in a manner which betokens trouble for democracy. But because ours is a political system of government it is no use politicians bewailing either the kind of civil servants we get or the power that they exercise. If they wish to change the system the remedy lies in their own hands. In defence of the politicians I simply say that it is easier to change a system which is understood than to change one which has been deliberately mystified down the years.

The majority of top administrative civil servants (i.e. those who advise ministers on policy) come from a narrow social class, went to public schools *and* to Oxford or Cambridge and obtained a good degree in an arts subject (see Chapter 6). The conventional wisdom (which I have never understood) holds that these are the best people to govern and administer the country.

The top civil servants that I met in the 1960s when I was myself a civil servant were personally charming, hard working to a degree and convinced that what they did was in the public good. Needless to say most of them were men. Yet what I could not stand and what is of more consequence to the way in which we are governed, was their bureacratic cast of mind. It came through in the way in which they dealt with their in-trays (an empty in-tray was a sign of failure), and in their precise almost self-deprecatory speech which contrasted sharply with the arrogant and subtle way in which they dealt with ministers when it mattered, for example by developing departmental policies that weak ministers could call their own, filtering information which ministers wanted, using delaying tactics, skilfully suborning powers of patronage that belonged to ministers; and it came through in the feeling they had that the reason why Britain was well governed was because they provided the cement which held our country together as politicians came and went. Even in those days, when there was a steely integrity in the civil service, they were politicians writ large.

The civil service machine was, as I saw it then, rather like a huge steamroller which was moving out of control down a gentle incline. Although there was nothing malicious in its movement it crushed everything that came in its unstoppable way.

The civil servant that I met ten years later as a politician was a slightly different animal although he had the same training and background. The bureaucratic cast of mind had hardened considerably. The effectiveness of inter-departmental committees had grown enormously. In particular the inter-departmental civil service committees which now parallel each Cabinet sub-committee were exercising great power. Often these official committees were being used to foreclose options for ministers rather than open them up. The civil service had learnt what trade unions learned long ago, namely, that unity is strength.

But there was another development difficult to pin down, impossible to measure and maybe easy to exaggerate in the light of one or two unfortunate experiences. I was left with the uneasy feeling that that central core of integrity which had characterised the civil service since the 1870s was beginning to crack. Instead of meeting obstacles head on, however difficult they were to overcome, it seemed to me that on too many occasions civil servants were now trying to skirt round them as though they were just another pressure group. At times I got the feeling of a bureaucracy that was overwhelmingly conscious of its own power and quite capable of using it not for the public good but to sustain itself and help its own members. I have always suspected that as countries or empires have moved into decline their bureaucracies have usually done fairly well for themselves. All this may in part explain the perceptible transfer of allegiance from Britain to the E.E.C. on the part of some civil servants that I met in the Foreign Office and Department of Energy who were working on E.E.C. affairs. They may have felt that in tomorrow's world the power of bureaucracy would be best expressed in the E.E.C. I say this not to denigrate the civil service but to serve as a warning of what could happen unless our civil servants can return to more Platonic ideals and more rigorous standards in their relationship not only with their ministers but with industrialists and others outside the service.

The suggestion that top civil servants can and do usurp political power and authority is not confined to politicians of any one political party. One Conservative former Treasury minister told me privately that whilst he hesitated to support me publicly his experience of civil servants at the Treasury accorded broadly with the views that I was expressing. In the debate in the House of Commons on the Expenditure Committee Report on the Civil Service on 15th January 1979 Nicholas Ridley, the Conservative Member for Cirencester and Tewkesbury, said (Hansard Vol. 960 No. 34 Col. 1384): 'I do not wish to go into the many . . . difficult points that I have described as the "battle of Sedgemore" – the matters that concern the relationship between ministers and civil servants about which the Hon. Member for Luton West (Mr Sedgemore) has such strong views. Indeed I rather agree with them.'

Mr Ridley, who in 1979 became a minister in Mrs Thatcher's Government, was also a Conservative minister at the Department of Industry when the Heath Government was in power 1970–74. He was responsible for drafting Chapter 13 of the Expenditure Committee Report on Civil Servants (Eleventh Report from the Expenditure Committee Session 1976–77) which expressed concern about the relationship between ministers and civil servants and which received the unanimous support of Conservative and Labour Members of Parliament on the Committee. The Committee wrote (paragraphs 137–142):

> All civil servants naturally say that they exist solely to serve the Government and that they take their policy instructions automatically from ministers. They could scarcely be expected to give your sub-committee evidence other than to this effect. However, many who have been, or who are, ministers believe that ministers do not always get the service which it is claimed that they get. They say that they find on their coming into office that some departments have firmly held policy views and that it is very difficult to change these views. When they are changed, the department will often try and reinstate its own policies through the passage of time and the erosion of ministers' political will. Many departments are large and it is not difficult to push forward policies without a minister's knowledge, particularly if there is any lack of clarity in defining demarcation lines between different ministers' responsibilities, as has been known to happen.
>
> Further it is often said to be extremely difficult to launch a new policy initiative which is not to the liking of a department. Delay and obstruction are said to be among the tactics used, together with briefing ministers in other departments to oppose the initiative in Cabinet or Cabinet Committee. The workload on ministers is immense and procrastination or repetition of the difficulties of a policy would be tactics that ministers would find difficulty in overcoming.
>
> In considering these allegations it is necessary to make two points which to some extent would justify these practices to the extent that they may exist. First, the workload of most departments is so great that all decisions cannot be taken by ministers. It is natural in these circumstances that ministers would want to delegate some matters for decision to the civil service. We merely observe that any such delegation should be decided by ministers, not by civil servants, and

the succeeding incumbents in the relevant ministerial offices should be informed of it.

Secondly, the civil service has a duty to preserve the overall consistency of Government policy when a minister embarks on a course conflicting with that of a minister in another department. It may be right for the one minister to be frustrated, and the other (or the Prime Minister) alerted, until such time as the two have met and argued the matter out to a decision, either in or out of Cabinet. In addition, when a Permanent Secretary considers that his minister is acting improperly he has a right to appeal to the Prime Minister and should do so.

Beyond these instances, however, there seems to us to be no justification for any of the practices mentioned in paragraphs 137 and 138. It is often argued that the civil service is entitled to prevent what is called 'the worst excesses of left or right' in the interests of stable Government policy. This point of view used to be argued, particularly in relation to the French civil service, but also in relation to Britain in the years following the last war. It is still thought by some to be a justification for the civil service resisting measures which ministers might wish to take, which in the opinion of the civil service are 'going too far'. In the opinion of your Committee the duties of the civil service should be limited to pointing out the possible consequences, including the political consequences, of any policy but should not include opposing or delaying the policy. If the policy indeed turns out to be unwise or destabilising, the political party in office pays the price. They carry the responsibility, they should have the power to implement their policies.

The danger with the argument of preventing 'the worst excesses' is that it becomes open to civil servants to decide what are and what are not 'worst excesses'. If they assume the right to do that, then the step to assuming views on all party matters is but a small one. Whatever the truth of the allegations discussed above may or may not be, it is relevant to consider the powers of ministers in relation to their advisers so that they may best discharge their responsibilities.

Civil servants did not take too kindly to this Chapter in the Expenditure Committee's report. They were even less happy with an amendment drafted by myself (see Appendix 1) which defined the issues more sharply but which was defeated by eleven votes to fifteen votes when the Committee considered the Report.

Astonishingly the view which Whitehall's civil servants took of this defeated amendment was that it was not meant as a criticism of them at all but was an attack on the policies of the Government. Lord Armstrong the former head of the civil service under three Governments

(1968–74) expressed this view publicly. And so did a likeable Deputy Secretary, Mr Philip Jones, at the Department of Energy. My diary note for 16th December 1977 records my conversation with him thus:

P.J. We think that you were attacking the executive not us.
B.S. That seems to be a collective civil service view first expounded by Lord Armstrong.
P.J. Tell me, why is it that you've criticised civil servants in many departments but you haven't attacked me.
B.S. That, Philip, was simply because I would have had to resign as Tony's P.P.S. before I could do so.
P.J. Why don't you ever come to me and get all that hate out of your system? Why don't the [political] advisers talk to me? Why don't we see their advice? Let's see it and then we can go into our respective quarters.
B.S. You make it sound like a boxing match, Philip.
P.J. If you want open government why don't you make the proceedings of the N.E.C. public?
B.S. What! And lay bare the soul of the Labour Party.
P.J. Has it got a soul?

In later chapters in this book I deal in some detail with the conduct of civil servants at the Department of Energy. Some of the incidents I describe might cause even the greatest of sceptics to raise their eyebrows.

It is of course wrong to think that the idea that civil servants wield or seek to wield political power in their own right is of recent origin. The late Richard Crossman, Cabinet minister 1964–70, in *Diaries of a Cabinet Minister (Vol. 1)* wrote of his experiences in the Ministry of Housing and Local Government and his battles with civil servants, led by the redoubtable Dame Evelyn Sharp, thus:

> At first I felt like someone in a padded cell, but I must now modify this. In fact, I felt like somebody floating on the most comfortable support. The whole department is there to support the minister. Into his in-tray came, hour by hour, notes with suggestions as to what he should do. Everything is done to sustain him in the line officials think he should take. But if one is very careful and conscious one is aware of secret discussion between civil servants below. There is a constant debate as to how the ministers should be advised or, shall we say, directed and pushed and cajoled into the line required by the ministry. Each ministry has its own departmental policy and this policy goes on while ministers come and go.

I was working as a civil servant in the Ministry of Housing and Local Government at the time when Crossman was minister there and for two years was Private Secretary to one of his junior ministers, Robert Mellish. Crossman deliberately created tension and friction with his civil servants. He would call huge meetings with the Permanent Secretary, Deputy Secretaries and all manner of senior people and then spend much of the time talking to some middle-grade architect – much to the embarrassment of everybody, including the architect. What Crossman wrote was a brilliant description of what was going on. If Crossman were alive today I suspect that the main change he would notice, to which I have already referred, is the replacement of departmental policies by inter-departmental civil service policies.

A Private Secretary in the civil service often has to make up his mind whether he is working for his minister or the department. Constitutional theory says that he is working for the minister but his promotion depends on the department. I took the decision that I was working for the minister and this got me into some trouble.

For instance there was one occasion when my minister, Bob Mellish, wanted to promote the idea in a speech of a national housing plan. I gave him a bit of help with the drafting and we put the appropriate passages into the official text of a boring speech which had been prepared by the department. The next thing I knew I received a call from the Chief Information Officer, Mr Peter Brown, a man who was good at his job, scrupulously fair and liked by everyone. He asked me if the passages in question had been cleared with the department. When I said 'No – the minister just wants to float the idea' he said that the speech should not be issued. I told him that I was sorry but that it was for the minister to say whether or not the speech should be issued and that he was definitely going to make the speech and wanted it sent out as a press release. After some argument Mr Brown agreed to issue a release of the speech. I deliberately refrained from trying to clear it with the department because I knew that if I tried it would have been stopped. The speech was quite a success. The *Financial Times* paid it the compliment of an editorial, Crossman asked Mellish about it and in due course a plan which made use of some of its ideas was published.

Some senior civil servants with whom I have discussed these matters admit to the existence of independent bureaucratic power but argue that it is incorrect to say that that power prevails over political power and authority. Rather they see a kind of dualism developing in the constitution in which there is political power and bureaucratic power which are sometimes in agreement, sometimes in conflict with each other. When conflicts arise sometimes there is a compromise, sometimes bureaucratic power prevails and sometimes political power prevails. I do not find this dualist interpretation of what happens very satisfactory but it does have the merit of being closer to reality than the conventional liberal fallacy which refers to an impartial, non-political administration carrying out the wishes of the Cabinet.

Every policy decision falls within a wider framework incorporating broader strategy, priorities and implicit values. In a democracy there are or should be competing frameworks. The question of who is responsible for determining the framework within which decisions are taken is critical. According to conventional constitutional theory it is the responsibility of ministers to decide on both the framework within which policies are decided and the policies themselves and it is the responsibility of officials to carry out the policies chosen.

In two important statements (quoted in *The Times* 15th November 1976) Lord Armstrong, who as Sir William Armstrong was head of the civil service, described a complete reversal of these roles. He said:

> Obviously I had a great deal of influence. The biggest and most pervasive influence is in setting the framework within which the questions of policy are raised. We, while I was in the Treasury, had a framework of the economy which was basically neo-Keynesian. We set the questions which we asked ministers to decide arising out of that framework and it would have been enormously difficult for my minister to change the framework so to that extent we had great power. I don't think we used it maliciously or malignly. I think we chose that framework because we thought it the best one going.

Later Lord Armstrong continued, throwing useful light as he did so on the way in which top civil servants are appointed:

> Choosing people, X and not Y to be the new Permanent Secretary of this department, or Y and not Z to be the Deputy Secretary of that department, then I reckoned it was my business to know these people and I would make a definite recommendation. I wouldn't say to the Prime Minister 'there is A, B, C, D and it's up to you to choose' because I think I knew them better than he did and so in that area I reckon I had greater power in that sense.

I believe that Lord Armstrong has slightly overstated the case for the power of civil servants and that the position is rather more complicated than he suggests. The more correct position is that the parameters within which the debate takes place and policies are made are set by the Prime Minister in conjunction with the civil service and that together they are constrained in the setting of those parameters by what is the conventional establishment wisdom at any given time. The conventional establishment wisdom at any given time is in no way to be confused with concepts such as the general will or the will of the people, still less with what people want.

4. Conventional Establishment Wisdom

One cannot understand how power is exercised in Britain unless one can appreciate the interaction of Prime Ministerial power and civil service power. In the exercise of that power the Prime Minister and the civil service both contribute to the formation of and express the conventional establishment wisdom. The civil service in particular ensures that the interests of its class and caste are expressed in that wisdom.

Developing this theme a little further I suggest that the only reason why our system of government functions at all harmoniously, operating as it does with two major political parties with different political and philosophical values and a determined civil service with its own view is not because our civil servants are politically neutral or objective in their advice and can abstract their birth, their past, their education, their caste and every other influence in life from their advice (nobody else does, so why should they?) but because all post-war Prime Ministers have held political views which encompassed but a small part of the political spectrum. I suspect that if the political parties really did operate on different political and philosophical principles the system would break down. Neither civil servants nor ministers would be able to cope. It will continue to cope – albeit badly – for just so long as the politicians do not move too far from the conventional establishment wisdom.

5. The Corporatist Nature of Government

The conventional establishment wisdom at the moment is corporatist in character and, in my view, likely to remain so for some time to come, despite the promise of the present Conservative government to break out of the corporatist consensus through a reversion to the economics of the classical economists and the evangelical individualism of Samuel Smiles and through what can best be described in the political and constitutional arena as social Darwinism. This sentiment has been eloquently expressed by Mr Peregrine Worsthorne, an oracle to the paternalistic right of the political spectrum. He put it thus in the *Sunday Telegraph* of 13th May 1979:

> Perhaps historians will come to see the Labour Government as having served, no doubt unintentionally, a profoundly conservative purpose, its radical smoke serving merely to disguise the reforming of Tory forces for a new counterattack . . .
>
> All indications suggest that the western world is about to pass through a period of contraction, of de-internationalisation. This will require more paternalism from government, not less, more concern and cosseting, not less. Never will the welfare state have had to play

> so crucial a role if necessary adjustments are to be peacefully accomplished. Far from it being possible to dismantle social services, the likelihood is that they will have to be strengthened and extended . . .
>
> Small shopkeepers, skilled workers and self-employed businessmen may be excused a blind retreat into Poujadist bigotry. But Mrs Thatcher's Government is not drawn from such men. Almost all of its members have done remarkably well under socialism. So by and large, has the old ruling order. Let them think twice before talking about cleansing the Augean stables. For if ordure there be, they waxed fat on it.

It is enough to make a corporatist smile and a radical cry.

I would hesitate to define corporatism. I would however characterise it as:

1. Government which seeks to reconcile the interests of big institutions and corporations with each other where they are in conflict in the belief that if this can be done then everyone else will have no option other than to accept what has been done and in the belief that in such circumstances dissent in society can be contained. Corporatism may not be the antithesis of individualism but it is certainly incompatible with it.
2. Government in which the leaders of the big institutions in our society see their role as that of bringing or keeping their members in line with government policy rather than necessarily expressing the views of their members. Democracy is a system of government which comes up from the people whereas corporatism is a system of government handed down from on high.
3. Government in which the leaders of the big institutions in society, in return for carrying out the role which has been assigned to them whether tacitly or overtly, and through a variety of pressures and inducements, are given a say in the decision taking process or more likely a veto over the framework within which policy is discussed as well as over certain government decisions.
4. Government in which the major bureaucracies in our society – the civil service, the E.E.C. bureaucracy, the C.B.I., the T.U.C – find themselves converging on one another. The theory of what I have called the convergence of bureaucracies, for which there is considerable evidence, stems from the realisation of bureaucrats that bureaucratic thought can best sustain bureaucratic power at any given time by moving towards the conventional wisdom and accepting the existing system of values in society. That the public never sees the inner workings of bureaucracies is one of the reasons why so many people do not understand how power is exercised in Britain.

For example, the public knows well that Governments make huge financial contributions to big corporations but it is only vaguely aware of the relationships that have grown up between civil servants and industrial management. It scarcely comprehends the merry-go-round of patronage which exists between top civil servants who hand out some 10,000 quasi-governmental jobs and positions on behalf of their ministers, many of them to industrialists and most of them to people of their own kind on the one hand, and between industrialists and people of their own kind who give top civil servants jobs on their retirement. That the links in the merry-go-round, resting on a system of shared views, are indirect rather than direct does not matter.

Some people say that the system of shared values is inevitable in a complex, interdependent society and mixed economy. I am not sure. But I am sure that such a system contains within itself the seeds of moral corruption and of its own destruction.

And just to show that I am not partisan on this issue of corporatism, I would add that not only is the public not aware but most trade unionists are not aware of the dangers of trade union representatives at all levels being sucked into the system through the work of institutions of corporatist consent such as N.E.D.O. and N.E.D.C. And when one Cabinet minister can refer scornfully to leading bureaucrats from the T.U.C. as 'failed Deputy Secretaries' because they are seen drafting sections of the T.U.C.'s annual Economic Review at the Treasury then the warning signals are there.

Under 3 above I spoke of the corporate state veto. The corporate state veto is both a threat and a promise. It is a threat to withhold co-operation from the Government, maybe even to bring it down (for example by precipitating a run on the pound) if the Government goes outside the agreed or understood corporatist parameters. It is a promise that reasonable co-operation can be expected from the institutions concerned if Governments stay within the parameters. In the last years of office of the Labour Government (1974–79) Labour ministers readily accepted that the City and the C.B.I. had a corporate state veto over such issues as the upper limits of the public sector borrowing requirement (PSBR), international trade planning and industrial democracy. Earlier the Conservative Government (1970–1974) was aware of the corporate state veto of the trade unions. The Prime Minister at the time, Edward Heath, though a corporatist himself made the mistake of ignoring the veto and was brought down by the miners. But the truth is that the bureaucrats at the T.U.C. came within an ace of reaching agreement with Mr. Heath on industrial policy. And it is well to keep in mind that secret meeting in the garden at Downing Street between Mr Heath and Mr Joe Gormley, the miners' leader, on 16th July 1973 during the miners' dispute, a meeting about which neither the Cabinet nor the executive of the National Union of Mineworkers were told. That was corporatism at work on what Lord Armstrong (in a 'This Week Special', *Miners – State of Emergency* on Thames TV on 15th March 1978) described as a hot high summer day'.

Mr Gormley was almost certainly right, if he was correctly reported on B.B.C. Radio (13th May 1979) to say that the miners should seek to work closely with the present Prime Minister, Mrs Thatcher, for a sensible energy policy. However I think he should know that in the last months of office of the Labour Government the Central Policy Review Staff, the Think-Tank, were tossing around ideas of pit closures which Mrs Thatcher might find less objectionable than the previous Prime Minister. It is not that I want to deny Mr Gormley further afternoons in the garden at No. 10, merely that he should beware the witches brew that may be put into his cup of tea.

Ministers, including Cabinet ministers, are downgraded in the corporate state. I once remember Frank Chapple, General Secretary of the Electricians Union, telling Tony Benn, the Secretary of State for Energy, that he and the Electricity Council and the Central Electricity Generating Board could run the industry perfectly well without the interference of the Government at which point the Secretary of State quietly reminded Mr Chapple that he *did* represent fifty million consumers and their interests could not be totally ignored. Similarly, when in February 1979 the Labour Government were drawing up the Concordat over pay policy with the trade unions every member of the T.U.C. General Council had a copy of the draft agreement – *The Economy, the Government and Trade Union Responsibilities* – including Ken Gill, General Secretary of T.A.S.S., who is a member of the Communist Party. When the Cabinet subsequently saw draft copies of the document before it was finally agreed, they were asked to hand their copies back to the Secretary of the Cabinet on the grounds of security! Tony Benn, incidentally, refused to do so.

Corporatism threatens Parliamentary democracy directly by by-passing Ministers, by-passing Parliament and by-passing the people. It can even be a threat to the rule of law when governments decide that they will copy the big institutions and replace lawful authority or the construction of consent through legitimate moral and political persuasion with threats of their own. And there were threats – made in secret of course – when the Government's pay policy in the winter of 1977 came under attack.

The note in my diary for 28th September 1977 summed it up succinctly:

> Corporatism is on the move. Tony Benn has been asked by his Cabinet colleagues to see if supplies of coal could be withheld from

coal lorry drivers whose pay settlement in the West Midlands has exceeded ten per cent and if he could interfere with the oil rights of the P & O Company because one of their subsidiaries has gone over ten per cent. He has in my view no moral or legal authority to do either. The Prime Minister has issued instructions that the phrase 'government sanctions' is not to be used. This sort of policy can never hold.

The matter of bribery by public and private companies in order to secure overseas contracts presented the country with an even uglier face of corporatism. For whilst the Government's public stand was that it would not condone bribery by publicly owned companies, privately it did precisely that. The issue arose over the disclosure of allegations that B.P., a partially publicly owned company, had been bribing Italian political parties to get contracts. John Prescott, M.P., for Kingston-upon-Hull, and I met a Treasury minister in his room in the Commons to discuss the matter. We were told, in the nicest possible manner, not to be naive and that of course British companies, including publicly owned companies, bribed foreigners to get business. They always had done so and would continue to do so. Morality should not be mixed up with trade.

Although I disagree with his main prescription, I thought that Sir Peter Parker, Chairman of British Rail, expressed well the dangers of the corporate state in the Rita Hinden Memorial Lecture, (given on 10th February 1979) when he said:

> We must have some protection of standards of justice and equality against the competition of corporations, who of their very nature – and I speak as the head of one – must be, however enlightened, self-interested and divisive. The threat of a corporate state emerges when the state's neutrality is at risk. The definition of a corporate state is one which has expanded its power on the basis of private corporatism, and has become a captive of the centralised private associations it sought or ought to control. It has lost the two fundamental principles of a democratic polity: that neither a tyrannical majority, nor an entrenched minority wielding critical power, should be allowed to dictate the common interest; and that brute force should be prohibited as a means of obtaining private wants. In other words, Madison's two great principles of a pluralistic form of government have been lost: that all interests should be included; and that all issues should be negotiated. The challenge facing us is to shore up these principles in our form of government, and extend them to cover the corporate forces themselves. That is my theme.
>
> . . . We have seen the growth of state power, the unattractive gigantism of industrial groups, private and public, the thickening

> bureaucracies of trade unions. And already there is a recoil against this encroaching corporatist style of state and society. In business there is almost a revivalist fervour of recovered faith in small scale units. In unions the rise of militancy on the shopfloor is plain enough. Peter Jenkins, in one of his penetrating pieces in the *Guardian* recently said: 'In the last few weeks we have seen the coming of age of syndicalism. If the country threatens to become ungovernable, it is not because of the power of the unions, it is rather because of their powerlessness to govern their own members'.

In his mammoth and fascinating book *Politics in Industrial Society – The Experience of the British system since 1911* Keith Middlemas suggests that corporatism in Britain arose out of the experience of the First World War which fundamentally altered the relationship between the state and its citizens, beginning with conscription and industrial discipline of unprecedented severity. Henceforth Governments were forced to adopt a series of compromises to maintain their authority. Middlemas argues:

> that a new form of harmony in the political system was established with great difficulty in the decade 1916–26; and that it lasted at least until the mid-sixties when the much-vaunted 'consensus' was seriously, if not fatally, disrupted. Is it unreasonable to assume that, earlier than in any other industrial country, British Governments began to make the avoidance of crises their first priority? That even before the era of full suffrage they had discovered how to exercise the arts of public management, extending the state's powers to assess, educate, bargain with, appease or constrain the demands of the electorate, raising to a sort of parity with the state the various competing interests and institutions to which voters owed allegiance? That they sought to avoid, by compromise, crises in sensitive areas like wages and conditions, public order, immigration, unemployment, or the position of women, abolishing Hobbes' 'natural anarchy of competing wills' not by invoking authority (at a time of declining faith and deference) but by the alternate gratification and cancelling out of the desires of large, well-organised, collective groups to the detriment of individuals, minorities and deviants? That they created in Britain a political *Gleichschaltung*, subtle and loose enough to be resented only by those deviants and minorities; in which, despite the appearance of crises in 1922, 1931 and 1940, party and Parliament declined in governing importance, while supposedly intractable economic conflicts were diffused, and the challenges of Conservatism and Socialism were alike dispersed in a common reformist policy justified by an unreal assessment of historical tradition? . . .

> The line of greatest social conflict . . . lay through industrial politics. Here the triangular pattern of co-operation between government and the two sides of industry . . . led to the elevation of trade unions and employers' associations to a new sort of status: from interest groups they became 'governing institutions' . . . I have called this process corporate bias, but it should not be confused with the corporate state of classical Fascism, nor the somewhat naive corporatism from time to time advocated by industrial theorists in the 1930s and 1940s in Britain, which centred on the National Industrial Council or industrial parliament . . .

Middlemas' analysis may be misleading both as regards the nature of corporatism and the way in which it has developed in Britain, particularly in the last two decades.

Firstly he argues that corporate bias is not an ideology: nor is it ideological in character. Yet the system which he describes operates in practice in a profoundly undemocratic manner. As such it is intensely ideological and goes to the root of perhaps the major ideological split in our society – that which exists between those who believe that governments should operate in a democratic fashion and those who do not.

Secondly, he plays down the role of governments in the corporate state, describing it as 'supportive' rather than 'directive'. In my experience the Government has always had a far clearer idea of what it wanted to do than either the trade unions or the C.B.I. Governments tend to have an overview which others do not, partly because of the resources at their command and their access to statistics and other information which enables them to make more sense of issues which are often exceedingly complex. Trade unionists, particularly at meetings with ministers, however cogently their views have been expressed in the minutes of those meetings, have tended to be defensive, often seeking to establish the limits of the permissible. Moreover it is difficult to see how 'prices and incomes policies', whether voluntary or statutory, which have been introduced by successive Governments since the early 1960s can be described as other than 'directive'. Much the same can be said of the Government's role in economic management as regards monetary and fiscal policies, including policies on public expenditure. Government action here is surely 'directive' rather than 'supportive' as regards actions by trade unions or industrial management. I would argue that the role of government, certainly in recent years, has become more positive than one might assume from reading Middlemas and that the role of the executive is pivotal to the corporate state.

Thirdly, Middlemas exaggerates the effectiveness of the role played by trade unions in the corporate state. Referring to other countries such as France, Italy, Spain, Germany, Belgium, Holland and Sweden he argues 'it is difficult on the evidence of the British case, to avoid the conclusion that trade unions' potential power will eventually predominate over that of management'. In expressing himself thus Middlemas may be a victim of the news manipulation which he rightly deprecates. The values of our society are certainly not set by trade unions and in the slump of the seventies managers acting on behalf of shareholders have shown that union power is virtually powerless to stop their members taking much of the blame for and the brunt of that slump. The corporate control of our economy is only marginally an expression of the negative power that unions wield. The rate of profit has fallen but can that really be ascribed to trade union activity and the assertion that real wages are too high in consequence?

Fourthly, Middlemas sees the role of political parties in the corporate state as that of mediating between competing wills in the economic sphere. As a member of a political party I find this description of what happens odd. Neither as a member of my local General Management Committee nor as an M.P. have I ever been aware that I was or was supposed to be mediating between competing wills. Nor do I know of others who believe that this is what they are about as members of the Labour Party. Of course Governments whose ministers come from political parties have in the nature of their role to decide between competing propositions, policies or ideas but that is something entirely different.

Lastly Middlemas fails adequately to answer the question why has corporatism developed differently on the Continent and in Britain? For example, in France it operates far more nationalistically in the field of economic regulation. Part of the answer may lie in the fact that some European countries have come under philosophical influences which have never taken root in Britain. Thus the way in which corporatism has developed in Germany and France may in part have been influenced by the philosophies of Rousseau, Byron, Kant, Fichte, Hegel and Nietzsche. This of course takes us back to ideology and the merging of method and ideology.

Corporatism as I characterise and describe it in this book lies somewhere between 'corporate bias' and 'classical Fascism'. Interestingly there have been echoes of what Middlemas refers to as 'naive corporatism' in calls, made in the 1960s and 1970s mainly by businessmen and newspaper proprietors, for a 'businessmen's government'.

If the evidence of this book is to be believed, the élite who run our country have been rather more flexible and skilful in ensuring the survival of the political system with its values, whatever they are worth, intact than Middlemas would give them credit. Few people would have thought in 1974 that the Labour Government would have been able to carry through policies which helped to create and then sustain over several years an unemployment level of over one million and do so with the active concurrence of many trade union leaders and the T.U.C. bureaucracy as well as with the support of the C.B.I.

Corporatism is a vehicle for sustaining a system of values, to stop ideas competing in society. In theory such a corporate system, or variations of it, could be used to sustain any set of values against any competing values, providing only that the values to be sustained do not entail democracy. In practice the particular system that I describe has grown out of historical developments in the constitution and the establishment's response to recurring economic crises and technological change. It can be seen in part as a crude response to one of the central dilemmas that faces our society – that of a prevailing philosophy that is subjective in character and that of a technology that is co-operative but authoritarian in its demands.

The dilemma runs right through our society. It is not concerned only with the problems of industrial production and distribution, the provision of vital public services and industrial relations, with the ease with which individuals or small groups, be they dealers on the foreign exchanges or workers on the shop floor exercising rights which belong to them as individuals, can disrupt or put at risk the very foundations of an increasingly inter-dependent society. It can be seen just as starkly in the way in which we educate our people. Liberal subjectivist philosophers have usually held that education is good in itself and that its purpose is to enrich the life of the individual rather than satisfy the demands of technology. In practice our educational system, except for the very few, has been a pretty utilitarian affair, leaving these idealised heights untouched. The growth of modern corporatism has added a piquant twist to this dilemma.

Thus it was disclosed on 21st August 1979 that the chairman of the University Grants Committee had written to Vice-Chancellors of Universities telling them to 'adopt a policy of restricting home undergraduate admissions for 1980 to 94 per cent of the number they are taking this autumn'. The letter itself stated that no precise levels of expenditure were known yet but concluded that it was 'inevitable that the target of 308,000 students in 1981–82 – and the indicated levels of grants associated with it – would be superseded'.

Taken at its face value, the chairman of the committee was writing a letter setting out the limits and consequences of public expenditure cuts yet to be made without the authority of the Department of Education, the Cabinet or Parliament.

Of course the letter could not be so taken. It was yet one more example of the way in which the corporate state works with the allegedly independent University Grants Committee acting as the agent of the Government. On the same day as the letter was made public the Department of Education admitted that there had been talks between them and the committee about the impending White Paper on Public Expenditure. The department went on to add that it had given no 'instructions' to the committee to send out the letter. One can accept that. In order to preserve a veneer of democracy, corporatism rarely functions through instructions.

The same day as the committee was taking on its new role a Government minister, Rhodes Boyson, flying in the face of liberal subjectivist philosophy, announced that the Government would be encouraging the 'contraction' of the teaching of some subjects. Technology demanded more mathematicians and 'hard scientists', less sociologists and arts graduates. Not only was the Robbins' principles, that those who could benefit from a university education should receive it, to be dropped but courses which were not functional, and especially those which were liable to create dissidents, were to be cut back.

It is doubtful whether the minister, who wanted university courses to be geared to the needs of industry and commerce and not to those of individuals, even recognised the dilemma contained in his utterances. The idea contained in his statement that the individual is subordinate to the whole of which he forms part has been well expressed in philosophical terms by Rousseau and Hegel. It may help technology but is inimical to democracy.

For the moment the technocrats are reigning supreme. Their technology which is becoming increasingly impersonal, monopolistic in its nature, oligarchic in its control and bureaucratic in its administration is given credibility by bogus philosophers who more and more are having to use mirrors to sustain the illusion of individualism. Some of these philosophers may even think that they have succeeded in creating in Britain Marcuse's one-dimensional man, seduced by and submerged in a mass culture that makes no demands on him as an individual, and renders him incapable of responding to ideas. That culture might survive if it were genuinely rooted in the people and their experience but the very fact that it needs corporate structures whose inner workings are secret and whose principles remain largely unexpressed suggest that that is not the case. Corporatism, once understood, exposed and explained by true philosophers may endure but will not last forever.

Although I have suggested that trade unions and the T.U.C. are part of corporatist government, I have been careful not to suggest that their values or the perspectives of their members feature in the conventional establishment wisdom. On the contrary that wisdom which seeks to sustain élitist and oligarchic government only accepts trade union perspectives in as far as it has to if society is to function at all. Thus whilst mention of institutions such as the City and C.B.I. conjure up favourable images in the mind of the establishment mention only the word 'trade union' and the stock market threatens to go haywire. So what real merit there is in T.U.C. bureaucrats going along with corporatism in the corridors of Great George Street (the home of the Treasury) is difficult to comprehend.

Again, society is unable to reconcile its subjectivist philosophy with its views on what should be the relationship between trade unions and individuals without becoming victim to hypocrisy. When an individual fights the closed shop he is generally regarded by the media as a hero upholding the rights of the individual. Yet most managements find the closed shop as convenient as trade unions find it necessary and one suspects that if there were more than a handful of rugged individualists in every large factory opposed to the closed shop the media would come to see them as trouble-makers. Contrarywise, if individuals or small groups refuse to follow the advice of their trade union officials and act unofficially then society tends to forget its individualistic ethic and casts such individuals or groups in the role of anarchists or politically motivated collectivists seeking to achieve their ends through anarchy, unless of course the individuals concerned are opposing official union support of strikes.

It may be that society, exasperated by its failure to relate subjectivism to the demands of modern technology, needs trade unions as a scapegoat to explain, in part at least, that failure. Put another way, it may be that our governing élite needs the illusion of much that passes for trade union and shop floor power to divert attention from its increasingly incoherent and contradictory subjectivist philosophy.

I hope I have said enough in this preliminary walk round the course to justify my assertion that our society is secretive, élitist, oligarchic and bureaucratic. If not I trust that the remaining chapters will repair the omissions. If, however, our constitution really operates in this fashion, the reader is entitled to ask why it is that so few politicians have portrayed it thus and why it is that not all of the text-books on the constitution have described it thus.

The first answer, at which I have hinted already, is that it is not in the interest of the relatively small number of people who do exercise power in the manner that I have described to admit that that is how they do it. Most civil servants I know regard Lord Armstrong's blabbing of the truth as a terrible mistake. He is not so well thought of at the Athenaeum and the United Oxford and Cambridge as he used to be.

Secondly, many distinguished and caring people think that our institutions and the values they represent serve us well at a time when it is becoming increasingly difficult for anyone to govern at all. So why should they concentrate on exposing, and, they would argue, exaggerating, those aspects of government which in their very nature cannot be as democratic as some would like. Many of our ablest commentators and some experts on the constitution too seem to adopt this view at least subconsciously. Theirs is not a conspiracy of silence: rather it is a mature understanding of the delicate gossamer thread that holds society together.

I dissent from the basic premise behind this argument and I believe that the longer we turn a blind eye to the truth the more likely it is that the gossamer thread which holds society together will snap. For we are a badly governed country – and our institutions must take some of the blame – whether the criteria be economic success, social stability and cohesion (what happened in the winters of 1972, 1974 and 1979 is likely to recur again and again), our ability to adapt to social change or bring about social reform, or our influence in international affairs. I also find it impossible to follow the argument that we should cherish what we have because, although it may or may not be democratic, it is efficient. And when people tell me that real democracy is too cumbersome and inefficient a system to work I reflect on the sleepy nature of our civil service Leviathan and all the delays, all the agonising that was a substitute for decision-taking, and all the negative attitudes that I have seen in government over fifteen years.

Thirdly, political theorists must take some of the blame for misrepresenting the nature of our system of government to the people. In his excellent essay *The Political Constitution (The Modern Law Review* Vol. 42 January 1979) J. A. G. Griffith, a professor of law at L.S.E., puts the case.

> It is still quite common to hear the constitution described – even lovingly described – as a piece of machinery cleverly and subtly constructed to enable the will of the people to be transmitted through its elected representatives who make laws instructing its principal committee, the Cabinet, how to administer the affairs of state, with the help of an impartial civil service and under the benevolent wisdom of a neutral judiciary. Not only is this the explanation given to thousands of schoolchildren but I have to tell you that it also finds its way – in a more sophisticated form – into the curricula of some institutions of further and higher education . . .

This theory which I heard expounded in the 1979 General Election on a public platform by a Labour M.P. derives in part from John Locke's view that sovereignty resides in the people who delegate it to politicians to hold in trust for them. I agree with Professor Griffith when he calls it 'a cover-up for authoritarianism'.

Simply to describe the constitution in critical terms is a negative, if fascinating, exercise. What should be done by way of reform is a question that must be answered and I make many detailed suggestions in the following chapters. But before moving on to them I would like to set out the framework in which they are made.

Reforming the System

There are a number of ways in which reform can be approached. Some people argue that we could protect ourselves from creeping authoritarianism if only we took the concept of 'rights' seriously. Ronald Dworkin in fact entitled his book *Taking Rights Seriously*. He argues that we need principles or standards above rules of law that should be observed not because they will 'advance or secure an economic, political or social situation deemed desirable' but because they are 'a requirement of justice or fairness or some other dimension of morality'. These principles would be interpreted in the courts. In philosophical terms Dorkin argues that the solution to our problems is to bring together the concepts of 'law as command' and 'natural law'.

The idea that political decisions can be taken in the courts and be based on a 'community morality', that is 'the political morality presupposed by the laws and institutions of the community', seems to me to beg the question of what the phrase 'community morality' means unless the proposition is circular and means 'that which will be obeyed' or unless the concept is meant to be metaphysical in which case its practical applications will be limited.

Neither in practical nor theoretical terms can I see how society can express political and philosophical ideas and the policies which flow from them in Bills of Rights. I can however see endless, even irreconcilable, conflicts in the attempt to do so. Just as Pythagoras failed in his attempt to bring mathematics and theology together through deductive reasoning so natural law and Bill of Rights theorists are forever doomed in their attempts to provide a deductive base for resolving political conflict, moving in the courts from axioms that are far from luminous to conclusions whose doubtful validity would be matched only by the defect in understanding that inspired them.

Politics in a democracy is about competing claims and the attempts of political parties to construct consent about the way in which decisions should be taken on the claims, and the criteria or values which should guide the process by which the decisions are to be taken. The role of political parties in our democracy is not to try to seek out some imaginary general will, still less is it to try simply to measure people's feelings or register their votes on particular issues: nor is it to mediate between competing wills: nor is it to throw up competing leaderships, as Joseph Schumpeter suggested in his book *Capitalism, Socialism and Democracy*, which can engage the electorate's attention for a short time, not concentrating on principles or policies but selling themselves and their products competitively as a department store would sell a new line of women's underwear with the buyers having an 'indeterminate bundle of vague impulses loosely playing about given slogans and mistaken impressions'. It is to construct consent or if you like *create* a favourable climate for certain policies which express certain values or criteria. Within political parties and the nation at large the debate should be first about the nature of the values and criteria themselves and then about the best way to give practical expression to those values and priorities. Only if it is conducted in this way does the democratic process offer the people a real choice. Bills of Rights might suffice in a one-party state but in a society where there is more than one party and where political parties operate on significantly different political and philosophical principles (in theory this happens in Britain though the practice is rather different) it is difficult to see how the idea could get off the ground. In such a society there can be no short cut to political decision taking through political control.

How could any Government in Britain, Labour or Conservative, function for example if a Bill of Rights enshrined 'equality' as a principle if such was thought to be part of 'community morality'? Any serious interpretation by the courts of such a principle would undermine the existing constitution completely, destroy the value system upon which the constitution is based and bring resistance that would be bound to bring defiance of such a nature that the law would be brought into disrepute. A Labour Government might claim that its election victory showed that there was such a standard of 'community morality' in existence but it would be a Pyrrhic claim. Social and economic revolution cannot be created by law. It can only be created by political control and political authority acting through the political process.

How would a future Labour Government be able to function if the present Prime Minister enshrined the concept of 'inequality' in a Bill of Rights? How could it function if the present Conservative Government enshrined what are generally referred to as 'liberal pluralist' principles in a Bill of Rights based on Lockean concepts of freedom which contrast sharply with positive concepts of freedom which form the bedrock of Labour Party thinking?

Similar objections apply to Lord Hailsham's ideas on the need for 'limited government'. Assuming that he believes what he writes he, Lord Hailsham, is now the Lord Chancellor in an 'elected dictatorship' whose party only received a third of the votes at the General Election 1979. In the *Dilemma of Democracy, Diagnosis and Prescription*, he writes that he is concerned about a position where 'a Government elected by a small minority of voters and with a slight majority in the House, regards itself as entitled and, according to its more extreme supporters, bound to carry out every proposal in its election manifesto . . . it seems to me that at any cost we must ensure that it cannot happen again'. To stop the Conservative Party from acting in an authoritarian fashion Lord Hailsham wants to 'institutionalise the theory of limited government' with a Bill of Rights (which presumably will not enshrine the principle of equality or the positive concept of freedom!), a proportionately elected second chamber, a limit by law on the right of Parliament to legislate without restriction and devolution to Scotland, Wales, Northern Ireland and the English regions in a federal structure.

Whereas Dworkins' Bill of Rights is to be based on 'community morality' a concept expressed in such a way as to embrace both legal positivism and natural law theories, Lord Hailsham's Bill of Rights seeks to resurrect the natural law in all its pristine glory, for his theory of 'limited government' is to correspond to nothing less than 'the general conscience of mankind'. It is an arrogant piece of metaphysics on the part of an old man who, having spent a large part of his life engaging in political argument through the political process, now seeks to allow the law to freeze that process.

The proposals together represent a value system which Lord Hailsham no doubt holds dear. It is the existing value system. But the function of democracy is neither to sustain nor destroy the existing value system but to express the value system that the people want when properly presented with the alternatives and given all the information they need to form mature judgments.

I am one of those who suspect the exercise of all power. I would advise the citizen to do likewise and to look for reform through democracy. In theoretical terms my proposals are simple – all the best ideas are.

I start from the premise that democracy without accountability is meaningless. Accountability requires:

1. that those who represent others can be replaced by democratic processes, including and especially elections;
2. that those who elect others to represent them at whatever level should know what problems are under discussion by their representatives *before* decisions are taken;
3. that there are arrangements by which people can make their views known to their representatives *before* decisions are taken; and
4. that those who wish to contribute to the decision-taking process should have full access to all the information they need to enable them to come to their judgments and put forward their arguments.

In short democracy is a continuous process and not a system of government based exclusively on trust where citizens go to sleep or are forgotten between elections.

Concern about the lack of accountability is now expressing itself in many spheres in a series of parallel power struggles. These power struggles all have a democratic theme running through them. They are in part an expression of concern and frustration with the failure of those in office to open up government to the people. In broad terms they can be summarised starkly and perhaps a shade simplistically as representing the struggles between the unelected House of Lords and the elected House of Commons, between the executive and the bureaucracy, between Parliament and the executive, between party political representatives and those who work for them and vote for them, between trade union officials and shop floor workers, and between managers and workers on the one hand and shareholders on the other. If life is not quite the conflict that I have presented here I do believe that reform lies in introducing more democratic and accountable practices in Parliament, in the work of the executive, in political parties, in trade unions, in commercial and industrial companies, in schools, on housing estates and in the health service.

Opportunities must be created in all these spheres for more discussion, more openness and more access to information. If there is some other way to solve the conflicts that exist between planning, individualism, representation and the dispersal and sharing of power I am not aware of it.

Nobody who does not want to is being asked to get involved. Everyone who does so want must be offered the opportunity. Only those who are authoritarian by nature will rest their argument for the status quo on the bland and silly assertion that most people are not interested in these matters. Most people seem to me to be very interested in what happens when their rubbish is not collected, when their taxes are raised, when their mother or their child falls ill, or their jobs are taken away from them.

On the face of it the proposals for reform that I put forward are modest. I suspect however that they will meet with stiff resistance. The spread of knowledge is likely in itself to encourage demands for shifts in the balance of power in a democratic direction. Yet our system of government is constructed to prevent precisely that. The main problem for those who wish to advance the democratic cause will be to convince people that debates about the constitution and the balance of power in our society are not arid and academic but are relevant to the problems that they face as individuals and as members of a highly complex interdependent society.

2 Prime Ministerial Power

He who does not understand the extent and irresponsible nature of the power of the modern Prime Minister does not understand the British constitution. Any idea that the Prime Minister is simply *primus inter pares* in the Cabinet is a million miles from the truth. His power (and there is no reason to believe that *she* would have it different) is the product of and is sustained by secrecy, patronage and the unitary and centralised system of government in Britain.

Prime Ministers in Britain are elected by very small electoral colleges. Citizens elect Members of Parliament who in turn elect their party leader who becomes Prime Minister when the party has a majority of seats or majority support in Parliament. One of the first tasks of any Prime Minister is to appoint his Cabinet. It has been said that at the moment of appointment the Prime Minister's power is almost supreme but that once he has appointed his Cabinet his power becomes constrained. I do not accept this traditional view. On the contrary, I believe that the operation of Cabinet government in Britain today serves to strengthen his power. Richard Crossman, whom one must admire for the way in which he lifted three or four of the seven veils which shroud government by publishing some of the official secrets from Cabinet meetings in his Diaries, took a similiar view; he saw Cabinet government fragmenting into government by inner Cabinet and then disintegrating into Prime Ministerial government.

Each member of the Cabinet – and indeed other trusted persons who are deemed fit to advise the monarch – is required to take the Privy Councillors' oath. This says:

> You do swear by Almighty God to be a true and faithful Servant unto the Queen's Majesty, as one of Her Majesty's Privy Council. You will not know or understand of any manner of thing to be attempted, done, or spoken against Her Majesty's Person, Honour, Crown, or Dignity Royal, but you will lett and withstand the same to the uttermost of your Power, and either cause it to be revealed to Her Majesty Herself, or to such of Her Privy Council as shall

advertise Her Majesty of the same. You will, in all things to be moved, treated, and debated in Council, faithfully and truly declare your Mind and Opinion, according to your Heart and Conscience; and will keep secret all Matters committed and revealed unto you, or that shall be treated of secretly in Council. And if any of the said Treaties or Counsels shall touch any of the Counsellors, you will not reveal it unto him, but will keep the same until such time as, by the Consent of Her Majesty, or of the Council, Publication shall be made thereof. You will to your uttermost bear Faith and Allegiance unto the Queen's Majesty; and will assist and defend all Jurisdictions, Pre-eminences, and Authorities, granted to Her Majesty, and annexed to the Crown by Acts of Parliament, or otherwise, against all Foreign Princes, Persons, Prelates, States, or Potentates. And generally in all things you will do as a faithful and true Servant ought to do to Her Majesty.

SO HELP YOU GOD

To be a Privy Councillor is regarded as a high honour by many. Yet the Privy Council is little more than a constitutional fiction to give status and dignity to the monarch. Further status is given to the monarch by one of the Government Whips in Parliament who is employed to summarise the proceedings of each day in Parliament for the Queen.

The real importance of the Privy Councillor's oath lies in the support that it gives to notions of secrecy. The oath, which dates back centuries before universal suffrage was established, was at first a device to protect the King and his advisers from Parliament; today it is a device to protect the Cabinet from Parliament and the public. It enables a Prime Minister to say of any other minister who releases confidential or secret information, albeit from the highest of motives and with wholly beneficial consequences, that that minister has broken an oath which should have been regarded as sacred.

If that is not enough the Prime Minister imposes further oaths and obligations of secrecy on his Cabinet colleagues. He requires every Secretary of State to take a further oath relating specifically to his departmental duties. I was present with Tony Benn at Nuffield College on 10th February 1978 at a seminar when he commented acidly that this further oath 'makes no reference to the constitutional requirement that Governments and ministers only remain in office while they enjoy support in the House of Commons and to the fact that they must be members of it'. That is not, of course, quite true. Even some senior ministers are members of the House of Lords.

A further obligation of secrecy is imposed on ministers by the Prime Minister under the 30-year rule which prevents the publication of official papers for that period. Thus Prime Ministers ensure that the conduct of wars and sterling crises remain hidden until long after any useful lessons can be drawn from them. Thus they seek to ensure that history cannot defame their memory with too great an accuracy until well after their death. Thus they ensure that in their retirement they can write lucrative and selective history in their own images. Again I turn to Tony Benn's words at Nuffield College:

> Under the 30-year rule the three page long memorandum issued by Mr Attlee on the obligations of a Cabinet minister has now been released. The present memorandum is six times as long. It cannot be printed because it is secret. Neither Parliament nor the electorate are allowed to know what obligations are imposed on ministers by the Prime Minister of the day. The Radcliffe Report on ministerial memoirs noted four separate statutes governing ministerial conduct including the Official Secrets, Copyright and Public Records Acts. By contrast, ministers have no statutory obligations to explain what they are doing, or why.

All Prime Ministers are very sensitive about secrecy, all are hurt by any suggestions that their administrations do not observe confidences. This may be in part due to the legitimate concern expressed in the introduction to the Government White Paper, Reform of Section 2 of the Official Secrets Act 1911 (Cmnd 7285). 'In the wrong hands certain information could undermine our vital interests or even our safety as a sovereign and independent country. Therefore for us, as for all democracies, there is an inescapable tension between the need to keep some information secret and the requirements of openness if people are to participate in government as they should.'

But most breaches of secrecy which wound Prime Ministers so much come nowhere in or near this category of information. The way in which the Cabinet sub-committee system works or the projected economic consequences of joining the European Monetary System or the information upon which civil servants at the Department of Education are deciding policy on the number of teacher training places that will be required in the 1990s hardly fall into that category. Indeed scarcely any information not concerned with internal and external security comes within that category.

Yet Prime Ministers are constantly setting up official enquiries into 'leaks'. These all have one thing in common, whatever the subject; the source of the leak is never discovered.

I became involved in my first 'leaks enquiry' in the mid-1960s when at the behest of the then Prime Minister, Harold Wilson, a man from security questioned a number of civil servants including myself, then in the Ministry of Housing and Local Government, about the leak of information in a Cabinet paper on housing policy. I was Private Secretary to Robert Mellish, a junior minister and responsible for the safe keeping of one of the copies of the Cabinet paper. All the civil servants questioned knew that the leak was the responsibility of the minister, Richard Crossman. None of us split on him. My last 'leaks enquiry' which concerned Cabinet papers on the European Monetary System is discussed in more detail in Chapter 9. As Prime Minister, James Callaghan expressed concern about various leaks, thought to have been occasioned by civil servants dealing with servicemen's pay, a Bonn summit and a letter and memorandum from Sir Douglas Wass, head of the Treasury, to Sir Peter Carey, Permanent Secretary at the Department of Industry, which related to government aid to industry and was thought to be electorally damaging to the Labour Party in the run up to the 1979 general election. (The suggestion that this document might have been stolen from the home of a civil servant can be discounted because civil servants are not allowed to take these documents home.)

On this latter 'leak' I put down three Written Questions to the Prime Minister on 7th March 1979. The enquiry revealed nothing or at least nothing that has been made public.

> To ask the Prime Minister, if he or any minister authorised the publication of the Wass memorandum concerning Government aid to industry; and if not, if he will make a statement.
>
> No. An enquiry has already been set up into the circumstances in which this document was made available for publication.

> To ask the Prime Minister, if he will set up an enquiry into the publication in the press of the Wass memorandum concerning Government aid to industry; and if he will instruct those conducting the enquiry to invite the editor of the *Guardian* and the *Guardian* journalist, Jane McLoughlin, to give evidence.
>
> An enquiry has been set up under the direction of an independent investigator who will be free to pursue his enquiries wherever he thinks it useful.

> To ask the Prime Minister, if he is satisfied with arrangements for the security of documents and vetting of personnel at the Treasury and the Department of Industry.
>
> Yes.

In view of other events at the Department of Industry described in Chapter five it would seem that the Prime Minister was too easily satisfied. The security of personnel and documents left much to be desired from 1974 to 1979.

One enquiry was, however, successful in tracking down the source of one leak, according to Tony Benn. He tells the amusing story of the 'leaks enquiry' set up by Harold Wilson into the disclosure, before any official announcement had been made, that Sir Don Ryder was to head the National Enterprise Board. The enquiry was placed in the hands of no less a person than the head of the civil service, Sir Douglas Allen. Sir Douglas's enquiry ended rather abruptly when he was told that the source of the leak was none other than the Prime Minister himself. He had been overheard by a Parliamentary Private Secretary and others talking loudly about the matter in the members' dining-room at the House of Commons.

I understand the general concern felt about leaking because it is a thoroughly unpleasant process which has little to do with open government. Leaks by their very nature are likely to contain slanted information, even misinformation. Cabinet meetings have barely ended at one o'clock on Thursdays before some Cabinet ministers (either directly or through others) and some senior civil servants are giving their interpretation of what happened and what should now be done. The press lobby in Parliament is always seeking to persuade ministers and their advisers to let them know what has happened. Often ministers need little or no persuasion. Most of the time I knew precisely which ministers and their aides were leaking which information to which journalists. Some ministers even took to the unpleasant practice of not only leaking secrets but in the process briefing against their colleagues. Tony Benn would never do that. Of course he usually gave an account of what went on in Cabinet to his advisers and myself because without such information we could not have discussed the issues sensibly with him. Even so he objected in principle to the disclosure of confidential information although I could not say that he never did it.

I can understand Prime Ministers disliking this process because it is essentially manipulative. But there one's sympathy must end because every commentator knows that all our institutions of government from the Prime Minister's office down act manipulatively. What is known as 'Downing Street guidance' which is a form of manipulative leaking pours out of the Press Offices of all Prime Ministers. When journalists phone up Members of Parliament and ask for comments on certain 'facts', the 'facts' have come to them in the form of 'Downing Street guidance'. Officially lobby correspondents are not supposed to admit to the existence of such guidance still less refer to it in any specific case. Yet on any serious issue I would ask the journalists what the guidance was. It might simply have been the Prime Minister's own version of what had happened in a Cabinet meeting; it might have been an attempt on the part of the Prime Minister to denigrate a colleague without the source being known; it might have been an attempt to assassinate the character of, say, the British Ambassador in America when there was a desire to replace him.

Newspaper readers would do well to reflect on the possible source of certain stories. A perceptive reader might be forgiven for believing sometimes that our reporters were psychic and in touch with each other by transcendental means. He might have found one Monday morning that all the newspapers were writing anti-Benn stories and all were implying that the source was the Prime Minister though none ever quoted the Prime Minister. The reality was not that the reporters were psychic nor that they had conspired together to make up the story but simply that they had been given 'Downing Street guidance'. The public may find the idea of a Prime Minister attacking a Cabinet colleague in this way as offensive as I do.

Mr (now Sir) Tom McCaffrey, a civil servant who was Mr Callaghan's Chief Press Officer, undoubtedly 'leaked' more information about government business than all the 635 M.P.s put together from 1976–79 (he would say that he was 'authorised' to give the information and to be fair it is part of the role of the Prime Minister's Press Officer to provide information either off the record or on an unattributable basis). Yet who outside the political cognoscenti has heard of him? His name was never linked to any of the stories and it was open to him to deny any story that appeared. Leaders of the Opposition do precisely the same thing and Mrs Thatcher employed Mr Derek Home for her manipulative business when in opposition. As Prime Minister she initially entrusted the task to Mr Henry James, a retired civil servant who was recalled on secondment from the Vickers Corporation. Now her Chief Press Officer is Mr Bernard Ingham, a former colleague of mine at the Department of Energy (see Chapter 4). The Leader of the Opposition is forced to leak directly to the press without the use of an intermediary since he or she meets the press lobby every Thursday for an unattributable and/or off-the-record briefing.

All post-war Prime Ministers would, I am sure, accept the doctrine on secrecy set out in paragraph 47 of the White Paper on the Reform of Section 2 of the Official Secrets Act:

> Legislation to put the Government under a statutory duty to disclose information on demand would have wide implications. First, resource costs. While there have been differing estimates of the cost of the U.S. legislation it is clear that it has been unexpectedly high. Perhaps more fundamentally, it is at least for consideration how far the analogy from foreign experience should be pressed. In order to achieve the reasonable objectives of open government in the British context, where the policies and decisions of the executive are under constant and vigilant scrutiny by Parliament and ministers are di-

> rectly answerable in Parliament, it may be neither necessary nor desirable to proceed to legislation of a kind which may be justifiable in other and often very different contexts – for instance, that of the United States.

Privately and publicly James Callaghan when Prime Minister made no secret of the fact that he was deeply suspicious of new-fangled ideas on 'open government'. Secrecy and discipline were concepts to be preferred. He would certainly agree with the views which Lord Peart, who was the Cabinet minister in charge of the civil service, expressed on behalf of Sir Ian Bancroft, the head of the civil service, when he replied in answer to a question from me at a hearing of the Expenditure Committee already quoted on page 17. 'You are asking me about matters which you say are secret and were discussed by Cabinet committees. I cannot reveal this. There are some people who would like to have it open, but I think it would be crazy.'

I doubt if Margaret Thatcher would dissent from the use of the adjective 'crazy' either. Against this background no one can be surprised that a Prime Minister will go so far as to deny Members of Parliament the findings of work done by the Central Policy Review Staff on unemployment which suggested that unemployment could, if policies were unchanged, rise to several millions by 1990. I asked the Prime Minister about this work and so did the Conservative M.P. and former minister, Maurice Macmillan. Mr Callaghan replied on 25th May 1979:

> As part of its normal remit to examine issues of major concern to the Government the C.P.R.S. has over the past months undertaken some work on unemployment, but this has not included a report. The detailed figures on unemployment and the labour market which formed the factual background to the C.P.R.S. work are widely available through Department of Employment publications, and a full survey was published in November 1977 by the Manpower Services Commission in its document *Review and Plan 1977*.

The Prime Minister's reply was little more than a play on the words 'report', 'study', and 'findings'.

I cannot say I was surprised, even when on 31st October 1978 I turned up to speak to a conference at Walton Hall near Stratford-on-Avon and heard Mr Jack Peel, the E.E.C. Director of Industrial Relations, talking publicly about the details of the C.P.R.S. work which the Prime Minister was withholding from Members of Parliament and, again, from most of his Cabinet colleagues. Incidentally Mr Peel, who was and is a European bureaucrat, called at the conference for the immediate formation of a coalition government 'not permanently but for a period of two to three or four or five years to deal with our economic problems'. Quite who these European civil servants are accountable to is not clear.

The present head of the civil service, Sir Ian Bancroft, and most of his colleagues are as much against open government as was James Callaghan and as is the present Prime Minister, Margaret Thatcher. Sir Ian expressed his own views and those of his colleagues in January of 1979 in a detailed paper to the Cabinet sub-committee which was considering the attitude of the Government to the Official Information Bill which was presented to Parliament by the Liberal M.P. Clement Freud, and given a Second Reading on 19th January 1979. The civil service response presented at the Cabinet sub-committee by Lord Peart was a lengthy denunciation of the Bill. In particular it wanted to destroy the heart of the Bill by removing the 'right' of the citizen to know. In their paper the civil servants expressed themselves particularly worried that they might lose their 'anonymity and neutrality' if the right were granted and if it became known what advice they were giving to ministers. Their so-called 'neutrality' is a concept discussed in Chapter 6. The document was described to me by one Cabinet minister on 23rd January as 'amazingly negative', yet 'so instructive that it ought to be printed'.

One former head of the civil service, to be fair, has taken a different attitude and since he comes in for some criticism in this book I think I ought to set out his views. The civil servant concerned is Lord Armstrong. He argued (in *The Times*, 30th June 1975) that open government, in the sense that a Government 'publishes the things it is thinking about and invites comment before taking a definite decision', is desirable. He favours 'telling the public more about the bases of its policies and the considerations behind future policies'. He calls for an extension of the Green Paper discussion documents as one way of doing that and suggests that the names of senior civil servants should be printed in the margins of Green Papers alongside policy analysis for which they are responsible so that they could be identified and questioned by Select Committees of the House of Commons and by the public. After a period of open discussion 'the Government would preserve the right to reach its final decision in strictest confidence with its officials'. He blames both politicians and civil servants for the current obsession with secrecy. The sting, however, in what seem sensible proposals lies in the tail when he suggests that politicians should present the public not with manifestos at election time but with Green Paper discussion documents. It is disappointing that in the end Lord Armstrong's proposals for open government add up to little more than a means of enhancing bureaucratic power at the expense of political power and authority. This last point apart, few Permanent

Secretaries in Whitehall today would agree with any of his proposals and no Prime Ministers have done so.

As potent as secrecy in sustaining Prime Ministerial power is patronage. Patronage corrupts. It corrupts the patron as well as those patronised. Lord Hailsham likened the modern Prime Minister in the exercise of his patronage to a spider weaving his web. I have in my mind's eye two images which tell me more about patronage than anything else. The first is of Prime Minister, Harold Wilson, walking through the voting lobbies in the House of Commons surrounded by a seething mass of sychophants so that the Prime Minister himself could not be distinguished from the blob which seemed to be moving down the lobby. The second is of Harold Wilson walking quite alone down the same lobby after he had resigned as Prime Minister, the sychophants having taken themselves off elsewhere in search of another patron.

The following tables set out the bare statistics of Prime Ministerial patronage.

CABINET AND NON-CABINET MINISTERS (1945–1979)

Prime Minister	Period in Office (Years)	Cabinet Ministers appointed	Non-Cabinet Ministers appointed (including paid Whips)
Attlee	6¼	50	188
Churchill	3½	33	118
Eden (3)	1¾	12	42
Macmillan (3)	6¾	62	224
Douglas-Home (3)	1	11	27
Wilson ('64–70)	5¾	73	280
Heath	3¾	41	183
Wilson ('74–76)	2	27	123
Callaghan (3)	3	35	117

Notes

1. The figures above have been calculated from the lists of ministries in *British Political Facts 1900 – 1975* by David Butler and Anne Sloman with later information up to Callaghan's defeat in May 1979.
2. The figures are derived from a straight count of names in Butler and Sloman's lists. It follows that they relate to *appointments* not to *different persons*. To take two examples from Wilson's 1964–70 period of office: Michael Stewart is counted five times as a

Cabinet Minister (First Secretary, Economic Affairs, Foreign Office (twice), Education); John Stonehouse is counted six times as a non-Cabinet Minister (Parliamentary Secretary, Aviation, Under-Secretary Colonial Office, Minister Aviation, Minister of State Technology, Postmaster General, Minister Post & Telecommunications).
3. Attlee, Churchill, Wilson (1964 and 1974) and Heath formed entirely new Governments and one can make a straightforward count of appointments they made. But Eden and Douglas-Home took over going concerns, as it were, and did not make very many changes. Macmillan also took over a going concern, but his changes and appointments on taking office in January 1957 were much more drastic. Technically perhaps Eden and Douglas-Home reappointed all those who stayed in post. But, following the arrangement in Butler and Sloman, I have not counted these and have only counted changed appointments to posts in their period of office. But I *have* counted all appointments made by Macmillan, including those who stayed in the same posts when he took over (see Butler and Sloman). I have treated Callaghan, who took over Wilson's administration, in the same manner as I have treated Macmillan.
4. Non-Cabinet ministers include paid Whips in both Houses.
5. The length of period in office is of general relevance to succeeding tables.

Chairmen of Nationalised Industries (1945–1979)

Prime Minister	Chairmen of Nationalised Industries appointed in period of Office
Attlee	14
Churchill	5
Eden	3
Macmillan	16
Douglas-Home	2
Wilson (both periods of office)	24
Heath	21
Callaghan	16

Notes
1. The number of appointments has been calculated from Butler and Sloman, with later information.
2. The authorities and boards covered are:
Defunct boards: B.O.A.C., B.E.A., British South American Airways; British Electricity Authority; Gas Council; British Transport Board; Transport Holdings; Iron and Steel Corporation; Rolls-Royce Ltd.
Nationalised industries – Treasury definition: British Airways Board; British Airports Authority; Electricity Council; Central Electricity Generating Board; North of Scotland Hydro-Electric Board; South of Scotland Electricity Board; National Coal Board; British Gas Corporation; British Railways Board; British Transport Docks Board;

British Waterways Board; National Bus Company; National Freight Corporation; Scottish Transport Group; British Steel Corporation; Post Office Corporation; British National Oil Corporation; British Aerospace; British Shipbuilders.
Others: UK Atomic Energy Authority; London Transport Executive; National Enterprise Board.
3. In some cases where a chairman has been designated long before vesting date the Government has in the meantime changed. This happened in the case of two new nationalised industries – British Aerospace with a vesting date in January 1977 but Lord Beswick was designated chairman in 1975 and British Shipbuilders which was vested in July 1977 but its chairman Sir Anthony Griffin was designated in 1975. However, on the basis that all the dates given in Butler and Sloman are dates of actual appointment, so that similar possible discrepancies are not apparent, I thought I should also place these two appointments in Mr Callaghan's period of office.
4. I have not counted the reappointment of Sir Derek Ezra of the N.C.B. in June 1976 as a new appointment.

ROYAL COMMISSIONS (1945–1979)

Prime Minister	Chairmen of Royal Commissions appointed
Attlee	7
Churchill	4
Eden	1
Macmillan	5[a]
Douglas-Home	1
Wilson (both periods of office)	16[b] [c]
Heath	1
Callaghan	3

Notes
[a] Includes National Incomes Commission
[b] Includes National Board for Prices and Incomes
[c] Includes two new standing Commissions: Environmental Pollution and Distribution of Income and Wealth.
2. The number of chairmen of Royal Commissions appointed in each Prime Ministerial period had been calculated from the list in Butler and Sloman with additional later information. *NOTES*: only one chairman had been counted for each Commission (e.g. the substitution of Kilbrandon for Crowther has not been counted). Long standing Commissions – such as those on Historical Monuments or Fine Arts – have not been included.
3. The Royal Commission on the N.H.S. was appointed in May 1976 but both it and the chairman's name were announced in January 1976. I have therefore put it in Wilson's administration.

Peerages (1895–1979)

		Creation of Peerages						
		New Hereditary Creations	Life Peers Law	Life Peers Other	Advanced in Rank	Total	Duration of Ministry (Years)	Average Annual Creations[2]
Salisbury	1895–02	42	2	..	n.s.	44	7	6
Balfour	1902–05	17	1	..	5	23	3½	7
Campbell-Bannerman	1905–08	20	1	..	..	21	2½	9
Asquith	1908–15	61	6	..	13	80	7	11
Asquith	1915–16	17	..	..	2	19	1½	13
Lloyd George	1916–22	90	1	..	25	116	5¾	20
Bonar Law	1922–23	3	..	..	..	3	½	6
Baldwin	1923–24	7	1	..	1	9	¾	12
MacDonald	1924	4	..	..	1	5	¾	7
Baldwin	1924–29	37	5	..	10	52	4½	12
MacDonald	1929–31	18	2	..	..	20	2¼	9
MacDonald	1931–35	43	1	..	6	50	3¾	13
Baldwin	1935–37	27	2	..	5	34	2	17
Chamberlain	1937–40	18	2	..	4	24	3	8
Churchill	1940–45	60	2	..	9	71	5¼	14
Attlee	1945–51	75	11	..	8	94	6¼	15
Churchill	1951–55	31	2	..	6	39	3½	11
Eden	1955–57	19	..	..	3	22	1¾	13
Macmillan	1957–63	42	9	47	6	104	6¾	15
Douglas-Home	1963–64	14	1	16	1	32	1	32
Wilson	1964–70	6	2	152	1	161	5¾	28
Heath	1970–74	..	4	30	..	34	3½	10
Wilson	1974–76	..	3	79	..	82	2	41
Callaghan	1976–79	..	2	58	..	60	3	20

Notes

1. These figures can be misleading as dissolution honours created by an outgoing Ministry fall, in fact, into the following Ministry. For example, of Wilson's new creations six were those of Sir Douglas-Home.

2. The table of peerage creations above is from Butler and Sloman. I have corrected an obvious printing error in the line relating to Macmillan, and have added a line for Wilson's second period as P.M. To maintain comparability, the added Wilson figures *include* Heath's resignation honours but *exclude* Wilson's own resignation honours (May 1976) which fall into Callaghan figures. There have been no hereditary peerages since October 1964 except for the six in Douglas-Home's final lists which technically (see above) fall into the Wilson period.

KNIGHTHOODS

New Years Honours List	Knights Bachelor in P.M.'s List
1949 (Attlee)	30
1953 (Churchill)	44
1956 (Eden)	32
1959 (Macmillan)	29
1964 (Douglas-Home)	30
1967 (Wilson)	31
1972 (Heath)	34
1975 (Wilson)	34
1977 (Callaghan)	29

Number of New Year and Birthday Honours Lists for which each P.M. was responsible

Attlee	12
Churchill	7
Eden	4
Macmillan	13
Douglas-Home	2
Wilson ('64–70)	12
Heath	7
Wilson ('74–76)	4
Callaghan	8

Notes

1. What I have done in these tables is to look at a *sample* New Years Honours List in the period of each P.M. From this list I have counted the number of *plain knights bachelor in the Prime Minister's List* (only). This seems to me the best measure of Prime Ministerial patronage; it excludes, for example, Foreign Office, services and overseas knighthoods. It also excludes appointments to the orders of knighthood which appear in the P.M.'s list. These are the knighthoods which 'come up with the rations' for Permanent Secretaries, etc., etc. If one multiplied the sample figures by the number of New Year and Birthday lists for which each P.M. was responsible, one would probably not be very far out, although the likelihood would be that the resultant figures are *too low*. This is because there are other lists (e.g. dissolutions and resignations) and odd knighthoods at different times (e.g. to newly appointed Law Officers before March 1974).

BARONETCIES (1945–1979)

Period of Office	New Baronets entered on Roll
Attlee	13[a]
Churchill	27
Eden	14
Macmillan	50
Douglas-Home	11
Wilson ('64–70)	3[b]
Heath	nil
Wilson ('74–76)	nil
Callaghan	nil

Notes
1. [a] Five of these were Churchill nominations of Conservative M.P.s; one was to the Speaker's secretary; the rest were to retiring Lord Mayors of London as was then customary.
[b] All three were Douglas-Home appointments to Conservative M.P.s. No baronetcies have been created after 1964.
2. The Home Office has supplied the above figures. These are by date of entry to the role of baronets. Thus (as with peerages) the figures falling within the time span of a P.M.'s period of office are not *entirely* attributable to the P.M. See notes above.

The extent of the Prime Minister's patronage is enough to make any democrat shudder. That one man should have so much power ought to be as worrying to him as it is to the rest of us.

The Prime Minister personally appoints every member of the Cabinet to office – nowadays some twenty or so people. He appoints all the junior ministers to office – some eighty or so people. Perhaps more important he is responsible for the appointment of all the heads of government departments (i.e. Permanent Secretaries). Few people seem to be aware that heads of government departments are neither appointed nor dismissed by their ministers. Technically the appointments are made by the head of the civil service but this is only done with the agreement of the Prime Minister. The importance of this is that all Permanent Secretaries know that their first allegiance is to the Prime Minister and the little satellite bureaucracies that surround him, and not to their ministers. Equally important the Prime Minister has a major say in and veto over the appointment of the chairmen of the nationalised industries who between them control a sizeable slice of the Gross National Product. The sponsoring minister makes the appointment after consultation with the Prime Minister. Therefore the chairmen of these industries know, like the Permanent Secretaries, that their tone and style and policies cannot diverge too far from those of the Prime Minister. As if that is not enough, he is similarly consulted and has similar powers in relation to the setting up of all Royal Commissions and the appointment of their chairmen. In his booklet, *The Case for a Constitutional Premiership*, referred to earlier, Tony Benn also refers to the power of the Prime Minister to appoint or be consulted about the appointment of ambassadors, chiefs of staff and the heads of M.I.5 and M.I.6: and the influence he can have over the names put forward for the 31 public boards in existence, or the 252 fringe bodies which themselves employ 184,000 people and spend £2,367,000,000 a year as recorded in the Civil Services Department Record published in 1978. The way in which some of these people are appointed is somewhat complicated and is discussed further in Chapter 6.

So far as security is concerned disclosures in 1979 concerning Sir Anthony Blunt, a former M.I.5. man, Surveyor of the Queen's Pictures and Russian spy who was granted immunity from prosecution in 1964, called into question the precise relationship between the Prime Minister and those who work for M.I.5. In theory the Director General of M.I.5. is directly responsible for his actions to the Home Secretary whilst the Prime Minister has overall responsibility for both the security and intelligence services. The affair also raised a number of constitutional and moral issues concerning the probity of the conduct of the monarch, Queen Elizabeth II, and her advisers in allowing Sir Anthony to retain his knighthood and royal appointment after it was known that he was a traitor. Secrecy and a lack of accountability were again dominant issues.

The Prime Minister also has a role to play in the appointment of some of the judges and the bishops of the Church of England. Significantly there has not been a Christian Socialist in the archbishopric at Canterbury despite the fact that Labour has governed for some seventeen years in the post-war era.

The Prime Minister's role in relation to appointments in the established Church has changed recently. Some months before Dr Coggan's retirement as Archbishop of Canterbury (January 1980) the Church of England set up a new Church Appointments Commission which chose two candidates and sent their names to the Prime Minister in order of preference, when the Queen's approval as 'Supreme Governor of the Church' was sought. Even in an age of civil scepticism Archbishops can be presumed to have some influence in setting values and standards. Dr Robert Runcie, the man chosen to succeed Coggan, once gave a sympathetic address to the Christian Socialist movement in the House of Commons. Paradoxically Dr Coggan, considered evangelical or lowbrow in ecclesiastical terms, preached a high Tory message for five years. His congregation on the council estates may not have been listening but it is likely that he reinforced prejudices in the suburbs of southern England. Dr Ramsay, one of Coggan's predecessors, told me over dinner on the eve of the Durham Miners' Gala on 14th July 1978 that the Lib-Lab pact, 1977–78, had provided Britain with the best Government it could have had in the circumstances of the time. He expressed himself genuinely pleased with its work. Disestablishment has not been a burning political issue for some time but it can hardly stay off the political agenda for ever as the formal relationship between the Church of England and the state fails to accord with the reality of disbelief.

The Prime Minister further controls the honours list and the existence of an advisory committee is not always a guarantee that favourite sons or dubious characters will not receive the highest honours. This control is not unimportant politically. It has been used and no doubt will continue to be used to solidify press support. Hence part of the reason why many papers support Prime Ministers personally but are not quite so keen on supporting the policies of the political parties they represent. We can now expect to see honours for the proprietors, editors and other members of certain newspaper groups from the present Prime Minister. The same happens with companies. In short, back-scratching is an institutionalised feature of the British constitution. In addition the honours system is a value system that tells the public that certain people are more desirable than others. A managing director of a firm that exports fruit machines has, for example, a far better chance of getting an honour than a nurse, a top civil servant a far better chance than a surgeon. Senior civil servants of course, get honours from the Prime Minister automatically however bad they are and just as there is hierarchy of tables, carpets and pictures in Whitehall so there is a hierarchy of honours. (Tony Benn tells the story of how he lured the Permanent Secretary at the Department of Industry into letting him take a picture of him wearing his medals and chains.) These things are important to civil servants. Finally the Prime Minister is responsible for the appointment of Life Peers. This is an extremely important weapon which enables him to retain in the House of Commons the support of ageing and sometimes bitter politicians who look forward to retirement in the House of Lords. The House of Lords can also be an attractive proposition for younger and more thrusting spirits.

Most, and maybe all, post-war Prime Ministers have used their power of patronage in the appointment of Cabinet ministers, ministers of state and Parliamentary under-secretaries partly to achieve political balance across the spectra which make up both the Conservative and Labour Parties, partly to get a geographical balance and partly to create administrations in their own image. As Prime Minister James Callaghan was particularly assiduous in this respect and in rewarding those who served him well behind the scenes, which was where he operated at his best. Mrs Thatcher's first set of appointments to office may not have been in her own social image in that twenty-four ministers are old Etonians and some of them are landed gentry by birth while she went to a grammar school and is the daughter of a grocer, but it has resulted in a Cabinet which expresses her own social and political views fairly well. Indeed it is interesting to note that once she had been elected Leader of the Conservative Party, the views of many of her more liberal frontbench colleagues seemed to move to the right towards her own views. It seems the promise of patronage was enough to do the trick.

The problem though is not one of personalities but of institutions and conventions. A Prime Minister who can make or break a hundred politicians from the majority party can in effect make or break in normal times just under one-third of the Members of Parliament in that party. If we assume that for every one person holding ministerial office there is one challenger then some two hundred Members of Parliament, or just under two-thirds of the majority party, come potentially within the Prime Minister's patronage. If thirty to forty Parliamentary Private Secretaries are added to this list then the number of backbench Members of Parliament in the majority party free of patronage or potential patronage is not large. The executive is largely being scrutinised by people who want to be part of the executive and who know that one man holds the key. These people know too the views of that one man. I am not suggesting for one moment that everyone in Parliament is caught up in gravy-train politics for I know that there are many outstanding men for whom office is not the main goal. Moreover the desire for office seems to me to be a good rather than a bad ambition in a politician. But there is a problem and it is that the desire for office, the desire to contribute to effective decision-taking should not be dependent on the whims of one person.

To take on the job of Prime Minister is to take on an extremely arduous and difficult task. Performing the role of a statesman in international affairs – and Prime Ministers, as James Callaghan never ceased to remind the Parliamentary Labour Party, effectively make international treaties single-handed because it is out of the question for Parliament not to sanction them – and dealing with crises which constantly crop up in government as well as presiding over Cabinet meetings would, one might have thought, have created enough tensions without building up unnecessary ones.

Yet most recent Prime Ministers, through the exercise of patronage, have cut themselves off from many of their Parliamentary colleagues and created quite unnecessary tensions for themselves. There is abundant evidence that this happened with Wilson, Heath and Callaghan. It is not long before Prime Ministers begin discovering challenges to their power real or imagined. It is not long before they begin to personalise situations which should not be personalised. They often end up by using the ultimate patronage threat – the threat to dissolve Parliament, a decision which rests in all but the most unusual cases with the Prime Minister rather than the monarch. Dissolution, of course, not only threatens the jobs of all ministers (though they stay in post in between the date of the dissolution of Parliament and the election) but also the jobs of M.P.s as M.P.s.

I personally heard James Callaghan threaten resignation (with an implied dissolution threat) on two occasions at meetings of the Parliamentary Labour Party and according to colleagues of mine in the Cabinet he did the same thing there on several occasions; according to other sources he also threatened it in order to get his way once or twice at meetings of the National Executive Committee of the Labour Party. On 2nd April 1979 he threatened to resign over the contents of the election manifesto. One would imagine that such threats would be the subject of diminishing returns but apparently not.

I remember Callaghan at his most brutal at a meeting of the Parliamentary Labour Party in Westminster Hall on 24th January 1978 when the P.L.P. met to discuss the proposed guillotine motion on E.E.C. Direct Elections. The Leader of the House, Michael Foot, began the meeting by saying, almost in tears, that loyalty to the Prime Minister came before loyalty to party and Parliamentary democracy. Michael Foot is one of our great democrats and Parliamentarians for whom my admiration remains undiminished. I am sure he did not mean what he was implying. I only record the point to show what pressures Cabinet ministers are under and how they can reduce themselves to ashes. And then – it was 5.50 p.m. according to my diary when he rose to speak – the Prime Minister said that he did not care how M.P.s voted at the meeting because he was going to go through with the guillotine motion (i.e. a time-table motion to limit debate when a Bill is going through Parliament, often used when M.P.s are suspected of filibustering) whether they liked it or not. He made it absolutely clear that not only did he have the power to dissolve Parliament but also that democracy as we used to know it had to give way to government by trust in the Prime Minister based on an understanding of the brutal use to which patronage could be put. It was a haughty, distasteful, unnecessary performance. On occasion such as this the payroll vote (i.e. ministers) is expected to turn up and support the Prime Minister. Given the numbers that usually attend such meetings a good payroll turn-out will usually win the day. On this occasion some eighty to ninety of them turned up to sustain the motion to truncate the debate against every decision taken by every organisation in the Labour Party. It was a sad but telling moment.

Besides these happenings the Prime Minister's attempt to use his powers of patronage in Cabinet seemed almost prosaic. On 16th February 1978 the Cabinet took a decision that North Sea oil revenues should not be channelled through a new special development fund and used for industrial and/or social purposes but would go into the general Exchequer account like any other revenues. As Secretary of State for Energy, Tony Benn had met some seven regional and interest groups of Labour M.P.s at meetings organised by myself at which from left to right across the Labour Party there was agreement that a special fund was sensible and would prevent the dissipation of the revenues – which has subsequently happened. Denis Healey was opposed to the idea in Cabinet although there were no technical (i.e. Public Expenditure Survey Committee or Public Accounts Committee) objections. His opposition stemmed from the fact that a special development fund would have taken away some of his powers to control expenditure. The Chancellor also argued that the revenues were already committed through P.E.S.C. exercises. When the issue had first come up in Cabinet a week previously the discussion suggested that the Cabinet was evenly split but the Prime Minister had summed up the meeting against setting up a fund. But at the Cabinet meeting on 16th February only three people – the Secretary of State for Energy (Tony Benn), the Secretary of State for Scotland (Bruce Millan) and the Secretary of State for the Environment (Peter Shore) supported the idea of a fund. The rest put their hands on their hearts and said that although it was a good idea it was not a practical situation. It is difficult not to believe that an understanding of the use to which patronage could be put had changed some minds in between the two meetings. In giving the Cabinet two bites of the cherry the Prime Minister was exercising his undoubted right as chairman of the committee not to allow a decision to be taken until he thought that the moment was appropriate.

An even more dramatic switch in attitudes on the part of even more Cabinet ministers arising out of an understanding of the use to which patronage could be put arose over Cabinet discussions in November and December 1976 over whether or not the Government were prepared to accept the terms and conditions of a loan from the International Monetary Fund: or, as some would put it, were prepared to accept the terms and conditions which the Treasury had asked the I.M.F. to impose. When the Cabinet first discussed the issue at their Thursday meeting the discussion showed that an overwhelming majority of its members were not prepared to accept the loan if it meant a major shift in economic policy involving substantial public expenditure cuts. No decision was taken at that meeting. Over the ensuing weekend an arm-twisting exercise took place and on behalf of the Prime Minister, Harold Lever, Chancellor of the Duchy of Lancaster, used his persuasive powers. When the Cabinet reconvened after a weekend of some excitement it decided to go ahead with the loan from the I.M.F. and accept the conditions that would be attached to it. Only five ministers, referred to by one of my colleagues as the 'magnificent five' made it crystal clear that they opposed what was being done. They were Peter Shore, Stan Orme, Michael Foot, Albert Booth and Tony Benn. Everyone that I have spoken to is agreed that the first man to change his position once the Prime Minister had made his own views clear was the Man of Principle, the Rt. Hon. Tony Crosland (see also Chapter 9).

Of course a good case can be made for supporting the Prime Minister in a crisis. If he signals to the international monetary world and to international statesmen that certain decisions are likely to be taken then terrible consequences *might* flow (e.g. a run on the pound) if those decisions are not taken. The survival of the Government might be at stake. That could have been uppermost in the minds of some members of the Cabinet. But it would be naive to assume that all members of the Cabinet adopted this high-minded approach and that none of them were conscious of the power of patronage. Moreover, it is possible to ask if it is right or democratic for Prime Ministers to signal Cabinet decisions in advance. Again in this instance the Prime Minister had used the power that any committee chairman has to put off the taking of a decision until he was sure of getting the decision that he wanted.

The Prime Minister's power of patronage in relation to top civil servants and especially Permanent Secretaries which was touched upon in Chapter 1 stems from his wider responsibilities in relation to the organisation of government. The Prime Minister is solely responsible for the structure of his administration. He can reshuffle not only ministers but ministries. He is responsible for deciding whether or not to have super-ministries run by overlords such as the old Department of Trade and Industry or whether to break down ministries and have a Department of Trade, a Department of Industry and a Department of Energy. In deciding which style to adopt he may be concerned with efficiency or he may be concerned with the power that attaches to ministries of certain kinds and their ministers. The Prime Minister is also responsible not merely for agreeing to the appointment of individual Permanent Secretaries; he is the only minister who has power to change the organisation and structure of a department. A Permanent

Secretary in a department has this power too but a departmental minister does not although some ministers and Permanent Secretaries work very closely together. It is clear that as Prime Minister James Callaghan intended to retain his powers in this field. Paragraph 83 of the Government Observations on the Expenditure Committee Report on the Civil Service (Cmnd 7117) stated:

> Within the framework of the collective responsibility of the Cabinet as a whole, the minister in charge of a department is responsible to Parliament for its policies, its organisation and its management. The staff of a department are Crown servants, the conditions of whose employment are governed by many factors, some a matter of law, some long established conventions and practical arrangements, endorsed either explicitly or implicitly by successive Governments. Paragraph 143 of the committee's report attributes to civil servants powers which they do not have; it also detracts from the role of the Prime Minister. The Prime Minister decides senior appointments and machinery of government questions himself, after consultation as appropriate with his colleagues and the head of the home civil service. Some major questions (e.g. the hiving off of bodies or the creation of new ones, and pay policy) are normally decided by ministers collectively. Collective Cabinet authority also governs the expenditure limits and staffing controls which are exercised by the central departments and to which the committee rightly attaches importance. None of these are matters on which civil servants take the final decisions, although their advice will normally be sought when appropriate.

A careful reading of this paragraph underlines what everyone who is conversant with running a department knows, that whilst it is the departmental minister who carried the can in Parliament when things go wrong, effective power over the organisation of departments lies with the Prime Minister, the head of the civil service and Permanent Secretaries.

The inability of ministers to appoint or dismiss Permanent Secretaries is a source of constant friction in Whitehall. If a minister wishes to get rid of a Permanent Secretary with whom he cannot work, whether it be for personal or political reasons, the issue goes to the Prime Minister via the head of the civil service to see if the Prime Minister would prefer to get rid of the minister. Permanent Secretaries know this and most survive attempts to get rid of them. Ministers are the more dispensable. Writing about this subject in a book on the fall of the Labour Government 1974–79 (*What Went Wrong – Whitehall's Short Way with Democracy*) Michael Meacher M.P., a minister in that administration, has this to say:

> But perhaps the most serious form of exposure to dependence on Whitehall lies in the obligation on a minister to work through a Permanent Secretary and senior officials whom he did not choose (and, in some cases, certainly never would have chosen) and who may have determinedly different political views about objectives or priorities. And it is exceedingly hard to remove such a person (though John Silkin's influence led to Freddie Kearn's departure from the Ministry of Agriculture, Fisheries and Food, Barbara Castle failed to remove Thomas Padmore from the Ministry of Transport when all the other Permanent Secretaries threatened to resign if she persisted).

Lord Pannell (Charles Pannell, at one time Minister of Public Building and Works) is convinced that friction between himself and his Permanent Secretary, Sir Antony Part, which came to the notice of the Prime Minister, Harold Wilson, was one of the reasons behind his political demise. Robert Mellish, also one time minister at the Ministry of Public Building and Works as well as my former boss, told me that he could never have worked for long with Sir Antony Part because of a clash of styles. Fortunately for Mr Mellish Sir Antony moved on. He reappeared as the Permanent Secretary at the Department of Industry in 1974. Unfortunately, the Parliamentary Under Secretary of State Michael Meacher, the Minister of State Eric Heffer, and the Secretary of State for Industry Tony Benn, all of them friends and colleagues of mine, found it difficult to appreciate Sir Antony's virtues. There can be no doubt that there was more sympathy between the Prime Minister and Sir Antony than there was between the Secretary of State and Sir Antony although theoretically the three of them were agreed on policies hammered out in a Cabinet sub-committee and in Cabinet (see Chapters 4 and 5).

Prime Ministers seem peculiarly sensitive about the advice they receive over the appointments of top civil servants as the correspondence below between myself and James Callaghan when he was Prime Minister shows:

> 5th March 1979
>
> Dear Jim,
>
> Civil Service appointments
>
> Conduct of top civil servants
>
> As you know, there is now considerable speculation in Whitehall and Westminster about changes in top civil service appointments. Rumour has it that Wass at the Treasury is to be replaced by Armstrong from the Home Office; that Hunt at the Cabinet Office is

to be replaced by Palliser from the F.O.; and that Palliser's job will go to Maitland, our man in Brussels.

I would not expect you to comment on these rumours, but would like to point out that changes along the lines outlined would in the view of many result in too many people who take too uncritical a view of the E.E.C. occupying top jobs. This could be particularly unfortunate at a time when there is a growing economic consensus that we may have to challenge some of the fundamental rules of the E.E.C. if we are to see our way through the serious economic crisis which we are in. I would hope that you would bear this in mind when making or endorsing any new appointments. Before leaving this subject I would be grateful too if you could let me know – 1. whether Mrs Thatcher, the Leader of the Opposition, would be consulted about such appointments, and 2. whether the Cabinet or the departmental ministers concerned would be consulted.

The other point I wish to raise is that of the conduct of top civil servants. Again, as you will be aware, there was recently a leak of civil service documents, apparently by civil servants and apparently carried out with the object of damaging the Labour Government. I am of course referring to the Wass/Carey correspondence. This is not the first leak of this kind. In these circumstances I would be grateful if you could let me know what action you are taking (the culprits will, I imagine, be sacked) and what steps you have in mind to make top civil servants more accountable to ministers and more respectful of the democratic process.

Best wishes,
Yours,
Brian

The Prime Minister's reply read:

14th March 1979

Dear Brian,

Thank you for your letter of 5th March.

You are right. I certainly have no intention of commenting on the rumours. But I am well aware of the importance of appointments to senior civil service jobs and of the appropriate extent of consultation. You may be sure that I also know what factors to take into account when approving such appointments.

As far as the leak of official information is concerned, you will know from my answers to your Questions on 7th March that an enquiry under the direction of an independent investigator has been set up. I have no plans to change the existing rules governing the work and conduct of senior civil servants.

Yours sincerely,
Jim Callaghan

Subsequently it was Sir Robert Armstrong who took over from Sir John Hunt as Secretary to the Cabinet. Mrs Margaret Thatcher made the appointment on the recommendation of the official committee on senior appointments consisting of the head of the civil service, the Secretary of the Cabinet, and the Permanent Secretary at the Treasury.

Similar considerations and similar problems arise where the appointment of chairmen of nationalised industries is concerned. No two people in public life have ever been on better terms than Tony Benn and Sir Francis Tombs (a man whom I personally hold in very high regard), the Chairman of the Electricity Council. In temperament and style they were very much alike – calm, rational, determined. When they argued the argument was real and born of mutual respect. Yet I remember one strange incident recorded in my diary on 8th November 1977 in the middle of the unofficial power workers' dispute and rota cuts and black-outs. It should be remembered that the Prime Minister in the E.Y.P. (Economic Strategy) Cabinet sub-committee and the Chancellor were adopting a tough confrontational stance with the workers who were on an unofficial work to rule. At a meeting with the Central Electricity Generating Board and the Electricity Council Tony Benn made it clear that in his view the Board should pay the men for the work done whilst on their work to rule despite their inclination not to. The diary note takes up the story:

> Tony was over deferential to the unions and for a while none too explicit to the Board. Eventually he got it out and said that it would be incomprehensible to the public if the issue was not settled because the Board wanted reprisals. If collective responsibility did not allow him to offer the men his 'sympathy' he nevertheless as the Secretary of State responsible for securing electricity supplies wanted 'speed'. And so he called for a decision by 12 noon. He then issued a brief statement for the department's Press Office to put out to the press saying that 'there were no problems for the government' just to make it clear where the responsibility lay . . .
>
> Immediately the meeting was over someone must have telephoned one of the Downing Street offices because within minutes of the end of the meeting the Prime Minister was like a cat on hot bricks. When Tony went to see Jim he, Jim, knew everything and he reiterated that he wanted a hard line adopted. This view seemed almost by metaphysical process to communicate itself back to the

> C.E.G.B. and the Electricity Council. For when Tombs returned at 12 noon he curtly told the Secretary of State to mind his own business, asked him to avoid making damaging press statements and said that the workers who had been warned would get no money at all. He clearly could not have adopted this line without knowing he had the support of No. 10. He knew it and so did we . . .
>
> As Tombs left the room I said to him 'I hope you know what you're doing. For your sake I hope the men go back because this is now your go-slow and the blame will lie with you if they don't!' He was absolutely confident that the men would go back and said so . . .
>
> Effectively what had happened was that political control expertly set up in the department through his junior minister John Cunningham and his advisers was being beaten by political control from Downing Street.

In this dispute, despite instructions to the contrary from the Prime Minister's Office, Joe Ashton M.P. for Bassetlaw was used as a go-between because he had direct contact with the workers involved. Without him the minister would have been devoid of any sensible information with which to make judgments and take decisions.

The Prime Minister's powers in relation to Royal Commissions operate in a rather different way. So far as I know, chairmen of Royal Commissions are not constantly or at all being briefed by Downing Street though some may know what is expected of them just as some chairmen of public enquiries know what is expected of them. The setting up of a Royal Commission is a useful adjunct to Prime Ministerial and ministerial power in that it enables decisions to be put off while the commission sits and often while the Reports fester after they have been produced. The Royal Commissions on the press, industrial democracy and the City, two of them set up by Harold Wilson as Prime Minister, the other chaired by him, have all been Prime Ministerial devices designed to alleviate the need for the Government to take action. It is not as though, as some people say, they substitute pragmatism for ideas. They often grow, live and die as if they have an existence independent of the political process.

The Prime Minister has a number of powers closely linked to his powers of patronage, some of them important in themselves, some of them not so important but of interest when taken together with all his other powers. The Prime Minister controls ministerial visits at home and abroad and says who can and cannot accompany ministers. He clears ministerial broadcasts and has the power of veto over such broadcasts. He clears ministerial articles in newspapers. He says which ministers shall appear on television when there are by-elections although strictly speaking this is a Party matter not a government matter.

More important the Prime Minister has quite illegitimately (the expression is certainly justified in the case of the Labour Party) taken over control of party political television and radio broadcasts. In the Labour Party such broadcasts should lie wholly within the prerogative of party and come under the jurisdiction of the National Executive Committee. Although the N.E.C. has sub-committees concerned with publicity and propaganda, somewhere and somehow the convention has grown up that party political broadcasts now come within the prerogative of the Prime Minister when Labour is in power.

When a Labour Government is in power there is inevitably tension between the N.E.C. which is the conscience of the grassroots of the party and between the Government which is constantly having to respond to events and which may for good or ill be out of sympathy with the radicalism of the grassroots. It is not my intention to go in any detail into the important arguments concerned but they cannot be ignored in this book in as far as they raise serious constitutional issues.

One such issue, illustrative of a variety of not dissimilar issues, was raised with the signing of the Lib-Lab Pact on 23rd March 1977, a move which in the Cabinet on that day was supported by twenty votes to four.

My diary note for 30th March 1977 records it thus:

> On his return from Brussels Tony Benn spoke to Francis Cripps and myself about the aftermath of the Lib-Lab fiasco. He referred to the fact that the Prime Minister had effectively, if temporarily, sacked him the other evening. It had happened thus – Jim really had been in a frightful lather about the Cabinet leak on the Lib-Lab deal – angry almost beyond repair. They had rowed. Then Jim phoned him up and said that Eric Heffer was trying to get signatures to summon an emergency N.E.C. meeting on the subject. Eric deserves the highest praise for this. This was on the Thursday. Jim told Tony that if he signed it he would be in breach of collective Cabinet responsibility – whereupon Tony told him, uninhibited as ever, that he had already signed the motion. Whereupon Jim called for his resignation. Jim criticised Tony about the leak and Tony criticised Jim about a deal known to the Liberal spokesman John Pardoe M.P. forty-eight hours before it was known to the Cabinet. Good sense prevailed and Tony's name was withdrawn. Existence after this can only continue on a day to day basis.

The doctrine of collective Cabinet responsibility is the doctrine that each Cabinet minister is deemed responsible for each and every Cabinet decision and expected to support it. He is expected to do this whether or not he agreed with it, knows what it is about, or was or was not consulted. Good government is said to rest on the doctrine. It enables the Government to present a united front to the public and it guarantees the integrity of the administration. It is conducive to harmony and understanding. It provides for a basis of confidentiality between ministers and their discussions in Cabinet which is absolutely necessary if governments are to function efficiently or at all.

One does not have to accept each and every one of these striking claims to accept that the doctrine is not without virtue. But no doctrine can ever be absolute. At its most basic ministers who oppose policies from a sense of deep conviction cannot be expected to endure a permanent lie in their public and private lives. Ministers can be expected to support each other in public without having to suggest that that which the public know is not true is true. The public today are aware that the major political parties are coalitions and that few big Cabinet decisions will be taken unanimously. They must know that the essence of a thriving political party is debate within the party. And since the Labour Party is constructed – at least formally – on far more democratic lines than the Conservative Party that debate is likely to be more formalised in the Labour Party. Much of it takes place inside the N.E.C. of which the Prime Minister and his deputy are ex-officio members and of which other Cabinet ministers are members by virtue of election. The N.E.C. argues not only about present Government policy but about future policies and this confuses the issue for its Cabinet members. Harold Wilson when Prime Minister took a very strict line and in October 1975 wrote a personal minute to Tony Benn, Judith Hart and Joan Lestor saying:

> I must ask you to send me in reply to this minute an unqualified assurance that you accept the principle of collective responsibility and that you will from now on comply with its requirements and the rules which follow from it, in the National Executive Committee and in all circumstances. I must warn you that I should have to regard your failure to give me such an assurance, or any subsequent breach of it, as a decision on your part that you did not wish to continue as a member of the administration. I should of course much regret such a decision but I should accept it.

Ironically, by allowing ministers to vote against the re-negotiated terms for the E.E.C. in 1975 it was Harold Wilson who did more than anyone to make a nonsense of the doctrine of collective Cabinet responsibility.

James Callaghan when Prime Minister resolved the dilemma to his own satisfaction by saying repeatedly that any member of Labour's N.E.C. could say or do what he wanted. It was just that if he were a member of the Cabinet he must be prepared to accept the consequences of what he said or did if the doctrine of collective Cabinet responsibility was breached. Although I myself do not believe that the matter can ever be formally resolved I would unhesitatingly come down on the side of legitimising dissent.

Governments have too many decisions to take for the full Cabinet to consider them all in detail. so much of the discussion takes place in Cabinet sub-committees which officially do not exist. Some preside permanently over specific matters of policy and meet regularly and are known by code letters such as E.Y., E.N., and R.D.; others are set up to deal with one specific issue and are usually in the GEN series.

Clearly who sits on these committees and who chairs them, for both of which the Prime Minister is responsible, are matters of some importance. If no member of the Cabinet concerned with the lack of accountability in public life sits on the Cabinet sub-committee which considers precisely that matter then the result is predictable. Who sits as chairman is important because official civil service committees composed of senior civil servants parallel each Cabinet sub-committee and produce papers for them, sometimes foreclosing options, often encouraging the chairman to move towards a specific conclusion.

When Harold Wilson was Prime Minister he specifically acted as chairman of the Cabinet sub-committee which dealt with energy matters so as to exclude Tony Benn from the post. James Callaghan when Prime Minister continued to chair this committee. On 15th September 1977 I was in Tony Benn's room at the Department of Energy when he received a telephone call from the Prime Minister. No one is still quite sure to this day why he took time off to make the call. The following note is, I should emphasise, a reconstruction as I only heard one end of the conversation:

'Hello Tony. I've made Eric Varley chairman of the Cabinet economic and industry committee. You see your ideas do take root sometimes.' (This is a reference to criticism by Tony that the Treasury controls the committee.)

'It's good of you to tell me that Jim. I'm most grateful. What about the energy committee?'

'Who's chairman of that?'

'You are Jim.'

'Oh am I?'

'Yes and Merlyn Rees is vice-chairman. I like Merlyn, mind you.'

'Oh! I'll look into that.'

James Callaghan's interest in the Cabinet sub-committee system picked up in 1978. In February 1978 in a minute to his colleagues he told them that he was not prepared to let the public know how the Cabinet sub-committee works. He felt that if the Government started telling the public how our constitution works 'it would be more likely to whet appetites than satisfy them'.

On page 17, I relate that when I asked Lord Peart, the Cabinet minister in charge of the civil service, about the contents of this minute at a hearing of the Expenditure Committee on 18th April 1978 he refused to comment. Fortunately the *New Statesman* takes a more open view of these matters and on 10th November 1978 it published the full text of the Prime Minister's minute, which was as follows:

The Prime Minister
Personal Minute
No. M6/78
Ministers in charge of Departments

Disclosure of Cabinet Committees

Consistently with the practice of all former Prime Ministers I have always refused to publish details of Cabinet committes or to answer Questions in the House about them. Hitherto this has led to some allegations in the press about Whitehall obscurantism but little interest or pressure in Parliament itself. There is however now some evidence that Select Committees would like to interest themselves in the committee system and may be seeking to erode the present convention. I have therefore been considering the case for taking the initiative and disclosing details of the committee structure.

I accept that the present convention has certain disadvantages for us. In particular non-disclosure makes it difficult to answer charges that the Government's policies are not properly co-ordinated. For example the Select Committee on Overseas Development has recommended the establishment of a Cabinet committee to co-ordinate political, trade and aid policies towards the developing world largely because the O.D.M. were not able to disclose that such a committee (R.D.) already exists. It is also arguable that non-disclosure is inconsistent with a policy of greater openness. In any case some parts of the committee structure are quite widely known outside Government: in these cases what is at issue therefore is a refusal to admit publicly what a lot of people know about privately.

It is important therefore to understand the reasons for the current practice of non-disclosure. They are as follows: the Cabinet committee system grew up as the load on the Cabinet itself became too great. It allows matters of lesser importance to be decided without troubling the whole Cabinet: and major issues to be clarified in order to save the time of the Cabinet. The method adopted by ministers for discussing policy questions is however essentially a domestic matter: and a decision by a Cabinet committee, unless referred to the Cabinet, engages the collective responsibility of all ministers and has exactly the same authority as a decision by the Cabinet itself. Disclosure that a particular committee had dealt with a matter might lead to argument about the status of the decision or demands that it should be endorsed by the whole Cabinet. Furthermore publishing details of the committees would be both misleading and counter-productive. The existence of some could not be disclosed on security grounds: others are set up to do a particular job and are then wound up. The absence of a committee on a particular subject (e.g. agriculture or poverty) does not mean that the Government do not attach importance to it: and the fact that a particular minister is not on a committee does not mean that he does not attend when his interests are affected. Publication would almost inevitably lead to pressures for both more and larger committees, and for disclosures of information about their activities.

I do not believe that we could in any event disclose the existence of the GEN groups. This is partly because of their ephemeral nature and partly because disclosure would often reveal either that very sensitive subjects were under consideration or that we had something in train about which we were not ready to make an announcement. Disclosure of the main standing committees would thus give a partial picture only. Moreover having gone as far as this I do not believe that it would be possible for me to hold the line and refuse to answer any further questions about the composition and activities of the committees. At the minimum we would be under pressure to reveal the names of the chairmen. This would make it harder for me to make changes: and it would have implications for the responsibilities of departmental ministers since Select Committees would try to summon the chairmen of Cabinet committees to give evidence in addition to the responsible minister. I should also be under continuing pressure to say that a committee was considering a particular subject (and often it would be a GEN group) and there would be questions about when committees were meeting, the work they were doing, whether particular ministers are on them, the details of under-pinning official committees, etc.

I have therefore decided that we should not change our stance on this matter. The present convention is long established and provides a basis on which we can stand. Any departure from it would be more likely to whet appetites than to satisfy them. I ask my colleagues therefore to rest on the position that the way in which we co-ordinate our decisions is a matter internal to Government and not to answer questions about the Cabinet committee system.

This minute also sheds light on how collective Cabinet decisions are taken when the Prime Minister has already made up his mind.

Prime Ministers exercise control over all ministerial meetings. I remember one occasion on 22nd November 1977 when one junior minister, Michael Meacher, tried to organise an informal meeting, if that is not a contradiction in terms, of those ministers who were against direct elections to the European Parliament. Suddenly Tony Benn received a letter from the Prime Minister together with a copy of a letter which Mr Meacher had sent out to other ministers saying he, the Prime Minister, had been given a copy of it by a Conservative M.P. who found it on the photocopying machine in the House of Commons basement (this seems an unlikely story since a Conservative M.P. would also have given it to the press and told them where he had found it. Neither of these things were done.) The Prime Minister went on to say in his letter that all meetings of ministers had to be cleared by him and that as this one had not been cleared by him it would have to be cancelled. I found this particular letter by the Prime Minister absurd and almost an attempt at thought control. The idea that ministers could never meet informally to discuss political issues without his consent was ridiculous. Reports were that the Prime Minister was getting so agitated about events that later that evening when I saw the Chief Whip Michael Cocks I stopped him and said to him 'I hope you'll stop your man pulling up the rug on Thursday. We don't want him to do anything silly, do we?'. The meeting went ahead as planned but word of the Prime Minister's ire must have got around because far fewer than expected turned up. The patronage threat was working again.

In the exercise of his power the Prime Minister is surrounded by a number of satellite bureaucracies all of which in one way or another are linked to bigger bureaucracies. The way in which these bureaucracies function and relate to each other and to the Prime Minister is the subject of a major work in itself. I can only touch upon a few matters. Anyone wanting to read about the practical operation of these bureaucracies should consult *The Politics of Power* by Joe Haines, former Press Officer to Harold Wilson when Prime Minister. Mr Haines' book is also very good on the Treasury and the Foreign Office.

The Prime Minister has his own Private Office. James Callaghan's Private Office contained a Principal Private Secretary, five Private Secretaries (one responsible for overseas affairs, one for Parliamentary affairs, and three for home affairs) and four Assistant Private Secretaries all of whom had the M.B.E. The Private Office is directly linked by a switchboard to all the other Private Offices in Whitehall. The Private Secretaries of the Prime Minister and the ministers make up what has been called a Private Secretary network whose antennae are sensitive and almost telepathically linked. They all serve two masters, the politicians and their civil service superiors. They are all, whether they would admit it or not, subject to competing tensions.

The Prime Minister also has his own Political Office, the financing of which has been the subject of some controversy with some Prime Ministers. In the case of Labour Prime Ministers, the trade unions, Transport House, business and the City have all at some time or another contributed funds. James Callaghan had a political adviser, Tom McNally, now Member of Parliament for Stockport South. A number of political advisers gravitate towards Parliament thereby guaranteeing for most of them at any rate that their power and influence diminish, unless of course the politicians that they served become or are Prime Ministers. Political advisers (the idea came from the Fulton Committee) consist of people appointed personally by ministers to help them with their departmental duties and to provide a link between ministers, political parties and Members of Parliament. They have full access to departmental papers. Technically they are civil servants and their salaries are paid out of public funds but their appointments are specifically linked to their minister's tenure of office. No departmental minister in the Callaghan Government had more than two such advisers, though subject to the Prime Minister's agreement there was no limit on their number and indeed in his book, *Final Term*, Harold Wilson speaks of one department having four. Most ministers seem to be agreed that the appointment of such advisers helped them considerably, though not all ministers had such advisers.

James Callaghan also had a senior policy adviser, Dr Bernard Donoughue, formerly an academic economist.

The Prime Minister also has a Press Office, linked to the Whitehall network of departmental Press Offices and a Parliamentary Private Secretary. Parliamentary Private Secretaries, sometimes referred to as dogsbodies, seem to be almost the only people in Whitehall and Westminster not on any organised network.

This was not by any means an excessive amount of back-up staff for a Prime Minister. Indeed it would be true to say that the country was providing the Prime Minister with his political back-up staff very much on the cheap. Such a situation is absurd and reflects a ridiculous distinction made by the establishment between party politics and the processes of government.

The Prime Minister's sources of advice, however, extend much wider than this. He is in charge of and directly advised by the Civil Service Department which is run by the head of the civil service and which contains the office of the Lord Privy Seal and, a Minister of State for the Civil Service. Indeed the Prime Minister's title is Prime Minister and Minister for the Civil Service. It is in and through this department that so much of the power which I have described is institutionalised. Relationships between the Prime Minister and the head of the civil service vary from one Prime Minister to another. The most remarkable relationship struck up in recent years was that between Sir William (now Lord) Armstrong and Mr Edward Heath. Lord Armstrong, both in what he did when a civil servant and in his many subsequent highly political statements (he criticised me most grievously in an interview with Lawrence Marks in the *Observer* on 18th September 1977!), gave the lie to the suggestion that civil servants were non-political.

I have already quoted (on page 32) his famous statement about the way in which civil servants set the parameters within which ministers can operate. More remarkably when he was head of the civil service he found himself advising Edward Heath, the Prime Minister, on the date of the election. It is difficult to believe that there is anything more political than that the head of the civil service at a time of national crisis, with a Conservative Government's existence threatened by the actions of miners who were supported by the Opposition, should be advising the Prime Minister on the date of the election. Lord Armstrong explained it away thus: now the question of an election or not is a highly political matter, something on which no civil servant would dream of having an opinion and yet it seems to me it was a move in the chess game that I had been playing with the Prime Minister and I couldn't refrain from giving him my opinion. (*The Times* 15th November 1976)

When at the hearing of the Expenditure Committee on the Civil Service on 18th April 1978 (Twelfth Report from the Expenditure Committee, Session 1977–78, Response to the Government's Observations on the Committee's Report on the Civil Service, Page 14) I asked Lord Peart, the Cabinet minister in charge of the civil service, if he could expect Sir Ian Bancroft, the present head of the civil service to be 'playing chess or ludo and giving advice to the Prime Minister on the date of the next election', I received the reply, which proves my point:

> *Lord Peart*: I would think that the people who would give advice to the Prime Minister on the date of an election would be the members of the Cabinet.
>
> *Sir Ian Bancroft*: Can I answer the question about whether I am playing ludo or chess and giving advice about the date of the next general election? The answer, categorically, is that I would not be playing ludo or chess or giving any such advice.

Sir William Armstrong played an important role in Edward Heath's corporate economic strategy which came to grief in 1974. He was referred to at the time as the 'deputy Prime Minister'. His immediate successor, Sir Douglas Allen (now Lord Croham), who trained at the London School of Economics was reportedly upset that he was allowed no such role in Harold Wilson's corporate strategy which foundered in 1976 when he resigned as Prime Minister. Interestingly Cecil King records in his *Diary 1970–74*, for Wednesday, 19th August 1970, Mr John Fforde, one time Chief Cashier and an executive director of the Bank of England, as saying over lunch that he 'thought Douglas Allen more intelligent than William Armstrong, and with a better grasp of national finance, but had no means of judging his quality in other fields'. Sir Douglas Allen's view that Permanent Secretaries should tell ministers when they are wrong, though unexceptional in theory, begged the question in practice: wrong in whose interest?

If the head of the civil service advises Prime Ministers on top civil service appointments and appointments to nationalised industries, the P.M.'s main advice on policy matters comes from the Cabinet secretariat and from the Central Policy Review Staff. When Sir John Hunt gave evidence to the Expenditure Committee on the role of the Cabinet secretariat on 14th February 1977 (Eleventh Report Session 1976–77 Vol. II (Part II) page 752) he claimed that the Cabinet secretariat was just a kind of refined secretary's office. These are his answers to my questions:

> *Question*: I wonder if you could tell us how the Cabinet Office recruits its members. Is it because they are bright, safe, or have certain political views? What actually does the Cabinet Office do? Is it providing a secretarial service for the Cabinet, giving advice that is meant to be superior to departmental advice, or seeking to come to a compromise between competing departmental claims? What do you do?
>
> *Answer*: I think that I manage a small but very busy activity which sees to all the arrangements for the Cabinet and Cabinet committees – getting the papers round in time, the agendas, briefing the chairmen, recording the discussions, sending out minutes, and chasing up decisions. That is its main activity. We have also brigaded under us, as we were saying earlier, the Central Statistical Office and the Central Policy Review Staff, and there is a history section, and so on . . . As regards recruiting staff, all the people in the secretariat, from Principal upwards, with the exception of myself, are on secondment from departments. In the case of Principals and Assistant Secretaries they come for two years, and Deputy Secretaries usually for three. This is a very deliberate policy for a number of reasons. First of all, the secretariat is organised according to functions – overseas, foreign affairs, defence, economic, home and social –and

you do need a spread of people who are closely in touch with departments from those areas. So that we are organised functionally. I think that it is also very important that we should maintain a secondment system rather than building up a permanent Cabinet Office staff precisely because, despite what I read in this morning's newspapers, the Cabinet Office does not have policies of its own. I think that if there was a permanent staff we would begin to develop an oil policy within the Cabinet Office, and a policy on this, and a policy on that. Our job is basically to see to the handling of business when it comes to ministers during a fairly short period – just before it comes to a collective discussion, during and just after.

Question: I was looking down the list of your members in the Cabinet Office – I have done that for some years – and they seem to be what civil servants call high fliers. Are you telling the committee that you pull all of these high fliers out of government departments, people who are going to become Permanent Secretaries, for the purpose of providing secretarial services just before meetings and just after meetings? What is involved politically in that bland phrase that you used about briefing Cabinet ministers?

Answer: Any chairman of a Cabinet committee is provided with what we call a handling brief, which is mainly a brief about the background, about the papers before him, the points that are likely to come up, and the issues to be settled. It is not primarily a brief of political advice: it is a chairman's brief.

Sir John did himself and his staff less than justice. The chairmen's briefs they draw up are powerful documents often leading in a certain and clear direction – often in the direction thought best by civil servants who have paralleled the committees which Sir John and his men service. Sir John himself has been used for major assignments by Prime Ministers. His office was a political force operating legitimately in the sense that politicians never asked for it to be different.

The Secretary of the Cabinet has one other vital role to perform. It is to provide the Prime Minister with a tactical briefing for Cabinet meetings which normally take place on Thursdays. The tactical briefing tells the Prime Minister amongst other things which of his ministers are likely to raise issues or cause trouble and on which subjects. Since the Secretary of the Cabinet does not get this information by contacting departmental ministers direct – any minister worth his salt would send the Secretary of the Cabinet away with a flea in his ear if he were asked by him what his position in Cabinet was going to be on any given issue – he must get it from the minister's civil servants. He is aided in this task by the fairly regular Wednesday morning meetings of the Permanent Secretaries which take place in Whitehall.

It must undoubtedly be useful for Permanent Secretaries to meet regularly and exchange views and ensure that they know what each of them and their ministers are thinking. The meetings must be useful in enabling them to draw up a common line for the many inter-departmental official committees which parallel Cabinet sub-committees. When Harold Wilson was Prime Minister he was so obsessive about this 'O' committee system that he would often refuse to let ministers discuss issues until civil servants had done so. Harold Wilson, himself a former civil servant, was a civil servant corporatist par excellence. These meetings of the Permanent Secretaries have been described as the real Shadow Cabinet meetings. On the negative side they are meetings which enable Permanent Secretaries to run down their departmental ministers behind their backs.

One of the interesting remarks of Sir John Hunt, quoted above, was that he had 'brigaded under him' the C.P.R.S., or Think-Tank as it is more widely known. The Think-Tank was first set up in 1971 to give the Prime Minister advice independent of the Whitehall machine on strategic policy matters. From 1971 to 1974 under a Conservative Government its Director-General and First Permanent Secretary was Lord Rothschild. From 1974–79 when Labour was in power Sir Kenneth Berrill filled the position. By the standards of Whitehall, it has a very small staff and for a long time consisted of little more than sixteen acute brains assembled from outside as well as inside Whitehall. Most of its reports have not been published despite efforts by Members of Parliament to get the Prime Minister to give his permission. In Chapter 1, I wrote about an important report on unemployment the very existence of which was not properly admitted by the Prime Minister when he refused to publish it. The reports are not universally made available to all members of the Cabinet. Some of its reports have been published including a highly contentious (to my mind admirable) report on the Foreign Office (C.P.R.S. *Review of Overseas Representation*) and a highly contentious report on the motor-car industry (C.P.R.S. Report. *The Future of the British Car Industry*. 1975).

I am in favour of the Prime Minister getting advice independent of the Whitehall machine though one senior minister did say 'it's time we abolished the Think-Tank and did some thinking for ourselves'. Concern has recently been expressed, confirmed by experience, that the Think-Tank has been sucked into the Whitehall machine and that the Cabinet secretariat has impeded its free access to the Prime Minister. One such expression of concern came from the Prime Minister's senior policy adviser, Bernard Donoughue when James Callaghan was Prime Minister. One astonishing admission that the Think-Tank was in danger of becoming a mouth-piece for Permanent Secretaries and departmental policies came from one of its own members when he referred to it as a kind of 'institutionalised Watergate' which bugged Government departments using departmental civil servants as the bugs. The account given in Chapter 4 of the ferocious battle over the choice of the thermal nuclear reactor lends weight to this view.

One place however where the Think-Tank voice can now be heard free of interference from the Cabinet secretariat is ironically enough in Cabinet sub-committees. Until recently officials were not allowed to speak at Cabinet meetings or Cabinet sub-committee meetings. Now, in a profound constitutional change members of the Think-Tank, who are civil servants, can speak at the latter. Quite who they represent is not clear – themselves, the Prime Minister, departments or something or somebody else?

The points I have outlined which go to make up Prime Ministerial power are far from exhaustive but do seem to be of some importance. Moreover something can be done about them. There are a number of ways, for example, in which the powers of patronage could be lessened. The first would be for the members of the majority party in Parliament to elect the Cabinet or part of it, leaving the Prime Minister to allocate individual posts. If that were done, ministers would not have to keep one eye constantly on the Prime Minister, always fearful sub-consciously if not consciously, that he might remove them at any time. Instead ministers would see their constituency as being in Parliament, not in 10 Downing Street, and they might be inclined to respond more to the arguments of the elected representatives of the people, within the context of Cabinet government.

Secondly, ministers should be allowed to appoint their own Permanent Secretaries so that they can work with them on the basis of absolute trust. I do not suggest that ministers should be allowed to dismiss Permanent Secretaries, save for misconduct, but they should be allowed to move them sideways when they cannot work with them.

Thirdly, Ministers should be allowed to carry out changes in the organisation and management of their departments. The ultimate responsibility of the Prime Minister and the head of the civil service should be revoked. This proposal goes somewhat further than Recommendation 41 of the Expenditure Committee on the Civil Service (Eleventh Report; Session 1976–77 (HC 535)).

Fourthly, ministers should be allowed to establish such political control in their departments as they think fit and should be free to adopt any organisation that they think fit for the efficient discharge of business (see Chapter 3). The Prime Minister's ultimate authority here should be revoked.

I should make it clear that in putting forward these last two proposals I am not suggesting that Britain should move to the American system – a system sometimes rather loosely and incorrectly described as an 'all in, all out' system for civil servants. It is not desirable, either from the point of view of good government or political accountability or good recruitment to the civil service, to switch to a political spoils system. Without fixed elections and the prospect of governments having two terms in office such a proposal would lead to chaos in the administration. What I do believe is necessary, and I shall argue the case in the next chapter, is that departments should be so organised that ministers have an alternative source of advice that lies outside that of the career civil service.

Fifthly, there should be major changes in the way in which chairmen of nationalised industries are appointed. The Prime Minister should no longer play a role in their appointment. Their posts should be advertised when they become vacant and interviews should be held by the departmental minister concerned. He should then submit his choice for approval to the House of Commons who would get up a Select Committee to confirm or veto it. The Select Committee would have powers to call for persons and papers, and interview the person concerned (and even hear the views of workers in the industry!). If the minister were unhappy with the decision, he could put the matter by motion before the whole House of Commons whose decision would be final.

It might be argued that such a system would frighten off capable candidates because the glare of publicity would be too great. I cannot accept that as a serious argument. Chairmen of nationalised industries *are* public figures, permanently in the political limelight whether they like it or not. They are often asked to explain themselves before Select Committees of Parliament and it is not unknown for them to appear on television. It would be a very weak potential chairman who could not manage to subject himself to the polite but probing questioning of a Select Committee of Parliament and maybe come under a little party political crossfire.

Sixthly, there is a need to make the bureaucratic satellites of the Prime Minister and especially the Think-Tank more politically accountable and more widely accountable. The Think-Tank should not be seen as the private preserve of either the Cabinet Office or the Prime Minister. Such political accountability could be achieved by bringing these bureaucracies under the control of a senior Cabinet minister working closely with the Prime Minister. Strategic policy matters are too important to be left to competing bureaucracies each striving for the Prime Minister's ear. Tony Benn has argued this case strongly whilst more surprisingly, the present Prime Minister, Margaret Thatcher, even hinted that she might do something along these lines – but that was when she was in opposition. It took only days in office to blunt her radicalism in this sphere and to allow mandarin rule to re-assert itself. Her Government should turn out to be a traditional one – secretive, élitist, oligarchic and bureaucratic. In that sense it could indeed be a classical Government.

Seventhly, there is the question of the method of election and appointment of the Prime Minister. In practice the Queen appoints as Prime Minister that person who has been elected leader of the majority party in the House of Commons. Many believe that M.P.s are the only people who can form mature judgments in this matter. Others would like to see more people participating in the process so as to get Prime Ministers more truly representative of the views of the political parties they lead. I do not regard the issue as critical (believing that it is the powers of the Prime Minister which most need change) though I am in favour of widening the electoral college in some way or other.

Eighthly, and it is my last point, there is merit in considering limitations to the Prime Minister's ultimate sanction of his colleagues – that of the threat of dissolution. Some have suggested that fixed elections are the answer. I do not favour that solution. I see the ability of a Government to go to the country to seek a fresh mandate whenever it wants as adding flexibility and strength to the constitution. Governments do get tired and lose their way. In these circumstances an immediate election may be the best expression of the democratic process. However, I believe that the decision on whether or not Parliament should be dissolved should be a collective Cabinet decision. I can see no reason for that awesome decision to be borne by one person alone. If the Prime Minister wishes to resign that should be his affair. It should be for the Cabinet, testing opinion amongst their colleagues, to decide whether the Government should continue or not. Prime Ministers may think that they are indispensable but they are not. There are always others to take their place. The future of a Government is too important a business to rest on the strength or weaknesses of one man.

Specific proposals for some of the other problems mentioned in this Chapter are dealt with in succeeding Chapters. Some of the problems I have mentioned here can only be resolved by an effort of political will on the part of Cabinet members and Members of Parliament. I have no prescriptions for strengthening political will in this book. Either it is there or it is not.

3 Ministerial Power

As the minister, or Secretary of State as most of them are called, walks up the steps of his new department he is aware that his power is not quite what it seems. He knows that his team of junior ministers has been appointed by the Prime Minister, not by him, though it is possible that he may have some small say in the appointments. He suspects that one or more of his junior ministers (called Ministers of State or Parliamentary Under-Secretaries of State) have been appointed by the Prime Minister precisely because he or she stands in a different part of the political spectrum from the Secretary of State. I have no hesitation in arguing that a minister should appoint his own junior ministers and that Prime Ministers who aim for 'balance' are acting foolishly. What a minister needs above all else, as pressures of work in his department and elsewhere isolate him from friends, colleagues, party and reality, is a group of people around him whom he can trust implicitly: a priceless asset often denied to Ministers. This thought occurred to me most forcefully one day when I was attending a meeting at the Department of Energy with Tony Benn in the chair and I suddenly began asking myself why I was so bored. The answer which came back immediately was that for ten years, whether as a civil servant (from 1962 to 1967) or as an M.P. (from 1974 to 1979) I had been attending the same meeting with the same people with the same values giving the same advice, whether the meeting concerned housing or energy or industrial matters, whether it was being held in London, Washington or Brussels or whether the speaker was talking in English, American or French. It is that atmosphere, that value system, which a minister finds it so difficult to break out of.

The new minister is immediately aware that it is precisely because his every need, his every whim, is apparently met that he is taken away from reality. Cars, aeroplanes, helicopters are at his disposal, literally within minutes. A constant stream of high-powered people come in and out of his office to give him advice. Yet as time passes, it must dawn on him that he does not see many of the people whom the whole edifice of power is designed to help. Even when he goes on visits around the country he is always meeting people in an artificial situation. More likely than not they will defer to him by virtue of his office. He finds that his time is not his own. The department organises meetings for him all day and every day and if necessary expands the work to fill in the time available. They regard his day as their day. One of the minor reasons why there was sometimes tension between Tony Benn and his civil servants was that he would not always use what the department regarded as prime time for their purposes. Often he would prefer instead to talk things through with his junior ministers, political advisers, P.P.S.s, research staff from Transport House, at what the department regarded as the most inconvenient times. The discussions might concern departmental matters or they might concern wider political issues. It was I imagine for this reason that James Callaghan once said to him that he had been told (presumably via the Whitehall civil service network) that he was lazy, an astonishing allegation to make against one who worked almost night and day.

The minister soon becomes aware that there is a departmental policy on most issues and that some Permanent Secretaries see their main role as sustaining the integrity of those departmental policies. The departmental policy may stretch back years (decades in the case of the Department of Trade) and the minister suspects that his civil servants bring a lifetime of experience to the problems that he meets, although the truth is that civil servants may move around as often as ministers. He has an uncomfortable feeling that he may be an intruder. He will do well, as the following figures show, to survive for three years as a minister before he is promoted, moved sideways or asked to resign.

MINISTERS' LENGTH OF SERVICE 1945–1979

	Home Secretary	Minister of Education ([a])	Chancellor of the Exchequer	Foreign Secretary ([b])
Counting reappointments as one				
Number of ministers	11	15	14	13
Average length of stay	3 years 1 month	2 years 3 months	2 years 5 months	2 years 7 months
Counting reappointments as two				
Number of ministers	12	17	14	15
Average length of stay	2 years 10 months	2 years	2 years 5 months	2 years 3 months

Notes

1. ([a]) Later Secretary of State for Education and Science.
   ([b]) Later Foreign and Commonwealth Secretary.
2. I have taken as my starting date the Labour Government which appointed ministers at the end of July and beginning of August 1975, and have counted all those serving up to and including the Labour Government which lost the election in May 1979 – a period of 33 years 7 months in all. Once confusion is introduced by ministers who served more than once in the same office. These were Roy Jenkins at the Home Office (1965–1967 and 1974–1976), Sir David Eccles (1954–1957 and 1959–1962) and Lord Hailsham (1957 and 1964) at Education, and Lord Home (1960–1963 and 1970–1974) and Michael Stewart (1965–1966 and 1968–1970) at the Foreign Office.

In the above table, I have shown two alternative sets of figures –first counting these ministers as having served just once, and secondly counting them each time they were in office.

Source: Butler and Sloman *British Political Facts 1900–1975*, updated.

Richard Crossman's diaries are massive testimony to what happened in the old Ministry of Housing and Local Government. In the *Politics of Power*, Joe Haines, Press Officer to Harold Wilson, gives his account of what goes on today:

> The determination that the opinion of the machine should prevail – and it exists in other departments, too, notably the Foreign Office but also in Defence and Environment – is anti-democratic. It is reflected in the contempt with which the manifestos on which a Government has been elected is held. (Whether that is a good thing or not is irrelevant; it is not a democratic thing.) From March 1974 Defence fought to spend more against a Labour commitment to spend less; Environment waged its war against the railway system when the Labour Party was pro-railway (and the re-establishment of Transport as a separate ministry in September 1976 will not necessarily change that attitude); and the Treasury persuaded the Government in February 1976 to retreat far enough away from its commitment to a wealth tax to ensure that it did not operate during the lifetime of the Parliament which began in October 1974. It was thought prudent at the time not to announce that decision, which at least gave a chance for second thought . . . The Department of Agriculture, Fisheries and Food, the most benign of Whitehall's ministries, has come to represent the producers' rather than the consumers' interests. The Department of the Environment appears more often on the side of the local authorities than on that of the taxpayer. The Department of Employment is still the old Ministry of Labour at heart; it is not only the channel by which the voice of the unions is transmitted to the Cabinet, it mimics the voice. Defence

represents the military establishment against the people, instead of the other way round, and the Foreign Office prepares new orchestrations of 'I surrender, dear' to every demand or démarche made to it. The Treasury for its part reflects the power of capital, business, finance, industry, foreign exchange and commodity markets, economists, monetarists, shareholders, stockbrokers, the City of London and the Governor of the Bank of England. If there is an ignorance greater than that of the politicians for the complexities of finance it is that of financiers and industrialists for the simplicities of politics . . .

The Chancellor would be asking Cabinet to consider an unabashed announcement of a statutory incomes policy, with no mention of sanctions against employers – which, if any statutory policy was embarked upon, ministers insisted was essential – and proposing nothing effective on prices. It amounted to a straightforward attempt by the Treasury to make the Government put its policies totally in reverse, abandon its manifesto commitments and commit suicide. Though it sounds melodramatic to say so, had they succeeded in the attempt, it would have been a civilian coup against the Government.

There can never be a final victory over the official machine because for them the game never ends, it is infinite. The civil service is occasionally defeated, but never banished from the field.

Civil servants, politicians and others have written in similar vein. The interesting thing is that every time someone writes from his experience about these matters the establishment issues a denial and continues as if nothing had happened. It is to pre-empt that denial that I have named names and documented some of the case studies so closely in this book.

In the *Guardian* on 28th October 1976 Peter Jenkins, the political columnist, wrote quoting an American Treasury official, whom he described as a 'wholly authoritative source', on the attitude of British Treasury civil servants. 'One of the problems is the axis between your Treasury and our Treasury. They seem to be agreed that the Labour manifesto is a manual for suicide . . . They are in constant touch with our people saying "Don't bale these bastards out."' When I put this matter to Sir John Hunt, the Secretary of the Cabinet, at an Expenditure Committee hearing on 14th February 1977 (Eleventh Report of Session 1976–77, Vol. II (Part II) page 757), it is worth noting that he did not as one might expect simply deny the allegations as absurd but preferred not to comment. As the Report puts it:

Question: The third is the rather more startling allegations, such as that the Treasury engineered a coup against the Government on July 1975 or indeed as I have heard it that they engineered a coup

between July 1976 and November 1976. From your position, you would be in a position to know whether the Treasury had engineered a coup against a democratically elected Government?
Answer: On the coup, I prefer not to comment, partly because I have not read the book that you are I think referring to and partly because from what I read in the newspapers – at any rate one point – I knew to my own belief that the whole story was not in it. But I really would prefer not to comment.

Few would regard that as a firm denial by one of Britain's leading civil servants.

If Adrian Ham is to be believed (he worked as Special Assistant to the Chancellor of the Exchequer from March 1974 to March 1976) the minister may wonder on whose side the civil servants are, although I think it fair to say that Mr Ham's experiences are probably coloured by the fact that he worked in the Treasury at a time when one crisis preceded another with alarming regularity and people seemed to be losing their heads. In *The Times* on 18th February 1977 he wrote:

> In my experience, the deliberate, calculated lie or distortion was not uncommon currency in civil servant dealings with ministers. Since ministers are not responsible for major appointments in their own departments, it is of course very difficult for them to do very much about this kind of thing. In fact, one of the greatest sins it appears that a Permanent Secretary can commit is to let his minister in on some confidence concerning official business passed on through the 'unofficial' Permanent Secretaries' network.

Sometimes ministers are at fault. Sometimes they simply do not want to interfere in the departmental line whether they agree with it or not. Indeed I remember Merlyn Rees, the Home Secretary, telling me on 8th February 1979, that ministers had deliberately not expressed a view when the department had been asked to submit evidence to the Royal Commission on Criminal Procedure. The department's evidence included such important proposals as dropping the right of silence for a suspect. Whether or not one agrees with that, it might seem an astonishing abdication of responsibility on the part of ministers, especially as Home Office evidence in an enquiry of this sort might be expected to carry a lot of weight. The Home Secretary seemed quite unaware that anything untoward had happened. He almost seemed to suggest that ministers might be 'biased' and that only the civil servants could give 'unbiased' evidence.

Even where the minister's officials want to support him in his dealings with his colleagues and the House of Commons the minister has cause for concern. He knows that his civil servants have had the advantage of seeing the papers of previous administrations but he is not allowed, because of some convention of the constitution which passes from Prime Minister to Prime Minister, to see those papers. So he is immediately excluded from a mountain of advice, discussion and information which is available to his civil servants. James Callaghan's official anodyne answer to suggestions that the convention (he called it a rule) should be ignored, given in Government's Observations of Expenditure Committee's Report on the Civil Service (Cmnd 7117, paragraph 89) was that the Government 'is not aware of any evidence that the operation of the rule has given rise to difficulties in practice; nor does it believe that the rule "increases the power of the civil service relative to ministers".' No reason is given for the existence of a rule.

The minister soon discovers that although he is responsible through the doctrine of ministerial responsibility for all the acts and omissions of his civil servants and all that goes on in his department in relation to its statutory duties, there is no machinery to enable him or his junior ministers or advisers to know even a fraction of what is going on. Indeed it is doubtful whether any institutional changes could enable a minister to be aware of everything that was taking place, given the size and workload of a Government department. This might be regarded as justification for a decline in the concept of ministerial responsibility, not in the sense that the minister can eschew responsibility for the work of his department but in the sense that few ministers hold themselves personally responsible for the mistakes of their department. Ministers rarely resign these days, however great are the departmental blunders for which they are responsible. I believe this is regrettable for it undermines the whole basis of political accountability. It may be that, in cases of departmental blunders, the civil servant concerned should get the sack but ministers should accept the responsibility. One of their prime tasks is to ensure that the work of their department is accountable to them in sensitive areas and to establish machinery and early warning systems to see that this does indeed happen.

As if all this were not enough the minister finds out that entry into the E.E.C. has complicated the running of his department. It is not just that two or three senior civil servants from the Department of Energy, for example, were permanently in Europe working on E.E.C. matters. If the same number from other Departments were similarly engaged, clearly a great deal of talent is permanently working in Europe in addition to the E.E.C. bureaucracy itself. Entry into the E.E.C., by imposing a huge new dimension to our constitution, has increased the burden on ministers. It has also enabled civil servants to develop contacts with their European colleagues in a way which has further circumscribed ministerial freedom of action. Certainly entry into the E.E.C. has brought a new network of committees for many departments which seem to distance ministers even further from the decision-taking process.

The pressures that came from these committees and from Foreign Office and Department of Energy civil servants were always for the minister to give way a little. It was not that Sir Donald Maitland, Britain's top civil servant in Brussels, or Mr D. le B. Jones, a Deputy Secretary at the Department of Energy dealing with E.E.C. matters, were unhelpful; just that they were working for two bureaucracies as well as for ministers. So inevitably there was tension. In May 1977 when there was an argument about whether Britain should have a separate seat at the World Energy Conference or be represented by the E.E.C. Mr Peter Le Cheminant, another Deputy Secretary at the Department of Energy (9th May 1977), said that the Foreign Office felt that our interests could be fairly represented by the E.E.C. Commission. This was not advice which found favour with the Secretary of State. On 20th June 1977 I remember Tony Benn writing three times on a minute 'NO, NO, NO,' when Sir Donald Maitland advised making some concessions on oil refinery policy, supplies of energy to our E.E.C. partners in times of crisis, and coal. I remember Sir Donald, a canny Scot at whose residence in Brussels I once spent a comfortable night, explaining what E.E.C. diplomacy was about. Apparently it was in order for Britain to object to E.E.C. policies so as to safeguard her interests so long as others (at least one other E.E.C. country) were against what was being proposed by the Commission. What Britain wanted to avoid was to find herself in a position where she alone opposed policies. For Britain to stand up alone for her interests was bad diplomacy.

My own visits with Tony Benn to the Council of Ministers' meetings on E.E.C. matters astonished me. The Ministers meet in secret with their advisers to take decisions and engage in what I can only describe as a lethargic form of barter with each other and with the chief bureaucrat from the E.E.C., the Commissioner, who dominated the proceedings despite the fact that one of the ministers was in the chair. The Commissioner in the case of energy was Mr Gido Brünner, a German civil servant with limited political flair, who was forever pursuing some abstraction which he called a 'European energy policy'. There was and could be no such thing. There were countries pursuing their legitimate national interests and there were important bilateral, trilateral and quadrilateral agreements in a number of vital fields. The sum of these policies was a 'European energy policy' but Gido Brünner could not see this and advised by Mr Leonard Williams (who had the grandiose title of Director of E.E.C. Energy Policies), a former British civil servant from the Department of Energy, he continued to chase his will-o'-the-wisp. The meetings of ministers went on for hours, broken up only for two to three hour ministers' lunches, while nothing happened, and then everyone went home tired. I do not think that we were bad Europeans: we simply did not understand either the objectives (unless they were simply to give the bureaucracy something to do) or sympathise with the secretive, bureaucratic form of government that was even more offensive than its counterpart in the United Kingdom.

I think it was Peter Shore (formerly Secretary of State for the Environment) who first spotted how it was that the E.E.C. bureaucracy was moving out of control. The method used by the Commission to develop its powers is delightfully simple. It gets the member states to agree to innocuous general resolutions for such things as the creation of a good urban environment or the secure and adequate supplies of energy for each country – resolutions, in fact, to which no one could object. Then when everyone has forgotten about them the Commission would come back and remind the member states that the resolutions had the force of law and pursuant to them it was not putting forward for approval such major projects as the joint development of Fast Breeder Nuclear Reactors. One could only marvel at the audacity of it.

If ministers and Members of Parliament are to establish more effective political control over the E.E.C. bureaucracy this would require at a minimum: 1. the Council of Ministers' meetings to be held in public when legislation is being discussed; 2. an amendment of the European Communities Act 1972 so as to give the House of Commons greater powers over E.E.C. laws which are now enforceable in the U.K. courts; and 3. the opening up of the activities of the Commission not only to the members of the new European Parliament but also to the Parliaments of the member states.

The pressures on a senior Cabinet minister who takes all his political roles seriously are very heavy indeed: Member of Parliament with work to do in the constituency, member of the Parliamentary Labour Party, member of the National Executive Committee of the Labour Party and member of the Cabinet running a Government department.

Tony Benn expressed it thus in his Nuffield lecture:

> Most of the day, from the time of arrival in the department at about 9 a.m. until leaving for the House of Commons in the late afternoon, is occupied with discussions with other ministers, political advisers or officials, or in meetings with outside groups.
>
> At about eight o'clock every evening my Private Secretary packs one – and sometimes more – official red boxes with papers to be dealt with overnight. These include papers requiring positive deci-

sions (policy submissions, letters to ministers, drafts of parliamentary answers or appointments), papers for information, invitations and engagements plus general reading matter. Work on these boxes may take from one to three hours each night and weekend boxes about the same. Comments and decisions on these papers, together with other instructions or questions to the department, are written up by my Private Secretaries and issued as Secretary of State Minutes (SOSOMs) to be sent to the appropriate officials. There were 1,821 such minutes in 1977.

The Secretary of State is under the Prime Minister, responsible for appointments to the nationalised fuel industries and to various committees in the energy field. In addition he is also chairman of the Energy Commission and of the Coal Industry Tripartite Committee and of an interdepartmental ministerial group responsible for North Sea policy. He is also a member of the National Economic Development Council. He attended eight meetings of these committees during 1977.

As the Crossman diaries revealed, there is a great deal of tension between ministers and officials in the formulation of policy. Open government allows those outside Whitehall to know what the issues are, allowing them to feed in a stream of advice representing alternative views which may help ministers in their task. Any Labour minister will want to maintain the closest contact with the Labour and trade union movement as part of this process. This strengthens his hand both in developing policy and in winning support for its implementation.

Unfortunately, having been a Cabinet minister Tony Benn is subject to all kinds of restrictions and unable in public at any rate, to go into the details of the way in which decisions are taken. In the next two Chapters I describe what goes on in Government departments and the way in which decisions are taken. Here for the moment I simply describe two incidents, using my diary: one concerned with a major party political issue (the formation of the Lib-Lab pact), the other with a major energy crisis at the department, in the hope that they will show the reader what politics and government is about. I have used the notes in my diary because although inelegantly and sometimes ungrammatically written they portray the immediacy of what was happening.

The note in my diary for the day in which the Lib-Lab pact was formed says this:

23 March 1977

Today a Labour Government gave way to a Lib-Lab coalition. The Prime Minister Jim Callaghan formally signed an agreement which was accepted by twenty votes to four by the Cabinet and then given to David Steel, the Liberal leader, to show his team who had signed.

At lunch I chaired a meeting of the Fabian Industrial and Economic Policy Group and then rushed back to the House to talk to Tony in his room where I found him with Frances Morrell and Ian Mikardo. Ian was drafting a letter to Michael Cocks, the Chief Whip, for signature by Labour M.P.s saying that we would support the Government in the lobbies but would not feel obliged to implement or be bound by any agreement between the Cabinet and the Liberal Party. Tony referred to 1931 and the possible re-alignment of British politics. He had a copy of the agreement which he had taken from the Cabinet room despite the fact that Jim had ordered all the copies to be returned. I read it and felt quite numb. It was a coalition without office for the Liberals. In Cabinet Peter Shore had described the agreement as 'offensive' and said that it would lead to serious long-term problems for the party. Bruce Millan, Stan Orme and Tony had all spoken strongly against the pact.

Stan Orme came into the room but was not quite as pessimistic as Tony. He said he would have preferred an election. Tony argued that the pact was unnecessary because the Liberals would never have committed suicide. Judith Hart came in and supported the agreement as a necessary expedient. Norman Atkinson arrived and finally Michael Meacher. Everyone except Judith saw it as a bad deal and good for Reg Prentice and the right.

In Cabinet Edmund Dell had described it as 'an historic step' and Shirley Williams had said that further steps like this would be needed in future to keep out right-wing Governments and Margaret Thatcher represented the worst form of potential right-wing Government. Healey grovelled to the P.M. and Roy Mason produced an historic gem 'this is the moment of truth'.

Bit by bit the meeting broke up until Tony was left with Frances Morrell and myself. The question of resignation arose . . . It was agreed, exceptionally, that I should tell the press what had happened. I informed journalists from *The Times, Guardian, Mirror, Tribune, Star, Labour Weekly, Mail* and *Express.*

The Tribune Group met and broadly favoured Ian Mikardo's letter. At 8.45 p.m. I informed Tony in his room in the Commons. He was looking woefully dejected. Both Stan Orme and I counselled against resignation. One strange feature of the agreement was that only one member of the Tribune Group in the Cabinet, Stan Orme, refused to sign it.

Talking much later to Bruce Millan he confirmed that he had been against the deal saying that whilst very little had been given away, a principle had been breached. But many people are unexpectedly going along with the deal . . .

24th March 1977

Jim was very upset at the Cabinet about the leaks and tore them all off a strip. Later Roger Stott, Jim's P.P.S., confirmed that Jim was crotchety and tired. At the Party meeting attempts not to raise the subject failed. Ron Thomas was howled down when he said he did not support the deal. Afterwards John Mendelson made an interesting comment. He said that too many people in the Cabinet thought of themselves as historically indispensable. Jim did. Michael Foot did. Mrs Ghandi did. Michael Foot even thought that Mrs Ghandi was indispensable. It led them all, said John, to cling to power. As ever John was being a bit unfair.

Politicians can always come to terms (eventually) with a political crisis. But a crisis concerning nuclear energy has to be dealt with immediately. It provides a true test for a statesman. There are indeed many lessons to be drawn from the incident I describe below. It shows how a serious crisis in government comes about, how a capable minister goes about dealing with it, how Prime Ministers always try to intervene (in this case from 3,000 miles away) and how ministers can be misled about the true nature of a crisis. The incident concerned unofficial industrial action at the Windscale nuclear plant which had led to its closure. The pickets were refusing to let nitrogen through into the plant and Tony Benn had been advised of the possibility of a critical nuclear explosion if the nitrogen which was needed to keep the atmosphere inert did not arrive. The Cabinet Contingencies Unit, the organisation which dealt with emergencies, had been meeting daily to review the situation. Their plan was to break the strike with troops, thus leaving Tony Benn as a sort of latter-day Churchill. The big question to which some of the best brains in Britain seemed unable to give an answer was 'What was the deadline?' The note for 10th March 1977 in my diary takes up the story:

10th March 1977

This is the day that the panic button was pressed. The nuclear inspector brings forward the deadline, which previously was stretching out in the other direction, for getting nitrogen into Windscale. Decisions on whether to use troops have to be taken by Saturday. The Cabinet Contingencies Unit has been meeting every day. Tony calls the Nuclear Inspector in for an explanation of the shifting deadline and gets an explanation of a sort. But everyone is suspicious by now. We drive to Northolt Airport, an R.A.F. pilot salutes the minister, and two Civil Aviation Authority pilots fly us to Carlisle in a six-seater jet. With Tony are James Bretherton, his

Private Secretary, Bernard Ingham, his Press Officer, a departmental nuclear man with a doctorate, Frances Morrell and myself. Frances Morrell is terrified of flying. High winds which make the flight bumpy don't help but everyone is very nice to Frances. Forty m.p.h. cross winds make the landing difficult if not dangerous and the plane hits the runway at Carlisle with a thud greater than I ever felt before and Frances looks even more horrified. We would have been diverted to Newcastle but for the hurry.

Thence by car we go to the Waverly Hotel, a no-star, no-bathroom hotel, in Whitehaven. Tony turned down a smarter place at Keswick in order to be on the spot. The hotel looks like those you see at Exmouth, Victorian and pale blue and actually fairly comfortable. It's now 10 p.m. and immediately Tony meets the local union officials who have been doing the negotiations, notably Thompson-Reed of the G.M.U. (the Municipal Workers) and Leo of the A.U.E.W. (the Engineers). Thompson-Reed puts it nicely when he wonders whether a visit by the Pope or the Queen, let alone the minister, will help but before the end of the meeting he becomes far more friendly. His point was well taken because the visit may exacerbate the gulf that has grown between the shop-floor and the union officials. It's almost another Leyland situation in which this gulf has been created not by the dispute but by the pay policy and falling living standards. The dispute, which began with locker men on a 24-hour lightning strike and was escalated by the management with lay-offs, has grown like Topsy and now falls into three parts.

1. General dissatisfaction with the management stretching over years: The scientists have bungled industrial relations.
2. Lay-off or strike pay. When the management laid off workers the B.N.F.L. (British Nuclear Fuels Ltd) staff side (1,500) were laid off on full pay, the A.E.A. (Atomic Energy Authority) industrial workers (100) were laid off on full pay, the contractors workers were laid off on full pay and even the bus drivers were laid off on full pay. But the B.N.F.L. industrial staff (3,000) were laid off without pay. The management claim they are now on strike. They've offered a lump sum payment of £50–£60 for six weeks.
3. A new demand injected by the workers for 30p per hour (or £12 per week) as a special allowance for working at Windscale. This is a none too subtle attempt to break the pay policy. Amazingly the management insulted the industrial workers with a 1p per hour offer. God save us!

Tony met the management of B.N.F.L. and the managing director Con Allday ('Con by name, Con by nature' say the placards) and Sir John Hill, Chairman of the A.E.A. It's likely that Sir John's contract will be renewed in September when the existing one expires. Con is having a rough time of it these days what with the planning application, the anti-nuclear lobby and now this.

At midnight Frances Morrell and I and the Doctor (he is a geographer) walk by the harbour. I've no coat. It's spitting with rain, there is a howling wind up, a crane is still working, a few lights reflect on a bizarre scene, the sea is producing huge curved waves like a moving glass sheet on the protected side of the harbour. At least we now know we've moved from London.

11th March 1977

Meetings begin at 7 a.m. and go on for ten hours without a break for lunch. I know of few other ministers who could have handled the situation because all day decisions are having to be made against an atmosphere of mounting tension. I'm exhausted just listening. But events do prove that it is useful for ministers to have friends around them.

At the first meeting with the management and the local nuclear inspectorate it is clear that we have arrived with a mine of misinformation on the safety aspect and have not been properly briefed on the dispute. Thackeray, the nuclear inspector, makes it clear there is *no* safety risk now and there is *not* an imminent risk. Although nitrogen is the primary source for providing an inert atmosphere to stop uranium and plutonium compounds from becoming unstable there are three back-up systems if the nitrogen doesn't arrive. There's special cladding, there's oil to produce steam, there's Argon that can be used and there's dry air that could be pumped in. Asked what would happen if dry air were pumped in, Thackeray replies 'If I was really pushed I would say I don't think anything at all would happen'. Yet in the next sentence he says, 'We have already passed and gone beyond safety standards which I consider necessary but the risk is small'. What we were discovering was that the management had been using safety (as well as the workers) in a nuclear plant as a bargaining weapon. But now that the minister has stepped in to exercise his statutory responsibilities they are running scared. At last they've realised that the arrival of troops to break a picket line of some 500 pickets could damage nuclear development beyond repair. It's not merely a Labour Government and a Labour Minister who stand to lose heavily. At last the civil liberties issues are becoming clear to the management. Indeed how could this dispute and the use of troops help them with their planning application? How could it help get Parliament to sanction further funds next week for Windscale expansion when the Nuclear Finance Bill comes back to the House on Report Stage? So now the management is playing a game of moving deadlines back. But we advise Tony to watch this because it is being done as part of a plan to starve the workers back to work.

An unhelpful telegram comes from Washington from the Prime Minister. It wonders if the Secretary of State's visit might create alarm. The P.M. wants it played in a low key. That's fair enough but somebody has to do something to stop the troops going in. And in any event the Contingencies Unit agreed that Tony should come. They've also agreed to a statement in the House today, interrupting business, but it's now clear that cannot be done. A long day is under way. Tony ignores the telegram. The P.M. may be able to walk on the water but he can't conduct negotiations from 3,000 miles away.

A statement is put out to defuse some idiot remark on the radio that an explosion is imminent. There is a risk that the local population will turn against the work force.

So now we've seen the national officials (over breakfast), the nuclear inspectorate and the management. Next we move to the G.M.U. headquarters to meet twelve convenors who have been dealing with the strike. As we go in there are shouts of abuse and derision. 'You'll never get in again Benn' is one cry. But as they've been on strike for six weeks one could hardly expect them to shake him by the hand. Bob Maxwell, G.M.U., outlines the development of the dispute in a highly articulate speech. He explains the utter confusion at the start of the strike, the management's refusal to allow the unions to address the men and their action in setting up a microphone system so that they could do just that and then the management refusal 12 hours into the 24-hour strike to offer lay-off pay if the workers went back and two similar refusals in the next 32 hours. And now they're losing God knows how much a week. He describes the situation as being 'planned and engineered with a view to burying them in the ground once and for all.'

Upstairs at the full shop-stewards' meeting (70 in all) grievances pour out. Bitterness is enormous. The stewards are in no way going to recommend that the nitrogen be let in. One says 'We're finished as a nuclear industry'. Another refers to a picket's remark that the whole of Windscale should be buried in concrete. Another speaks of years of destruction in the field of industrial relations. Another says that 'you people from London only come up here when there's war or you want our vote' and the applause is tumultuous. Another aims it straight at the Government with 'You are crucifying us. You are the worst Tory Government we have'. And another aims it straight at Tony personally with 'You sanctioned the lay-offs. It's your fault. It's a deliberate political move'. I tell the man privately he's barmy if he believes that.

The meetings go on as Tony sees everyone again. It's clear the management will have to pay a larger lump-sum as lay-off money or a plant re-commissioning sum or the strike could go on forever. Some promise of a review of management's performance may also be needed.

Back with the national officials Tony makes a serious mistake. He starts talking about starting tripartite talks today with himself in the chair – not to negotiate but to see how the three major issues can be dealt with. But whatever he says he will be seen as starting negotiations. How can he present an increased award to his Cabinet colleagues if it starts with him being part of the negotiations? I have visions of reading the morning's papers 'Last night in Cumbria near Windscale the social contract disappeared. A Mr Benn is helping police with enquiries'. When we have a quiet moment Bernard Ingham tells Tony he is now being used. Frances Morrell and John Cunningham (the junior minister) tell him he must not start tripartite discussions. He must bollock the management rigid and make it clear that they must start negotiations immediately again with the unions and without saying that they must offer more he must make that clear. They will know that the lump-sum payment can and should be increased.

This he does. In the nicest possible way he rebukes Allday and Hill and instructs them to reopen negotiations. He then tells the national officials they must start talking and despite the desire to drag him in they must do it on their own. From that moment things go well. The national officials see a chance of getting credit from the men for negotiating more. Tony convinces the stewards that something will be done before Monday 9 a.m. at which time he has instructed Sir John Hill to be at his office (We've got to be there at 8 a.m. !!!) and they applaud him though outside they're still jeering. He says he's got no money to lay on the table but nobody believes him fortunately.

Then Tony does well with the media and concentrates on how responsible the men are and how there is no real safety risk. He comments on the impending Parliamentary debate and the planning application.

We drive back to Carlisle, get in the plane and unbelievably Tony keeps an engagement in Newcastle. The rest of us fly from Newcastle to Heathrow. Frances is terrified again so she drinks double gins and we drink double scotches and we all certainly need them. In the car on the way back from the airport we assess the situation and end up talking about television cops. Reality is with us again.

What had we learned or achieved? First that even at ministerial level there is a mine of misinformation around. Second that disputes like this cannot be settled in London still less by Downing Street Press Officers worried about their memoirs (they had ordered that T.V. be avoided), still less that they can be solved from Washington. Third, that management has to be told that they are not trusted by ministers on occasions like this. Fourth, that Labour ministers have to show whose side they are on. And fifth, that prayer may still be needed to stop the troops going in.

Drive back to Luton from House of Commons.

The troops were in fact never needed. The minister had effectively settled the dispute and an acceptable offer was made and nobody lost face. I am still haunted by the thought of how difficult it would have been for that minister if he had had no friends with him, with whom he could talk in between meetings and against whom he could bounce off his ideas.

Most ministers could do more to help themselves. They could make better use of their junior ministers, most of whom do no more than help keep the administration afloat. Some junior ministers are hardly kept in touch with what is going on in the departments outside their own work still less are they encouraged to contribute to policy. Some junior ministers who do seek to contribute to policy are by-passed by their civil servants who go direct to the minister or Secretary of State. Alex Lyon, an excellent junior minister at the Home Office when Roy Jenkins was Home Secretary found his civil servants trying to by-pass him because they did not like his policies on immigration. Rather than try to get the civil servants to act properly it was decided to sack Alex Lyon for being a bad team man. Some ministers have no political advisers and hold no regular minister's meetings or lunches at which policy can be discussed. All this is their own fault.

But what a minister most needs is an alternative source of advice to that which he gets from permanent officials. If party political democracy is to have any meaning this advice should come from political offices set up inside each Government Department. In the case of the Conservative Party the political office would be linked to the Conservative Central Office and in the case of the Labour Party to Transport House. If such offices were set up it would make it all the more imperative for the major political parties to organise themselves on a more democratic basis. These political offices would be staffed by whoever the minister wanted – industrialists, academics, journalists, trade unionists, shop stewards, maybe M.P.s. The people working in the political office would have to be given an executive function and departmental advice would have to go through them and civil servants would not be allowed to by-pass them and go direct to the minister. A political office is, of course a bureaucracy but I do not believe that a small temporary and political bureaucracy with countervailing power to a large permanent departmental bureaucracy would damage democracy. I accept that there are some difficulties in having M.P.s in political offices which would have to be thought through, but they are not insuperable. There is already a precedent: the local government committee system in which the information available to most committee members is not so different from that available to the chairman of the committee (who corresponds to the minister) works reasonably well.

4 Power Struggles at the Department of Energy

Tony Benn was Secretary of State at the Department of Energy for the period I am describing. Under him were three junior ministers, to whom he genuinely delegated work. I cannot ever remember him as Secretary of State having to override any of their decisions. The Minister of State was the effervescent Dickson Mabon. Some thought that Dickson Mabon as a social democrat was put into the department by the Prime Minister as a counterbalance to Tony Benn's left-wing Christian Socialism. John Cunningham, in charge of electricity, gas and conservation policy was a former P.P.S. to James Callaghan. I have no hesitation in saying that he was one of the ablest junior ministers I came across whether as a civil servant or a politician. There was a thoughtful, purposive manner about him: he not only wanted to establish political control, he did so. He was of enormous help to the Secretary of State at times of crisis and in particular in the power workers' dispute of November 1977 and the Windscale nitrogen crisis in March 1977. Windscale was in his constituency and he was able to bring knowledge where civil servants could only bring guesswork and ignorance. The third minister, in charge of coal and nuclear matters, was Alex Eadie whose advice was always eagerly sought and most of the time accepted.

The Secretary of State's two political advisers were Francis Cripps, a Cambridge economist, and Frances Morrell, both of them very able and highly effective in their work. They demonstrated the immense contribution at a political and at a technical level which political advisers can make. Indeed Sir John Hunt, the Secretary of the Cabinet, once told me after an Expenditure Committee hearing in the House of Commons on 14th February 1977 that Francis Cripps was his idea of what a political adviser should be. Sir John came across the work of Francis when he helped to prepare a paper on the alternative economic strategy for the Cabinet in 1976.

Tony Benn's method of operation on most issues was to talk things through with his ministers and political advisers. Sometimes he would argue with them, sometimes he would use them as sounding boards.

On some of the big issues concerning nuclear power one could follow his highly rational thinking over countless such meetings. He rarely engaged in such discussions or debates with his civil servants.

The department was a relatively small one, employing some 1,300 civil servants. Nevertheless it was an important policy-making department and it sponsored most of the giant industries which supplied power. Coal is publicly owned. All nuclear development takes place in the public sector. Gas and electricity are public concerns. And even in the field of oil supplies the British National Oil Corporation plays a significant role.

At the head of the department was Sir Jack Rampton, the Permanent Secretary. Under him were four Deputy Secretaries, 16 Under Secretaries and 51 Assistant Secretaries (23rd May 1979). They all did their best and most of them did their work well. There was particular harmony between the Secretary of State and those working on the oil side under Mr John Liverman, a Deputy Secretary, and between him and Sir Frank Kearton, chairman of the British National Oil Corporation. The problem in that field was with the oil companies and the Treasury. Notwithstanding a remark made to me on 2nd February 1977 shortly after I had become Tony Benn's P.P.S. by Mr Jasper Cross, an Under Secretary, that 'too many coal miners are leaning on their shovels', the Secretary of State found the coal division responsive to his wishes. There is no doubt in my mind that the same could be said for gas and electricity matters where the Secretary of State was on excellent terms with Mr Glyn England, the chairman of the Central Electricity Generating Board, and Sir Francis Tombs, the chairman of the Electricity Council, and on reasonable terms with Sir Denis Rooke, the chairman of the Gas Council. The areas where there was most friction were E.E.C. matters and nuclear power. This chapter deals in the main with some of the struggles that took place in that field.

The Permanent Secretary, Sir Jack Rampton, was a man concerned to sustain the integrity of the departmental policy. Permanent Secretaries not only advise ministers, they also run great departments of state. Inevitably their modes of operation will be different. But in my experience most of them make it their business to stick pretty closely to their ministers. With Sir Jack Rampton it was different. He was absent, of his own volition, from many meetings which I would have expected a Permanent Secretary to attend. After he lost the battle with his Secretary of State over the choice of thermal nuclear reactors his presence seemed even less noticeable than before. Indeed occasionally and good-humouredly I would tell Tony Benn with mock excitement in my voice that I had seen him disappearing up the corridor. I was sure it was he. The more serious point was that the battle over the choice of thermal nuclear reactors finally established political control of the department. After that there was no doubt that the Secretary of State was in charge. That was where Richard Crossman never quite succeeded at the Ministry of Housing and something that Tony Benn never managed at the Department of Industry.

In addition to the Permanent Secretary and his administrative mandarins the department had a Chief Scientist to advise the Secretary of State. At first the Chief Scientist was Dr Walter Marshall, subsequently it was Sir Hermann Bondi who moved over from the Ministry of Defence. Dr Marshall expressed himself with a certainty on the awesome issues of atomic and nuclear power that I found unnerving. On the issue of whether Britain should develop the Advanced Gas Cooled Reactor (AGR) or go for the American Pressure Water Reactor (PWR) Dr Marshall was PWR man. I felt that he had too many conflicting roles and the responsibility for this lay squarely with the Secretary of State. Dr Marshall was not only the Chief Scientific Adviser at the Department of Energy, he was also deputy-chairman of the Atomic Energy Authority (who could hardly have been said to take up a neutral role over the development of atomic power) and safety adviser to the Shah of Iran's nuclear programme. When I first heard of this latter point from Dr Marshall himself on 17th May 1977 I could not believe it. Here in the U.K. the Secretary of State had taken no decision on whether to proceed with the AGR or the PWR but the Shah of Iran had no doubts that he wanted to build PWRs and a U.K. civil servant was advising him. There had been talks between Dr Marshall and the Iranian Foreign Minister about the possible purchase by Iran from Britain of 20 PWRs, a decision which was to be dependent on the U.K. opting for the development of PWRs for its own use. It seemed a dubious deal to me because the Shah had previously wanted France and Germany and the United States to tender for his contracts. Those countries had refused because they wanted a negotiated contract into which they could write their own profits. At the meeting on 17th May 1977 Dr Marshall spoke of Iran's new 'maturity'. He was at that moment, he said, testing the safety of French and German reactors that might be built in Iran and added 'I would see no safety problems with a British system'.

Now that the Shah has been deposed one might wonder at Iran's new 'maturity' and now that the U.S.A. has experienced the Harrisburg PWR fiasco can one really be as confident as the Chief Scientist, Dr Marshall, was about safety matters? Part of the Shah's interest may have been in the bomb.

Tony Benn realised that the situation was unsatisfactory and so when Sir Hermann Bondi came to the department he was given one role only – that of Chief Scientific Adviser to the Secretary of State.

Personally I preferred Sir Hermann's quieter more relaxed and more sophisticated style to that of Dr Marshall. The fact that he, Sir Hermann, seemed to incline towards the PWR made me think that there might be something to be said in its favour, although in public and in private I continued to support the AGR as much because the Secretary of State supported it as for anything else and because of the opposition which he met from his civil servants. It is to this that I now turn.

Power struggle No. 1

Quite the most astonishing and deliberate attempt by civil servants to frustrate ministerial power and authority occurred over the question of the future development of nuclear power in Britain. The whole Whitehall machine came together to defeat ministers and used tactics which would have made self-respecting civil servants of yesteryear weep. The tactics were indeed such as to suggest the disappearance of that central core of integrity which once characterised the working of the civil service machine.

The argument was eventually resolved in favour of ministers when the Secretary of State for Energy made the following statement in the House of Commons on 25th January 1978 (Hansard, Col. 1391):

> With permission, Mr Speaker, I wish to make a statement about nuclear reactors for the British power programme.
>
> The House will recall that on 28th June 1976 I announced that I was taking stock of progress with the Steam Generating Heavy Water Reactor (SGHWR) programme at the suggestion of the United Kingdom Atomic Energy Authority.
>
> Since then we have carried out a thorough review of thermal reactor policy. The National Nuclear Corporation (N.N.C.) has submitted its comparative assessment of thermal reactor systems, which has been made available to the House. The Nuclear Installations Inspectorate (N.I.I.) has given its advice on the generic safety issues of the pressurised water reactor, which has also been made available to the House. There has been extensive consultation with all the main parties.
>
> It is the unanimous advice of all concerned that in the changed circumstances of today the SGHWR should not be adopted for the next power station orders. The Government have accordingly decided that it would be right to discontinue work on the SGHWR.
>
> The Government agree with the Electricity Supply Boards that two early nuclear orders are needed and that these must be advanced gas-cooled reactors. The Government have therefore de-

cided to authorise the Central Electricity Generating Board and South of Scotland Electricity Board to begin work at once with a view to ordering one AGR station each as soon as possible.

The decision will enable our nuclear industry to build on our extensive experience of gas-cooled technology. The generating boards have already begun to accumulate operating experience with the AGRs which have so far been commissioned. The completion of the remaining stations in the existing AGR programme and the successful construction of the next AGR orders will be the first priority in our thermal nuclear programme.

The Government also consider, having regard to the importance of nuclear power and present knowledge of the different systems, that the United Kingdom's thermal reactor strategy should not at this stage be dependent upon an exclusive commitment to any one reactor system, and that in addition to the AGR we must develop the option of adopting the PWR system in the early 1980s. This view is also supported by the electricity supply industry.

The electricity supply industry has indicated that, to establish the PWR as a valid option, it wishes to declare an intention that, provided design work is satisfactorily completed and all necessary Government and other consents and safety clearances have been obtained, it will order a PWR station. It does not consider that a start on site could be made before 1982. This intention, which does not call for an immediate order or a Letter of Intent at the present time, is endorsed by the Government.

All future orders beyond those which I have indicated today will be a matter for decision at the appropriate time. Our aim is to establish a flexible strategy for the United Kingdom nuclear power programme in the light of developing circumstances. We believe that these decisions will do so.

During the previous months Whitehall's civil servants fought tooth and claw to achieve a different result. They did not want to see the cautious development of nuclear power based on the building of two Advanced Gas Cooled Reactors. They wanted the Government to throw caution to the winds and order at a cost of some £20 billion some thirty or so American Pressure Water Reactors. Had the expenditure of £20 billion of PWRs gone ahead it would have meant the Government embarking on the most costly project ever in times of peace. It would, as we now know but did not then, have meant ordering some thirty reactors not dissimilar to the Harrisburg reactor which went critical in America, had to be closed down and could have been a serious hazard for thousands of people living in the area where it stood.

Sir Jack Rampton, at a meeting at the Department on 11th January

1978, said of a Pressure Water Reactor which he had seen in the U.S.A. that it was 'aesthetically beautiful'. That is hardly the expression which would have first come to the mind of pregnant mothers living in the Harrisburg area as they packed their belongings for fear of radiation poisoning.

The Permanent Secretary's views, which represented the collective wisdom of the Department of Energy, were set out in a memorandum, *Nuclear Reactor Choice*, to the Secretary of State on 15th November 1977. The memo begins by apologising for any 'drafting imperfections' that might have been occasioned by the urgency in producing the memorandum on account of having to wait for the results of the discussions of the previous week. The following is an outline of Sir Jack Rampton's main points.

Nuclear Reactor Choice

1. The situation we were now faced with had similarities with 1974. In 1974 we dropped the High Temperature Reactor and chose between the Steam Generated Heavy Water Reactor and the Pressure Water Reactor. This time we were dropping the SGHWR and we were left with the Advanced Gas-Cooled Reactor and the PWR. The SGHWR, of which incidentally Frank Tombs was probably the strongest advocate, was a wrong decision. We had lost three critical years, wasted resources, and in the meantime created despondency in both the electricity supply and manufacturing industries.
2. To go for the AGR now as our main system would be to make the same mistake as we did in 1974. In 1974 we backed a commercially unproved system. The AGR was still an unproven system. Eighteen months was not sufficient or adequate experience on which to decide to adopt it as our main future system. It was possible that the AGR would prove a reliable and dependable system. But at this stage we could not be sure. Even if it did behave satisfactorily, its likely export prospects, higher cost of electricity production and its on site problems, still made it less attractive than the PWR as the main system on which we should rely, as well as depriving us of a real international presence.
3. It was said that the PWR was not a proven system. This was not so. The 200 Reactor years operating experience of the PWR had to be compared with our very limited experience with the AGRs which only began to come into commercial operation last year. (i.e. 1976)
4. It was also argued that it would take a long time to produce 'a British' PWR. He believed this was a very exaggerated point. It had been one of the curses of U.K. behaviour in the nuclear and other high technology fields that we always wanted to 'improve' other people's established designs. Minimum change was called for and British for the

sake of being British made no sense. Nor was it credible that somehow it was much more difficult for the U.K. technically to introduce a PWR than the wide range of other countries that had done so, particularly when you considered which those countries were, many with not half the industrial know-how and back-up that we had.

5. The economic, industrial and energy supply considerations all pointed decisively in his view in favour of our adopting the PWR as our preferred main system for the future. If one went for AGRs with minimum delay and possibly deferred effort on PWRs without any commitment not to build any, we would have really taken a decision which would make it impossible for us to have a PWR capability in meaningful time. This was not true in reverse since, if necessary, we could always fall back on the AGR on which experience would go on accumulating.

6. He was in no doubt that the best course would be to move direct to the ordering of PWR. If we concentrate, with full and positive Government support, our own resources and resources made available by the U.S. the ordering timescale for the PWR suggested by the Central Electricity Generating Board could well prove pessimistic. On this basis he did not believe that the PWRs need be any later on the ground than AGRs.

7. If however, the C.E.G.B. and the National Nuclear Corporation were unable to accept this even on the premise set out in point 4 then there might be a case for one or two more AGR orders. But, if it were decided to order more AGRs, it was most important that there should be the absolute minimum of change to the existing design for Hinckley 'B' (an AGR power station) and it should be on the clear understanding that we were adopting the PWR as our main system for the long term, and that nothing should hinder their development in the shortest possible time.

8. A policy based on PWRs might well need a bigger effort of public explanation and political determination. But what we were trying to do at this stage was to make a judgment on what was likely to be most in the longer term interest of the U.K.'s economic, industrial and energy supply future. Getting this wrong could have far-reaching consequences. His own strong advice was that the Government should:

(a) firmly commit itself to the PWR as the main system:

(b) reconsider with the C.E.G.B. whether, with full political and industrial support, a PWR could be got on the ground at least as quick as an AGR;

(c) allow only such further AGRs as may be absolutely necessary to meet the immediate situation.

9. There was a final word on the commercial Fast Breeder Reactor. There could be no final decision on this at least until the end of next

year, given the commitment to a full enquiry. It was not possible at this stage to be sure whether the resources needed to get the PWR system into series ordering plus possibly one or two more AGRs would defer the possibility of building a U.K. FBR. That would have to be carefully considered further. But what did seem clear was that, far from inhibiting an early decision to collaborate with the French/Germans or the U.S., the prospects would actually be improved; and in his view the resources would certainly be available for that.

The important points to consider are:

1. The paper set out not ministerial policy but the policy of the department.
2. The department knew that what they were proposing conflicted totally with the views of the Secretary of State and his junior ministers.
3. The paper was produced at a very late stage in the discussions although the department's mind had clearly been made up much earlier; in the department's defence it could be said that they felt it necessary to wait not only till they had all the written evidence from a variety of sources but also till they could take account of what was said in the various discussions which the minister had been holding. The bizarre concern with drafting errors tells a story in itself about what civil servants consider important. (When I was a civil servant in the Ministry of Housing and Local Government all my colleagues were obsessed with the need for perfection in drafting. It was the one skill I picked up in the service which I did not have when I went in.)

The Permanent Secretary's memorandum which was seen as a direct challenge to the Secretary of State and which was to precipitate a crisis of confidence, should be contrasted with the memorandum submitted by the junior minister directly responsible for nuclear power, Alex Eadie. This said:

> 1. We would find it difficult to defend a decision to pursue two thermal reactor systems even if the AGR was presented as a short term project and the PWR as a longer term investment.
> 2. It means a diffusing of financial and scientific resources. This could lead to inefficiency and delay in commencing the building of our next thermal nuclear station – this is something we cannot afford. What is perhaps worse is that I believe such a decision would receive a political hammering and that, at this time, would not be helpful to the industry and would be ammunition to opponents of nuclear power.
> 3. To go for two systems would, I believe, mean inevitable delay in our ability to commence work on a Commercial Fast Breeder (if we

decide to go ahead with a FBR in due course). I think that if we are pursuing two thermal reactor systems we would not be able to make available the necessary resources to develop the FBR.
4. I have looked at the claims in favour of PWRs and I am not impressed by the argument that it would have export potential. It would be a considerable time before we could have a PWR functioning in Britain and it is not possible to forecast accurately what the future world markets for PWRs would be. History has shown us, particularly in the energy field, how difficult it is to make predictions.
5. I think that to go for a PWR system could trigger off more opposition to nuclear power because it would be seen as a foreign reactor, we cannot afford to run this risk because we need thermal nuclear stations for the 1980s.

Having been present at some of the meetings you have had with members of the industry I have come to the conclusion that the AGR offers us the best prospects of nuclear power within the time scale in which we need it.

The statement that the running life of our AGRs is limited has been used as an argument against fully adopting the system. We will of course gain more experience as our five AGRs become operational. A British PWR could be more of an unknown quantity for we do not know yet what precise safety standards the N.I.I. will finally insist on. They have said of the PWRs that on safety grounds they have no objections to the system 'in principle'.

The country needs nuclear power and it is essential that the industry gets an immediate order for a nuclear power station. Whatever choice we make we cannot be guaranteed a completely smooth passage but I believe the AGR offers us the best prospects, for our next thermal reactor.

My diary of 16th November 1977 picks up the story.

The bombshell is contained in the department's recommendation on the choice of thermal nuclear reactor system. This is to opt wholly for the PWR against the advice of not only the minister but also the customers (i.e. the Electricity Council, the C.E.G.B. and the S.E.G.B.), the National Nuclear Corporation and the bulk of the supplying industry. Rampton takes the lead at the meeting – his first appearance for some time – and all the civil servants back him, including the new Chief Scientist, Hermann Bondi, who has come over from the Ministry of Defence. The paper is openly critical of Tombs. The only argument I can see justifying their proposal is that of the reliability of the AGR. Rampton wants a PWR ordered immediately for 1982 and says that work could begin on site before then despite the fact that everyone else says that this cannot be done. He has no evidence for his assertion. Although the first PWR, if one was built, would not be on stream until 1989 the series ordering of PWRs would have to start in the mid-1980s i.e. before there was any British experience of a British version of the reactor in operation.

Tony makes it clear that he will never accept the department's recommendation and asks why twenty-one years of British experience in Gas Cooled Reactors should be cast aside. Answer – because the PWR is a proven system. Tony asks them if they are advising him to go for the PWR even if the AGRs prove successful. Answer – yes. The PWRs, have, they say, 200 years operational experience. This statement turns out to mean that some 1,100 megawatt stations have been in operation for about three years.

When Rampton says that the PWR option will be closed unless firm orders are placed Tony suggests that such is the desire for PWRs on the part of civil servants in the room and elsewhere that the option could never be closed. He comments acidly on the lateness of their recommendation bearing in mind that he has to go to Cabinet in a week's time. The Cabinet have asked for a week to consider the paper. Perhaps more extraordinary Sir Kenneth Berrill, the head of the Think-Tank who is preparing a paper on the subject for the Cabinet, has asked Tony for notes on all the advice he has received from various sources. Such a request is unprecedented and suggests considerable mistrust on Berrill's part occasioned by briefing from civil servants from the Department of Energy behind Benn's back.

Certainly the whole Whitehall machine is about to go into action. A phenomenal battle is about to start.

Nine Scottish M.P.s arrive to discuss the oil reserves . . .

In the Lobby Alex Eadie says he would like to see the back of Rampton. I suggest that there are three possible explanations for Rampton's attitude on nuclear energy –

1. that the department is trying to vindicate its advice last time round when it wanted the PWR and not the SGHWR;

2. the department really does believe PWR is the best choice today; and

3. there is something else. Alex opts for 3. He says that the reason why the SGHWR failed was that at the time (and he was there) there was a disagreement between Tombs from the Electricity Council and Sir Arthur Hawkins, head of the C.E.G.B. and that the industry were determined that the SGHWR should not be a success. He says that Tombs told him from the first that because of the opposition of the C.E.G.B. and G.E.C. and others the SGHWR would never be built.

The following day unsuccessful attempts were made through the head of the civil service, Sir Douglas Allen, to get Mr John Liverman appointed as a joint Permanent Secretary with Sir Jack Rampton. Liverman was an extremely able and helpful civil servant in charge of negotiations with the oil companies.

On 28th November unhappy events threatened to turn nasty. The Secretary of State's political advisers who had been asked to prepare a paper for the Cabinet setting out the Secretary of State's view found the department unwilling to co-operate when a civil servant declared that he could not really help because the department could not accept the Secretary of State's terms of reference for the paper. These were: 1. that the paper should show that there was a need to order two AGRs and; 2. that it should set out the options thenceforward – AGR or PWR or both. The civil servant was not to blame and must have been acting under instructions. So much for the theory that once a minister had made up his mind a department does all it can to help him.

This incident ended with a flurry of comings and goings designed to re-assert ministerial control from which came agreement that the Assistant Secretary in the nuclear division would lend his services to the Secretary of State. Indeed the Assistant Secretary under the guidance of the political advisers produced a very good and helpful paper with excellent appendices.

But this did not mean that civil servants had returned to their constitutional role of working for and helping their minister. For the Think-Tank was busily preparing another paper for the Cabinet not dissimilar to Sir Jack Rampton's earlier memorandum. This paper was to call for the expenditure of some £20 billion on the series ordering of PWRs. It could only have been prepared with the help of the Department of Energy and possibly G.E.C. Not to put too fine a point on it, civil servants at the Department of Energy were briefing the Think-Tank so that it could oppose their minister. Civil servants at the department and the Think-Tank were advocating the expenditure of billions of pounds of public money on a PWR reactor before it was known if the nuclear inspectorate would clear it on safety grounds and they were advocating the expenditure at a time when there was no reliable evidence presented to the minister on the future supply and demand for energy that could justify the expenditure.

The situation had all the makings of a public scandal. It was difficult to see how even a PWR addict could justify such an ordering programme. My diary note for 15th December 1979 asks:

> Why not wait until 1981 when the nuclear inspectorate may have cleared the PWR on safety grounds? Why not one PWR for the moment? Why not see how the AGRs develop? Why? Why? Why?

> . . . What is the curious role of the Treasury in all this? They seem anxious to commit enormous sums of money on nuclear power in general and on the PWR in particular. Their normal stance is to save pennies rather than commit themselves to the expenditure of billions of pounds . . . Fortunately the Think-Tank paper is not well argued and the Secretary of the Cabinet has congratulated the department (in reality the political advisers) on their paper.

On 15th December 1977 the Prime Minister had a meeting with Sir Arnold Weinstock, the Managing Director of G.E.C., and forgot to mention the meeting to the Secretary of State for Energy when he, the P.M., chaired a Cabinet sub-committee meeting on 16th December 1977 to discuss the choice of nuclear reactor. A minute of the meeting between the P.M. and Sir Arnold, which may have been accidentally delayed, arrived at the department after the Cabinet sub-committee meeting had already started. My diary note for 16th December 1977 comments:

> What sort of way to govern a country is this? One might have expected the P.M. to tell the Secretary of State for Energy that he was meeting an industrialist to discuss energy policy *before* the meeting took place. Now in the past few days the P.M. has seen both Weinstock and Rampton (prior to the P.M. discussing energy policy with Giscard) without telling the Secretary of State concerned that he was to do so.
>
> Tony for once has supporters in the Cabinet so he may win this argument whatever the P.M.'s views. At this morning's meeting he was supported by David Owen (against his Foreign Office brief), by Shirley Williams, by Peter Shore, by Bruce Millan and, though absent, by Roy Hattersley. This may be due to the fact that Tony's political advisers had spoken to the political advisers of the various ministers before the meeting. They really are doing an excellent job.
>
> Against a sane approach are the Chancellor, Denis Healey, the Chancellor's Chief Secretary, Joel Barnett, and Harold Lever, the Chancellor of the Duchy of Lancaster. They are talking about an AGR for Scotland only but the Scottish Electricity Generating Board will never wear that and become the only people on earth developing a new AGR. The Cabinet sub-committee has asked Tony to draw up another paper on why the industry needs two AGRs now if it is to survive and asked him to take further advice on how to proceed.

Following on the disagreement in the Cabinet sub-committee a second round of consultations took place.

The role as well as the competence of civil servants in this burgeoning affair was called further into question at meetings held on 10th January 1978. My diary note for that day develops the story:

> This morning Tony saw Sir John Hill, chairman of the Atomic Energy Authority, and then Sir Kenneth Keith and Mr Wyghfield from Rolls-Royce who see themselves as PWR specialists having built 50-megawatt tiny-bobber PWRs for 'submersible vehicles', a phrase which I take to mean nuclear submarines. I was not at either of these meetings.
>
> I did attend the meeting at 4.30 p.m. with Lord Aldington, chairman of the National Nuclear Corporation and a G.E.C. man, and Mr Ned Franklin from the Nuclear Power Corporation held in Tony's room in the House of Commons because of a three-line whip.
>
> Lord Aldington gives two reasons for having a PWR back-up to the AGR that would take the form of a Letter of Intent to Westinghouse, the American firm which designs PWRs that the C.E.G.B. would order a PWR if all the various hurdles were successfully surmounted.
>
> First, that was the only way in which Westinghouse would release the necessary technology. Then he added a proviso that although it might be expensive it might be possible in the future to persuade Westinghouse to sell the information needed to build a PWR without placing an order or Letter of Intent. This proviso was news to me, news to the political adviser and news to Tony himself. None of us could remember it being made at previous meetings with Lord Aldington. But when challenged Lord Aldington insisted that he had given the advice previously and had confirmed it in writing in a letter of 10th November.
>
> The point is important because if the advice had been given before orally at *meetings* his civil servants had subsequently not shown him any confirmation in writing.
>
> Aldington and Franklin gave as their second reason for wanting to order a PWR the loss of morale of the staff of the Nuclear Power Corporation. They, the N.P.C., were currently losing trained staff at the rate of 1 per cent per month and this would continue unless they believed that there was a realistic prospect of a PWR order which a Letter of Intent would give. It was also important that British industry should have experience of building a PWR here, if it was to be a genuine option.
>
> When asked how the organisation would look if the N.P.C. were producing AGRs and PWRs Aldington and Franklin became vague. They were equally vague on the time that it would take to build PWRs and cost escalation and efficiency. They could not even say if the reactor that would be ordered would be a single shaft 1,300

megawatt reactor or a two shaft 1,300 megawatt reactor with each shaft producing 650 megawatts. For people seeking to spend billions of pounds of the public's money they seem to have few of the answers.

Then it emerged that there was no single shaft 1,300 megawatt reactor in action anywhere in the world and nor was there any two shaft 1,300 megawatt reactor in action anywhere in the world of the type that would be required. This was astonishing news because the whole PWR thesis up to now has been that we are ordering technology which exists.

The meeting had in effect produced three criticisms of the department's civil servants. They had misled Tony whether accidentally or otherwise: 1. in telling him again and again that Britain could not obtain the information they would require from Westinghouse to build a PWR without building a PWR; 2. in not telling the minister that there were no PWRs of the type the C.E.G.B. would want in existence and; 3. in not finding out what the proposed structure for the N.P.C. was. These are very serious criticisms indeed of the civil servants concerned.

If anyone could have pulled it off for the PWR lobby, which by now was sensing defeat, it was Sir Arnold Weinstock. He arrived at the department at 11 a.m. on Wednesday 11th January 1978. Sir Arnold had made a basic mistake in his campaign. While it had been a good move to see the Prime Minister, it had been a bad error to allow the G.E.C. case to be put by Lord Aldington if only because Lord Aldington's first duty, which he carried out to the best of his ability, was to put the case for the National Nuclear Corporation. Sir Arnold's view that what is good for G.E.C. is good for Britain was not shared by everyone at the N.N.C. and this came through in Lord Aldington's approach, despite his efforts to keep the PWR option firm.

Sir Arnold's approach at the meeting was in part impressive, in part theatrical and in part ruthless. He begun like someone with a deep rational commitment to the PWR. He said that he had originally favoured the AGR and had given evidence to a Commons Select Committee to that effect. He had then been talked out of his view by Mr Robert Peddie of the C.E.G.B. way back in 1972 and had become converted to the proposition that the PWR was the better bet in an industrial context. He had subsequently visited the Westinghouse operations in the U.S.A. and had been impressed by their capacity for the factory production of key components. After that he had negotiated a collaborative agreement with Cruesot Loire and Framatone in France which would have involved a joint programme with the pressure vessels being produced in France and the reactor internals being produced in the U.K. This agreement had, of course, not been implemented because of the decision of the Government to go for an SGHWR programme but Cruesot Loire had recently confirmed that there was still scope for co-operation if the Government decided on a PWR programme. In the meantime he had put pressure on the Nuclear Power Corporation to ensure that when they did need to order components for the AGR programme from abroad, such as special types of steel, these came from French sources. If a collaborative agreement could be confirmed then a joint selling organisation could be created which would soon, given the size of the French programme and the diminishing American influence in it, tackle Westinghouse from a position of strength. There was however no truth in the rumour that G.E.C. might buy up Westinghouse's interests in Europe. The nature of their pension scheme would make it an unattractive proposition. The Government should switch entirely to a PWR programme immediately. G.E.C., he stressed, was not set to make enormous sums of money out of a PWR choice. What they wanted was a system which would enable them to sell their turbines and reactor internals abroad more effectively and this could only mean a PWR.

Effectively Sir Arnold was putting forward an industrial argument for the PWR which the civil servants at the Department of Energy had up to then clearly not understood. This argument had first surfaced in the Think-Tank report. His basic interest was not in PWRs at all but in developing a new turbo-generating industry with 3,000 r.p.m. turbo-generators. These he could export. But he needed to test the new technology involved and this could only be done if the Government ordered a PWR and allowed him to supply the generators for testing. He made it clear that although the aim was for a series of PWRs using new single shaft 1,300 megawatt generators the first PWR would have to have two 650 single shaft generators in reserve in case there were too many problems with the single shaft. In short he wanted the Government to pay for the development costs of his new technology.

All this was very impressive and soundly argued from G.E.C.'s point of view.

Then came the theatrical performance. My diary note puts it thus:

'We could do it you know', said Sir Arnold. 'We're a good company. We could become world leaders. We're not a nasty, greedy, parasitical organisation like people make us out to be.' And then changing tack completely he said to everyone's surprise, 'We helped the Government out over Meriden and didn't even get a letter of thanks'.

I could almost see the tears coming as Tony replied that he could not be held responsible for G.E.C.'s publicity needs. 'We didn't want publicity. Just a letter of thanks for the people who did the work,' he replied.

The ruthless performance came when Sir Arnold was discussing personalities and the need to recognise both the N.N.C. and the N.P.C. Eric Varley, Secretary of State for Industry, was described as one of a 'mad group' who sanctioned the SGHWR. Mr Roy Berridge, the chairman of the Scottish Generating Board, was a 'prize nincompoop' who held the illogical view that he could only buy the AGR if someone else bought it too. 'Either he wants it or he doesn't.' Mr Ned Franklin of the N.P.C. was a man with 'too big an idea of his own importance. You can't run a business by committee as Franklin does. He lets financial controllers discuss physics. There are too many people talking about subjects of which they know nothing.' The 'Atomic Energy Authority mafia', he said, 'would have their comeuppance. They had developed the AGR and want to develop the Fast Breeder. Everything they do is a flop.' Scorn too was poured by Sir Arnold in the idea that Rolls-Royce were capable of building the PWRs.

After the meeting Sir Arnold complained that one of the advisers of the Secretary of State had talked to a journalist from the *Observer* and to everyone's complete surprise was backed up by Sir Jack. Quite why the Permanent Secretary should have taken the side of the managing director of G.E.C. against the minister's political adviser is difficult to know. In any event Sir Jack must have been aware that someone in the department was giving the press pro-PWR briefs.

On 12th January at a further meeting the C.E.G.B., S.E.G.B. and the Electricity Council made it clear that they would not be prepared to order PWRs and drop the AGR programme. They wanted to order two AGRs and have a Letter of Intent to order a PWR subject to certain provisos on safety, design etc. As they were so firm and united in their views and they were the customers it was clear that the PWR lobby could not win. They also made it clear that if Sir Arnold Weinstock pulled out of the nuclear business (i.e. out of the N.N.C.–N.P.C.) as he threatened to do it would make no difference. All he does, they said, is to supply generators and he will not stop doing that. They made it clear, too, that they would not be disappointed if Sir Arnold and G.E.C. pulled out of the N.N.C.–N.P.C.

At this stage and with victory in sight in what had turned out to be one of the biggest Whitehall-Westminster battles ever fought, the Secretary of State made what I would regard as two minor and unaccustomed errors. Up to this point his performance had been brilliant. At meetings he displayed all his outstanding administrative and political skills in probing the PWR arguments and getting the PWR lobbyists themselves to damage their own case. Moreover, thinking back on these meetings and checking through my diary I cannot remember, and certainly have not recorded, one single intervention by his civil servants which was designed to help him. If behind the scenes he had the backing of the two ablest political advisers in Whitehall and one competent Assistant Secretary one could still only reflect on the isolation of the minister.

His first error, like the second, of no practical consequence, was to call an unattributable press briefing. He rarely did this for the reason that he believed very strongly that politicians who had something to say should be prepared to stand up and be named as well as counted. Nothing of consequence emerged at or from the meeting but the record the following day was not much straighter than it had been the day before. The press experts on energy matters who turned up showed themselves to be more confused than malicious about the issues. One could hardly blame them. It was a complicated subject and most of the people feeding them with information had axes to grind. As the argument had developed I myself had been constantly surprised by new facts and interpretations which had come forward. Nothing that the department produced, unless one included the Cabinet paper prepared by the political advisers and the Assistant Secretary, contained any clear step-by-step analysis.

Then on 16th January Sir Arnold Weinstock asked for a meeting with the Secretary of State from which his political advisers were to be excluded, although the Permanent Secretary and Secretary of State's Private Secretary were to be present. When I said that it was a bit odd that Sir Arnold should be able to say who the minister could and could not bring to meetings Tony Benn replied that he could hardly refuse Britain's top industrialist a private meeting if he wanted one. At the meeting Sir Arnold, presumably knowing that he had lost the battle, made it clear that he was going to be helpful whatever happened. No note of the meeting was taken.

My diary note for 17th says rather shamefacedly:

17th January 1978

I intended to go to the meeting with Westinghouse this morning but I woke up late. I heard later that Westinghouse had been most helpful and had said they would help in any way they could and would be prepared to re-negotiate the agreement if necessary. As the German concern the Kraftswerk Union had been equally helpful the previous day one could not but wonder about the soundness of the advice which Lord Aldington had been giving.

19th January 1978

Everyone is happy as it seems that the thermal reactor choice battle has been won. Weinstock, Rampton, Varley and everyone else have been outflanked. Varley has agreed the paper that should go to the Cabinet sub-committee next Tuesday.

24th January 1978

At E.Y. [Economic Strategy Committee] today the battle was won. A civil servant seems surprised when I tell him that I'm agnostic as between the AGR and PWR and only supported the AGR because Tony did. One of the political advisers comments 'I don't care whether we have AGRs or PWRs. The point is we've won'. The P.M. who chaired the meeting was angry about leaks. There is to be a statement tomorrow in the House pending which there is to be 'a total publicity black-out'. The PWR lobby will be furious. It is well represented on the Tory benches. It will be fun.

25th January 1978

The thermal reactor announcement is made in the Commons and the triumph is complete. There were some minor changes in the statement. The ability of some ministers to copy their civil servants in trying to iron out alleged drafting imperfections is alarming. A great victory for Tony against great odds.

A battle of this magnitude inevitably leaves behind a number of questions and allows for lessons to be drawn from it. How did Tony Benn win? I put the question that way because it was very much a personal victory in the sense that I could see few other ministers in similar circumstances holding out as he did. Normally a combination of the Whitehall machine, departmental civil servants, the Think-Tank, the Foreign Office, the Treasury, the Ministry of Defence, backed by the country's leading industrialist with the sympathetic ear of the Prime Minister, would win any battle. Indeed that is a central thesis of this book.

Tony Benn won the argument for the AGR:

1. because of his own skills and those of his political advisers. He had one advantage over civil servants not normally given to ministers. His ten years' political experience dealing with industrial matters, including the problems of nuclear power, meant that he knew far more about the subject than did his Permanent Secretary, Sir Jack Rampton, or any of his departmental civil servants. Usually the reverse is true. This experience enabled him to expose their arguments in a way in which a minister would not normally be able to do;

2. because the customers for the power stations – the C.E.G.B., the S.E.G.B. and the Electricity Council – all wanted AGRs first because AGRs would come on stream in advance of PWRs (though if the truth was told they wanted PWRs as well). This one fact forced them to argue more strongly for the AGR than they would normally have done;
3. because the supplying industry who would build the reactors wanted AGRs for the same reason. Jobs would be lost if they had to wait for PWRs;
4. because the spending ministries and ministers did not want to see large sums of public money tied up in nuclear power which they might otherwise spend.

Can anything be said in defence of the actions of the civil servants concerned at the Department of Energy? The short answer of the democrat must be 'no'. The official explanation would however run something like this. The Department of Energy is charged by statute to see that the country has secure and adequate supplies of energy. The PWR would have assisted that aim. It would have brought nuclear power on stream in the 1990s when oil supplies were running out and it would have lessened our dependence on coal which in the light of the 1974 confrontation between the miners and the Heath Government was a desirable aim. The energy produced would have been cheaper than that produced by coal or oil or alternative sources. So the department stuck to its guns although it knew that in so doing it was opposing the policy of the minister in charge. If politicians wish to put at risk energy supplies either to save jobs, or develop British technology, or save public money in the short term that is their affair. The department carried out its statutory duties and for that we should be grateful.

One does not have to be a logician or a constitutional theorist to see the inherent flaw in the above argument. When the statute charges the Department of Energy to see that there are secure and adequate supplies of energy it is placing an obligation not on civil servants in the department to do so, but on ministers. It is for them to judge how this can best be done – accepting or rejecting the advice of their civil servants and others as they think fit.

The points to which I would draw to the attention are as follows:
1. Civil servants in a Government department sought to frustrate the policy of their minister and substitute for it departmental policy.
2. Civil servants from a Government department found themselves combining in part at least with private industrialists to secure this end.
3. Civil servants from a Government department combined in part at least with other civil servants in other departments and with civil servants from the Think-Tank to secure this end. The Think-Tank in

effect put in to the Cabinet the paper that the departmental civil servants would have liked to have put in.

4. When the head of the civil service, and therefore the Prime Minister, were asked to authorise departmental reforms to combat what was happening they did not help.

5. Prime Ministers should inform departmental ministers before the event when they are seeing departmental civil servants and private industrialists about departmental matters. This was not done in this case.

6. The so-called expertise of the civil servants was very suspect in as far as it took the help of two political advisers to get a sensible analysis of the alternatives.

Of course the issue is not over. A Conservative Government is in power. The Conservative Party has in the past been in receipt of money from G.E.C. There is a powerful pro-nuclear, pro-PWR, pro-G.E.C. lobby in the Conservative Party in Parliament. G.E.C. and Sir Arnold Weinstock may themselves seek to reopen the issue. Sir Arnold is a shrewd operator and he may sense that threats of oil shortages will enable the debate to start all over again. Civil servants do not give up easily either. They will almost certainly want to reopen the PWR argument now that there is a change of Government.

Sir Jack Rampton and his senior colleagues were not invited to the party which Tony Benn threw on 26th January 1978 for his Private Office staff, the Assistant Secretary, his political advisers and myself to celebrate victory in the battle for the thermal nuclear reactor. But in the final week before the General Election on 3rd May 1979, Sir Jack and his senior colleagues had the last laugh. Acting in his capacity as Secretary of State Tony Benn instructed his Private Office to send a memo to Sir John Hill, Chairman of the Atomic Energy Authority, to stop all preparatory work on a PWR (the work is being done so as to keep open the option announced in his statement in the House of Commons of 25th January 1978) until a full report of the Harrisburg accident had been received and studied. The memo was not sent but returned to Tony Benn. When he asked Sir Jack Rampton why it had not been sent Sir Jack replied that the department thought that he did not have the authority to send the memo.

The governing institutions of the corporate state finally triumphed on this issue on 18th December 1979 when the Conservative Secretary of State for Energy, after only months in office, announced that a multi-billion pound nuclear programme, based subject to safeguards on the PWR, would go ahead. Sir Jack Rampton and Sir Arnold Weinstock and others in the PWR lobby could indeed afford to smile. From first to last Parliament had taken no part in the decision-taking process. Worse, Parliament had at all times been an idle and ignorant bystander. Perhaps one day Parliament will be asked to rubber stamp the decision.

Power struggle No. 2

The second issue which I deal with very briefly concerns not the conduct of civil servants but the conduct of the scientific establishment towards the democratic process. The issue itself is that of the Fast Breeder Reactor.

Civil nuclear power in Britain developed slowly out of the military use of atomic and nuclear power after the last war and as it did so it brought with it all the secrecy that accompanied the development of military atomic and nuclear power (e.g. Attlee when Prime Minister not telling his Cabinet colleagues about the development of the atomic bomb). One of the contributions of Peter Shore as Secretary of State for the Environment and Tony Benn as Secretary of State for Energy has been to open up the nuclear debate and make civil nuclear issues as publicly and politically accountable as other issues. If the thesis of this book is right that is not asking for much. Peter Shore helped by setting up the Windscale enquiry into the reprocessing activities there and then subjecting the matter to Parliamentary debate. Tony Benn has made much more information available than hitherto partly through the release of departmental information and partly through the Energy Commission which is a new and relatively open forum on energy matters whose proceedings are published. Some nuclear scientists resent this. Some like Sir John Hill, the Chairman of the Atomic Energy Authority, see it as giving their cause a new legitimacy.

Yet even now all is not well as a cursory examination of the development of policies on the Fast Breeder Reactor shows. Fast Breeder Reactors differ from thermal nuclear reactors in that they use plutonium, the stuff from which nuclear bombs are made, as a fuel and also breed their own fuel – again plutonium. They provide or will provide, if and when any are ever built, an efficient way, so say their proponents, of using uranium. I am not concerned with the argument for or against fast breeders.

In Britain there is a prototype Fast Breeder Reactor at Dounreay in Scotland. For years a research project has been in operation there with millions of pounds of public money spent each year on the project. Over £50 million a year has been spent on the development of the FBR for some years now. The figure is expected to top £100 million a year from 1980 onwards. Yet although the expenditure of the money is authorised by Parliament the Cabinet, to the best of my knowledge, has not met for years to decide on whether it was getting value for money, on whether the development should continue or on whether to build a commercial Fast Breeder Reactor. I have little doubt that what we have so far witnessed is part of an inexorable process which will end up with the building of a commercial Fast Breeder Reactor, particularly now that all that money has been spent on research.

I thought the matter was nicely put by Sir John Hill, the delightful Chairman of the Atomic Energy Authority, on 27th July 1978. Sir John congratulated the Government on their handling of the matter thus far. He felt it right that first the decision on the choice of thermal nuclear reactor should be taken and then the Windscale matter should be disposed of. He felt he needed a year to prepare a case for the development of the commercial Fast Breeder Reactor which would be put to a public enquiry. The preparations for the enquiry he thought would take about two years. The important thing was to retain staff in the interim period so that there would be no difficulties when the go-ahead was given. Sir John almost unwittingly had described an inexorable process leading to a certain conclusion. I believe that he had stated the future accurately. That is what will happen because that is the way the establishment works. The chairman of the enquiry will understand this as well as anyone else. The role of the Cabinet and Parliament will be to rubber-stamp the decision at the last moment.

Not surprisingly the Secretary of State pointed out that Sir John had missed out a step. That was whether a commercial Fast Breeder Reactor fitted into any overall pattern of U.K. energy supplies and what were the options. Moreover development work in the U.S. on a commercial fast breeder had stopped with the death of the Clinch River project. And of course Parliament might take an interest in the matter. Undeterred Sir John made it clear that he needed more money. The doctrine of historical inevitability may make bad history and bad philosophy but it makes scientific sense.

Power struggle No. 3

Sometimes the pressures of work, the way in which advice and explanations come to ministers (often in background notes which they hardly have time to read) as well as the desire to push departmental policies forward lead to misunderstandings between ministers and their civil servants. The third power struggle to which I refer relates to one such issue and concerned the re-processing work of the Windscale atom plant in Cumbria.

The note in my diary for 8th February 1977 is self-explanatory:

> There is an explosion at the briefing meeting with civil servants just before the Second Reading of the Nuclear Fuel (Finance) Bill.

There is, as we all know, to be a planning enquiry to deal with Windscale's application to re-process Japanese nuclear waste. But what happens in the interim to contracts which the B.N.F.L. are entering into at home and abroad. Tony discovers to his horror that the civil servants have written to B.N.F.L. only yesterday saying that they can continue to enter into contracts for pond storage with home or overseas customers and embark on cumulative storage. Although there is a proviso that if the planning enquiry goes against B.N.F.L. the waste will have to be returned this could build up enormous trouble with people arguing on one side that 'It's gone too far now' and on the other that 'the minister has prejudged the issue'. Tony is furious and says, 'I was not aware I said specifically to the company "you can go on receiving fuel and you can go on receiving new contracts"'. I wondered why Peter Shore said he was surprised that the pressure from B.N.F.L. had disappeared. Now I know'. The civil servants insisted that all this had arisen from a letter sent by Tony to Peter Shore with the implications set out in a background note. Tony conceded 'It may be all my fault' but he did not believe it and told me so afterwards. He continued to the civil servants 'the full inwardness was not open to me' and added 'Freeze the whole thing and tell B.N.F.L. I want to think further'. Trust between him and his civil servants is not all that it could be. He decided after calming down a bit that they could not now be frozen but that he would insist that all future contracts be subject to his personal approval. It was an eye-opener watching the civil servants glancing uneasily at each other.

Tony's speech which he re-wrote himself, staying up into the early hours of the morning, went down well in the House. Yesterday he had been very unhappy with the highly technical speech drafted for him by the department. He had also upset some of the civil servants by suggesting that the huge background brief which accompanied the draft speech should be circulated to all members of the Standing Committee which would consider the Bill after its Second Reading. Giving Parliament facts gratuitously seemed offensive to some of them.

Power struggle No. 4

I have already referred briefly in Chapter 1 to the problem of the need to move large quantities of plutonium nitrate from Windscale to the prototype fast breeder plant at Dounreay so that the plant could keep running. The movement of this dangerous substance had been completely banned in the United States. But here the Minister was told that unless the plutonium nitrate was moved very shortly the prototype Fast Breeder Reactor plant at Dounreay would have to close. At a meeting at the Department of Energy on 27th July 1978 with Sir John Hill, Chairman of the A.E.A., and civil servants, including the Chief Scientist, Sir Hermann Bondi, Tony Benn said that it was unfortunate that the problem had not been drawn to his attention a long time ago. He felt that he was considering it under some pressure, given the threat that if he did not agree to transport the nitrate then the prototype fast reactor would shortly have to close. Whereupon to his astonishment, Sir John Hill said that the Department of Energy had been told some time ago, thus making it clear that it was not his fault if the Secretary of State had not been informed. A check on the papers then showed that the civil servants in the department had indeed been given this information some months previously but they had not seen fit to inform ministers. Apparently they could see nothing politically sensitive or of interest to the minister in the movement of the nitrate by land and by sea and the risk of theft or accident. That at any rate was the official explanation. More likely the civil servants deliberately kept the information from the minister for fear that he might ask awkward questions about the movement of the nitrate (interestingly enough the official note of the meeting makes no mention of the emergence at the meeting of the fact that civil servants in the department had been informed some months earlier of the possible need to move the nitrate. The note of the meeting was of course made by a civil servant).

The Secretary of State was further told that an accident at sea had been simulated and a dummy flask had been dropped into the sea some 15 miles from the nearest ship. The flask emitted a continuous signal and had been recovered almost immediately. When questioned on what the term 'almost immediately' meant Sir John Hill replied 'in two hours'.

To objections that movement of this substance had been banned in the United States the Chief Scientist, making it clear that such a movement would have to take place every four or five years until and unless an expensive mixed oxide plant was built at Dounreay, said that the movement was very similar to earlier movements in the U.S.A. before the ban.

The movement of the nitrate eventually went ahead with clearance from the Health and Safety Executive and the Commission for the Environment but Tony Benn was not at all happy with the way in which the matter had been handled.

During this struggle it emerged that leading figures from the Atomic Energy Authority were pleased with the suggestion that G.E.C. might withdraw from the nuclear industry and simply act as one supplier of generators. Yet the A.E.A. was one of those organisations which found it easier to give than take criticism. Sir Brian Flowers, the Rector of Imperial College and the author of the Flowers Report, a cautionary tale on the environmental dangers and problems for civil liberties that might accompany the development of nuclear power, was to find this out in stark and shocking form. As my diary note for 15th June 1978 puts it 'According to Sir Brian some members of the A.E.A. had referred to him as Judas Iscariot'. Sir Brian was himself a member of the A.E.A. and was not anti-nuclear. He was merely concerned for the future of the planet.

Power struggle No. 5

The fifth power struggle to which I intend to refer at the Department of Energy brings out a different point about the conduct of civil servants. It arose out of the seemingly technical problem of producing accurate forecasts for energy. The problem is far from technical for Government policies will depend on which forecasts the Government accepts out of a range of forecasts or on what the Government thinks the legitimate range of forecasts is. These policies could, for example, involve no extension of the provision of nuclear power, a limited extension of the provision of nuclear power or the massive extension of the provision of nuclear power. Similarly policies on oil depletion or even international relations with Arab countries could depend on which forecasts the Government was using.

On Thursday 13th October 1977 some concern was expressed by the Secretary of State that the working paper which was to go to the Energy Commission showed a demand for energy that was less by some 90 million tons of coal equivalent for the 1990s than was shown in a paper issued by the department only a few months earlier. If one considers that a Fast Breeder Reactor saves some four million tons of coal equivalent it is easy to see how billions of pounds could be at stake in the change of forecast. Tony Benn's concern was that until the previous day no civil servant had pointed out the change and he felt that Mr Philip Jones, the Deputy Secretary, ought to have done so. This incident led by accident, as it were, to further enquiries into what was involved in departmental forecasting and it emerged that there were some thirty-four different scenarios from which, depending on which scenario was used, almost any policy advice could be given and justified. Mr Jones kept talking about 'keeping options open' which the Secretary of State thought might be another way of saying that the U.K. should develop nuclear power with all due speed.

Tension on this issue broke out again when one of the political advisers, Frances Morrell, went to see the Chief Statistician and Forecaster, the helpful Mr F. W. Hutber, to find out how the 10 per cent fall in demand had come about (it was mainly due to lower estimates of economic growth and partly methodological). Mr Philip Jones got to hear of this visit and made it clear that in his view the adviser should only have seen the Chief Forecaster in his presence. Then there was an argument between Mr Jones and Mr Hutber about whose forecast was right. Something was obviously wrong somewhere because the 10 per cent fall in demand was being equated with 90 million tons of coal equivalent whereas according to the rules of arithmetic this amount represented a fall in demand of 15 per cent. But these figures had already been released as official. Another source of trouble was that the Secretary of State had not been consulted over the press release because, as civil servants saw it, it had no political import. At one stage in this incident Mr Jones made it pretty clear that he was upset with the way things were developing in the department. To his credit he later apologised to the Secretary of State for his behaviour.

Power struggle No. 6

The sixth incident concerned the White Paper which the government were eventually to publish in response to the Flowers Report on the environmental aspects of nuclear power, a subject which was in the main the responsibility of the Secretary of State for the Environment.

It is summed up in the note in my diary for Friday 13th May:

> The day before he left for Moscow Tony's civil servants put up a draft White Paper which to some extent misrepresented the Flowers Report. The draft seemed slanted towards a rapid and somewhat unchecked development of nuclear power. Tony had agreed three small but major changes with Frances Morrell and Francis Cripps and these went to the department while he was in Moscow.
>
> On his return he found that the civil servants had effectively ignored his points in the re-draft. In the end Tony told Philip Jones, the Deputy Secretary in charge, that the behaviour of the department would not do, only to be met by the reply, which turned democracy upside down, that some of the civil servants did not trust the minister.

The necessary changes were eventually made in the draft White Paper. To this day there is something about Mr Philip Jones that I remember with affection.

Power struggle No. 7

The Whitehall machine is so large that often its left hand does not know what its right hand is doing. This can cause confusion amongst civil servants as well as amongst ministers. The civil service is not as compartmentalised as it used to be and there is now more integration between administrative staff and professional and technical staff. The lawyers, however, still remain a breed apart and I recall one occasion when they failed to brief their administrative colleagues over the meaning of a licensing agreement they had drawn with the Shell/Esso oil companies when the Government was negotiating legally binding Participation Agreements with them and using North Sea oil exploration and development as the lever.

The problem came to light at a meeting between Tony Benn and his officials and senior representatives of the two companies at which I was present on 15 June 1977. My diary records it thus:

> From 2.30 p.m. to 5.30 p.m. another slogging session with the oil companies – this time Shell/Esso – over the completion of the legal documents on participation. The meeting opens in chaos with the company men producing a document on licensing drawn up by the department's lawyers which Tony and the officials have to disclaim as not being Government policy. 'The lawyers' he says at the meeting 'have led us up the garden path. They are not responsible for our oil policy'. Then after Tony has been opposing arbitration for half an hour over licensing disputes the company men produce the heads of agreement which allow for arbitration, but all the time the civil servants had not intervened to point this out to the minister as they should have done. Then there is a misunderstanding over whether the arbitration arrangements cover future legislation by the Government. That odd idea – that a foreign arbitration court might be able to stop the Government changing taxes or royalties – cause concern. But it's a false alarm. Frank Kearton is being very tough, almost obstinate. Tony tells the company men again and again as we go through self-destruction, arbitration, access clauses, etc., that he represents a nation-state and that whilst the Participation Agreements are not confiscation neither are they optical illusions or mirrors. They have to be real. On the option and buy-back provisions one of the oil men says that the companies are worried about being 'nickled and dimed to death by the Government' which quaint phrase refers apparently to the possibility of the Government destroying their operations bit by bit by refusing to let them buy-back B.N.O.C. oil which they need for their own refineries and overseas customers.

An unsatisfactory meeting with an ineffectual performance by the civil servants is adjourned until tomorrow.

Power struggle No. 8

Industrial disputes are a recurring feature of the energy scene. The miners helped to bring down the government of Edward Heath. Disputes in the electricity industry have led to power cuts. Strangely, therefore, the Department of Energy has never armed itself with civil servants who understand industrial relations or who are in close contact with trade unionists. They could always contact the management in the nationalised power industries at a moment's notice but were helpless when it came to advising ministers on how trade unions felt in the middle of disputes. The idea that they might employ trade unionists at the highest levels was unthinkable. So ministers, Conservative and Labour, have had to fend for themselves in order to establish trade union contact and ascertain their negotiating positions. This was particularly noticeable in the power workers' dispute of 1977–78 which led to cuts on a rota system.

When these critical disputes occur the Government prepares for emergencies through its Civil Contingencies Unit, a Cabinet unit set up in 1972 to replace the old Emergencies Committee and headed for some years by Sir Clive Rose, a man once unkindly described as Britain's 'principal strike breaker'. The Unit's planning relies heavily on powers granted to the Government in the Emergency Powers Act 1920 and the Emergency Powers Act 1964. This latter Act enables troops to be used in industrial disputes without Parliamentary approval providing that their use has been duly authorised in a Defence Council Instruction. Intense secrecy surrounds the work of the Unit.

The Unit was constantly meeting when Labour was in power and preparing behind the scenes for troops to break strikes. It made preparations for every conceivable kind of civil emergency. In the case of the electricity industry it discovered in the 1977–78 dispute that the Central Electricity Generating Board did not consider that troops had the expertise to run or even close down the national grid in a crisis. They might even destroy it if they attempted to do so. The following note in my diary for 18th January 1978 recalls some of the problems. The unofficial power workers' dispute of November 1977 had ended but the Government were still worried for the future.

> In a talk with Tony and Frances Morrell and Francis Cripps on contingency plans for a power workers' strike we discussed the scenarios which the Contingencies Unit were considering. If we get a repetition of the unofficial action we had before Christmas there will

be rota cuts. If the action escalates even marginally above that we get the three-day week. Marginally above that we get operation Grasshopper at 50 per cent capacity with all domestic heat and light cut off all the time and shops and small businesses closing. After that comes total disaster and operation Herringbone. The need is to get the Cabinet to accept the 7 per cent formula, which the Electricity Council is calling a 'productivity deal', as coming within the wage guidelines in order to avoid operation Grasshopper. Tony feels Jim may want to fight it through, banking on the unpopularity of the power workers and public support for the pay policy.

He comments acidly on how useless his civil servants are in a dispute like this, how little they know about industrial relations and how much they are creatures of the employers, in this case the management of nationalised industries. He is contemptuous of their belief that the troops are always the answer and their failure to consider the political implications of their use.

It was in March that subsequent discussions were to reveal differences of opinion between the electricity industry and the Contingency Unit on the advisability and effectiveness of using troops. We shall never know who was right unless and until the day of doom comes nigh.

In France the day of doom never comes nigh because there they have developed the concept of the 'regulated' strike, in which unions agree to guidelines designed to keep life going in a crisis. The concept of the regulated strike, beautifully French in origin, is one that I suspect we shall see more and more in Britain. The guidelines for secondary pickets agreed by trade unionists in the troubles of the winter of 1978–79 are perhaps an example of this development.

Power struggle No. 9

Britain's energy policy is largely in the hands of Whitehall, the oil companies, the scientific nuclear establishment and management and unions in the nationalised industries. Inevitably the E.E.C. in seeking to ensure adequate supplies of energy for all its member states is bound to encroach on that energy policy. Sometimes the E.E.C. operating through the Commission and the Energy Council of Ministers seemed to be looking for a grand design; sometimes it seemed to be responding rather helplessly to events, such as the oil crises; sometimes it seemed to be searching for something to do and would come up with plans as far apart in scale and implication as minor hydro-carbon research and the joint development of Fast Breeder Reactors. I never noticed any country take the grand design theory seriously if its own vital national interests were threatened and any idea that Britain was somehow more nationalistic than other countries will not stand close examination. Britain was simply more open about its nationalism. Tony Benn made no secret of the fact that he thought that a European energy policy was not one which could be created or laid down by the Commission in the interests of the E.E.C. Members but was the sum total of the policies of the states concerned. Sometimes these states went their own way. Sometimes they combined although not always on an E.E.C. basis. For example while the fusion research project (JET or Joint European Thorus) at Culham was an E.E.C. collaborative project most of the others such as the Anglo-French cross-channel link bringing the two national grids together were not E.E.C. projects at all.

Tony Benn made this point again and again to his own civil servants, to Mr Gido Brünner, the E.E.C. Energy Commissioner, and to the energy ministers of the E.E.C. member-states both privately and at their Council of Ministers' meetings. It must have been difficult to understand because everyone else talked as though E.E.C. energy policy was something else. Commissioner Brünner found the point impossible to understand. On Thursday, 2nd March 1978 he came to the Department of Energy to discuss Britain's refinery policy, agreed in legally binding Participation Agreements with the oil companies. My note of the meeting suggested that there was an unbridgeable chasm between the policy of the Commission and the policy of the British Government as stated respectively by Gido Brünner and Tony Benn. It reads:

> Next comes Commissioner Brünner. At the briefing meeting which preceded his arrival Tony tells D. le B. Jones, Miss Brown and the Foreign Office man who is invited at the last minute that he intends to take a strong line with Brünner over refinery policy. Brünner arrives with his personal assistant, a likeable man, and Williams the Director of the E.E.C. Energy Policies.
>
> The meeting is a clash of minds which do not understand each other. To Brünner, Tony is obstructive and over-suspicious about his plans to get the oil companies to agree to voluntary restraints over projected increases in refinery through-put. To Tony, Brünner utterly fails to comprehend the fact that the U.K. is not going to be a bystander to an E.E.C. oil policy that overrides the U.K. national interest. Brünner explains his modest and seductive plan which is for a small cut-back in the number of oil refineries in the E.E.C. and maybe a few closures. Tony counters by 1. asking that Frances Morrell be allowed to be present when Brünner meets the trade unions in Brussels on 6th March and that Liverman be present when Brünner talks to the oil companies on 10th March and 2. suggesting that the Commission set up on an E.E.C. basis tripartite talks

> between national governments, trade unions and oil companies out of which agreement might come. He explains to Brünner that he feels that he is trying to rush ahead too quickly and that consent will only be constructed painstakingly and slowly. He further explains to Brünner that his proposals are unworkable and unacceptable to the U.K. Government. He says that the oil companies find them unnecessary, unworkable and possibly illegal under U.S. anti-trust laws and that the U.K. unions want a U.K. presence at any talks. Visibly irritated Brünner again outlines his modest proposals. He has nothing against tripartite talks 'in the long run' but he doesn't want the steam to go out of his plan. As for a U.K. Government presence at his talks that might make the participants dry up. Tony even more explicitly, with his voice slightly raised and taking on a more rhetorical flavour, is insistent that the U.K. Government cannot be treated as a bystander who is informed of what is going on when it pleases the Commission. He explains that he will not support the Commissions's approach. Re-statements of the relative positions are then made again by both parties. Miss Brown is looking unhappy. The F.O. man could be sick at any moment. D. le B. Jones can offer nothing to bridge the gap. The meeting ends with Tony saying to Brünner 'I ask you once again to let U.K. representatives be present at the meetings'. Williams makes a joke about having tried to get Frances Morrell to Europe before and the meeting ends.

The meeting had been the classic clash between a bureaucrat who was politically accountable to no one and an elected minister anxious that agreement should be constructed by consent rather than as part of a behind-the-scenes fix between civil servants and private companies.

Power struggle No. 10

Power struggle No. 10 threatens to be between the present Conservative Government and the public over nuclear power. At a meeting of the Economic Strategy Committee held on 25 October 1979, chaired by Margaret Thatcher, it was suggested that a crash nuclear programme could best succeed if the public were told as little as possible. As the Cabinet paper put it: 'But a nuclear programme would have the advantage of removing a substantial portion of electricity production from the danger of disruption by industrial action by coal miners or transport workers . . . Opposition to nuclear power might well provide a focus for pressure groups over the next decade and the Government might make more rapid progress towards its objectives by a low profile . . .' The account given on pages 98 to 103 of this book shows just how illusory is the idea that nuclear plants are immune from industrial dislocation.

5 Battles at the Department of Industry

Battle No. 1

Many Labour Members of Parliament believed in February 1974 that the work of the Department of Industry would play a significant role in strengthening Britain's manufacturing base. By 1979, when Labour lost the election, the Department of Industry had become known as the Department for the De-industrialisation of Britain. Long before that, however, Labour's industrial strategy had been destroyed. Much has been written about the period and it is not my intention to go over familiar and contentious ground. But I think it is important to understand the nature of the power struggle that was going on and how the various parties concerned operated. On the face of it, it is difficult to understand why the industrial strategy failed. There was a manifesto commitment. The Wilson Cabinet was committed to the policy. And all the ministers at the Department of Industry backed it – Tony Benn, Eric Heffer and Michael Meacher.

The strategy failed for four reasons, all of them holding lessons for those who believe that our institutions and those who run them always work honourably.

Firstly, while Harold Wilson, the Prime Minister, supported the policy publicly, as chairman of the Cabinet sub-committee which dealt with the issues and the work leading up to the Industry Act 1975 he systematically worked for its destruction and encouraged others to do so. As a result not only were the provisions of the Bill watered down but no attempt was made to work many of them (for example those concerning the release of information and planning agreements) once the Bill had become an Act.

Secondly, there were some Cabinet ministers who were against the policy and found collective Cabinet responsibility too much for them.

Thirdly, two ministers found the policy so offensive and thought it so potentially damaging that they were discussing (whilst they were ministers) the formation of a new political party. I first heard of this treachery on the grand scale when the Private Secretary to one of the ministers, a civil servant, told me about the proofs of an editorial for a national newspaper attacking the industrial strategy which were on the minister's desk for correction the day before they were printed. Subsequent enquiries revealed that these ministers were engaged in discussions about the possible formation of a new political party.

Fourthly, a number of senior civil servants at the department were hostile to the policy. They knew, as did everyone else, what the Prime Minister's view was. In part their opposition may have been due to the fact that they knew they were not competent to oversee an interventionist policy. Their expertise in industrial affairs was largely illusory (one minister recalls the occasion when the civil servant who was advising him on the machine tool industry in an adjournment debate had recently come from another department where he had been expert on the rate support grant). In part, their opposition may have stemmed from the fact that the policy simply did not accord with their values and views.

What is interesting is that all of these groups from the Prime Minister down to the civil servants were making frequent use of the press. From 1974 to 1979 the Department of Industry leaked like a collander. At various times a journalist from the *Economist* and the *Financial Times* was the favoured recipient of leaks. Some of the leaks, which on occasion amounted to full-blooded stories, referred to the details of Cabinet sub-committee decisions and were too accurate to have come from ministerial sources.

None of the three ministers who were appointed in 1974 felt that they had the enthusiastic support of senior civil servants. The most charitable thing that any of them could say about the work of their senior officials was that they approached it with sullen acquiesence. One tells of how a senior official asked him right from the start 'you don't really intend to introduce the proposals in your manifesto, do you?' Another recalls with disgust how when he asked a senior official to contact the Secretary of the Confed. (i.e. Confederation of Shipbuilding and Engineering Unions) the official replied 'I am sorry, minister. You have the advantage on me there. What is the Confed.?' This ignorance of union matters on the part of civil servants whose contacts had been almost exclusively on the management side was a constant source of friction and trouble. So, too, in a different way was the constant appearance at the department of groups of shop floor workers. It was an exercise in democracy that civil servants did not like.

Any lingering suspicion in the minds of ministers that senior civil servants were even-handed disappeared over the issue of the accounting officer's minute, which concerned loans and grants to the various co-ops – Kirkby and Meriden. Workers' co-operatives, aided in part with public funds under the provisions of the Industry Act 1972 and, with the encouragement of Tony Benn had been set up in these factories by the workers when they were threatened with closure. This was a complicated business but briefly the sequence of events was as follows.

A Permanent Secretary, as accounting officer, in a department has a responsibility to Parliament for the efficient management of the department. This is not a responsibility delegated to him by the minister. It operates through the Exchequer and Audit Acts. It is his own responsibility. In the case with which we are concerned the accounting officer involved was effectively telling the minister that monies were being improperly or illegally spent in that the criteria required by the Act of Parliament under which the money was being provided were not being or were not likely to be met. It was a very serious allegation indeed.

The New Year of 1975 had only just begun when the accounting officer at the Department of Industry, Sir Peter Carey, put in an accounting officer's minute relating to the viability of the Kirkby co-operative suggesting that the criteria laid down under the Industry Act 1972 could not be met and complaining in effect of the Secretary of State's conduct. Then an astonishing thing took place.

A senior civil servant leaked what was happening to the *Financial Times*.

There are two ways of interpreting the action of that civil servant. The first is that out of a sense of duty he felt impelled to make known what was going on to the readers of the *Financial Times* quickly, indeed, immediately. The other is that the civil servant wanted to discredit the Minister or the co-ops or both. The story which appeared in the *Financial Times* on Monday, 6th January 1975, by John Bowne, the lobby Editor under the head line, 'Official Objection to Benn Move on Kirkby Co-operative' was as follows:

> At least one senior civil servant has taken the most unusual course of placing 'a formal written objection on file' to a decision of his minister.
>
> The controversial decision is that of Mr Anthony Wedgwood Benn, Secretary of State for Industry, to provide funds of up to £3.9m to the Kirkby (Liverpool) IPD workers' co-operative, an act already criticised by his advisory board on industrial grants.
>
> The civil servant is Mr Peter Carey, Second Permanent Secretary in Mr Benn's Department of Industry and No. 2 to Sir Antony Part, chief civil servant in the department. Mr Carey is also the accounting officer responsible for government expenditure under the Industry Act.
>
> Mr Carey's objection is that the £3.9m is an imprudent use of

> public funds. The 'written objection' procedure is provided for under civil service rules in order to protect civil servants whose advice has been rejected by a minister from any censure or criticism by the Commons' all-important Public Accounts Committee.

For some inexplicable reason the *FT* did not follow up this grand scoop. The source of the leak was never officially discovered.

The Prime Minister read the *Financial Times* story and as one would expect asked Tony Benn what was going on and if the story was true. At that point Roy Williams, Tony Benn's Private Secretary, a civil servant, came to the rescue. He told the Secretary of State to stall for 24 hours while he checked the files. When he did precisely that he discovered that Tony Benn had acted to take account of the accounting officer's worries on each occasion in the past when the accounting officer had expressed concern.

In the meantime a trawl of Whitehall failed to reveal the presence of any other accounting officer's minute for ten years. It was that serious. But that presented a puzzle. Rolls-Royce, which had been taken into public ownership by the previous Conservative Government using the same Industry Act, could not possibly have been seen to be viable or likely to meet any required rate of return because it was in the hands of the receiver at the time. And Concorde was losing hundreds of millions of pounds (by 1978 £800 million had been written off as a loss) whereas sums less than £5 million were involved in the case of the co-ops. Yet no accounting minutes had appeared in either of those cases.

On 7th January Tony Benn spoke to Sir Antony Part, the Permanent Secretary about the issue. On that day too the *Sun* and *The Times* took up the story in editorials. The *Sun* editorial, one of the results of the leak of information by the senior civil servant at the Department of Industry, said among other things:

> A SPANNER IN WEDGIE'S WORKS
>
> The Sun salutes the courage of civil servant Peter Carey, the man who has thrown a spanner in the works for Industry Secretary, Wedgie Benn . . .
>
> Many hard choices will have to be made.
>
> We would be happier if we thought they were being made on the basis of advice from experts like Peter Carey rather than the political whims of the devious Wedgie Benn.

Some will doubt if the proper constitutional role of senior civil servants is to obtain editorials like that for their ministers.

The Times editorial was more circumspect and said:

A QUESTIONABLE JUDGMENT

> It is a quite proper aspect of the Whitehall system that it does not comment on confidential advice to ministers. Reports, however, that a Permanent Secretary at the Department of Industry has formally expressed his misgivings about the action taken by Mr Benn in relations to the Kirkby workers' co-operative raise important issues of public policy . . .
>
> There remains a doubt as to whether the writing of a formal note of dissent for the record, which is reported to have been the action taken, in fact completely covers the position. The formal action which the accounting officers are required to take in such situations is to send a minute to the Comptroller's department, recording that they consider expenditure is improper or imprudent in terms of a specific Act of Parliament . . . On the one hand the job of a civil servant is to interpret the political wishes of his ministers. On the other he has to observe administrative proprieties.

On 11th January Tony Benn drafted a minute to the Prime Minister in reply to his queries. The minute pointed out the action he had taken as a result of the worries of the department, and the partial nature of the operation of the accounting officer's minute system, as he saw it. He concluded that the issue was not about viability but that it seemed that if big business tried to defend itself and if high prestige projects were involved then that was all right, but if workers tried to defend themselves then no accounting officer's minute appeared.

On 13th January Tony Benn spoke to Sir Antony Part again. Shortly afterwards, on 17th January, Sir Antony Part had a heart attack. Almost the last time Tony Benn saw him was in hospital. The trust between a Secretary of State and Permanent Secretaries which is essential if a department is to function at all was gone. I set out my own views on the role of the accounting officer's minute in the next chapter.

Battle No. 2

Civil servants at the Department of Industry seemed almost frightened of the workers' co-ops because they were a new way of doing things and because they challenged concepts of management, control and ownership as conventionally understood. The campaign against them was ceaseless. In the case of the Meriden motorbike co-op there was a development so odd that I still find it difficult to believe that it happened.

I am often asked what I mean when I say that civil servants sometimes seek to foreclose options rather than open them up. Fortunately

Mr A. J. Suich, the Principal in charge of the motorbike section of the Department of Industry, has provided the perfect minute to illustrate the point. His minute dated 12th October 1978 argued a powerful case for winding up the Meriden co-op and giving effective control to a Japanese company called Kawasaki by presenting ministers with three options two of which had been argued away in the minute. The minute shows that civil servants were actively engaged in working in conjunction with others on a proposal to hand over a private sector British company to a Japanese firm and were doing so behind the back of the managing director of the firm (Geoffrey Robinson, Labour M.P. for NW Coventry) and the shareholders who happened to be the workers in this case. This whole affair was improper to a startling degree. Many private firms get much larger sums of Government money than Meriden, for example Imperial Chemicals and Vauxhall, but ministers and civil servants would not dream of discussing with others behind the backs of all concerned their take-over by foreign companies.

Mr Suich's minute, which in fairness to him I set out almost in full, was addressed to the Private Secretary to the Minister of State, Alan Williams, with copies to the Private Secretaries of other ministers, the Permanent Secretary, and other civil servants. I have left out the detailed financial figures in paragraph 6.

Kawasaki and Meriden
The Proposition

1. Mr John Williams, N.E.B., [National Enterprise Board] reported to Mr Bell on the results of his trip to Japan at which he discussed with Kawasaki the possibility of their setting up manufacture in the U.K.

2. Mr Williams said that Kawasaki were very interested in setting up manufacture here in partnership with an appropriate U.K. organisation. The partner-designate would be Mr David Brown, he has no experience in motorcycle manufacture but there is no one in the 'U.K. motorcycle industry' who could be regarded as appropriate. Mr Williams had suggested that the project might be looked at as tripartite between Kawasaki, David Brown and N.E.B. and that it should be clear that Mr Brown was the U.K. principal and N.E.B. would be helping him but not the other way round. Mr Brown and Kawasaki envisage a green field plant in the North East (definitely not in the West Midlands) to make 100,000 machines a year over the whole range of motorcycles from 100cc upwards, basically to Kawasaki designs. The plant would have the marketing rights for Europe and North Africa and would work in co-ordination with existing Kawasaki assembly plant in the U.S.A., a proposed assem-

bly plant to be set up in Brazil and Japanese plants. It would not merely be an assembly plant but would manufacture though a surprisingly large part of the total cost of the machine would be bought out (85% mentioned). An investment of some £20m is envisaged to which H.M.G. would be expected to contribute, presumably through R.D.G.s [Regional Development Grants] and Section 7 assistance. Employment of the order of 1,000 was mentioned. All of these figures are of course very tentative at this stage.

3. As regards Meriden, Kawasaki were very interested in obtaining the Triumph trademarks. They also recognised the political sensitivity. The proposal therefore was that the new enterprise should buy out the Co-operative. This would put money into the pockets of the Co-operative members which could be used by them to set themselves up in some other area of engineering. Kawasaki/Brown/N.E.B. (KBN) might be prepared to sub-contract to the new Co-operative, e.g. frame-making though Mr Williams recognised that this could give employment to only a fraction of the 680 currently employed at Meriden. It could also serve to quieten political objections and opposition.

4. The question now is when and how to raise the matter with Meriden; Mr Brown is likely to seek a meeting in the near future with the minister to discuss the proposition. We agreed to send to Mr Williams such information about the Co-operative as we are free to give and I am sending copies of the 'Trust Deed' setting out the Co-operative's constitution, the accounts up to 30th September 1977 (the last published accounts; any monitoring information we have had from Meriden since then we have had in confidence) and copies of the agreements between Meriden and the department which govern our relationship.

Assessment

5. The assumption is that KBN would buy from the Co-operative's Trustees the three issued shares at a negotiated price (£x). Presumably this money would then rest with the Trustees who with the agreement of the Co-operative members at the time, would decide what to do with it; whether to use it to set up a new (non-motorcycle) Co-operative operation or whether to share it out (my guess is that the members will opt for a share-out and most of them would take the money and get jobs elsewhere).

6. KBN would then take over Triumph Motorcycle Meriden Ltd complete, with its factory and plant, stocks and other assets, its marketing subsidiaries and with its liabilities. Since they do not intend to manufacture in the West Midlands they would then pre-

sumably wind the company up, realising the assets and meeting the liabilities. What they would buy would be: [Here the Assets and Liabilities are listed].

7. These figures must be treated with caution but they indicate that KBN would have bought a net liability of £y which, with the £x paid for the shares, means that they would pay £z for the Triumph trademarks plus political acceptability. They may argue that the price they pay for the Meriden shares represents their view of the value of trademarks and acceptability to them, therefore the Government should meet the cost of liquidation by accepting only the surplus after all other liabilities but those to the Government had been met.

8. Presentationally it might be argued that this would be no different from the position should Meriden have failed and been forced into liquidation; indeed to the extent that a winding-up under KBN might be expected to be a more orderly affair than a compulsory liquidation the Government might be marginally better off. However there could be considerable criticism of the fact that the Co-operative members, after running an operation which cost several millions of taxpayers' money and none of their own over the years of its existence, are nevertheless able to walk away with a substantial bonus in their pockets. There may be pressure for action to recover that money from the Co-operative members as a contribution towards the losses (but without such a handout the Co-operative members are not likely to agree to a KBN takeover).

The Alternative

8. The progress of the Co-operative's affairs suggests that ministers will shortly be faced with having to decide whether to put more money into Meriden, and substantial sums are likely to be needed, probably with the writing off of assistance already given, or to allow the Co-operative to collapse and go into compulsory liquidation.

9. If Meriden is saved once more the possibility of obtaining public acceptance to Kawasaki setting up here in competition must be regarded as very doubtful and the prospect of Kawasaki withdrawing altogether must be considered high.

10. If Meriden were allowed to collapse (which would leave Kawasaki free to buy the Triumph name from the Liquidator) the political climate for gaining acceptance to KBN may also be very difficult and there could be accusations that the Government withdrew support from the last remains of the British motorcycle industry in order to let the Japanese company in.

The Options

11. On the very sketchy information we have so far the options are:
a) Further substantial support for Meriden and no possibility of a KBN operation in this country.
b) Liquidation of Meriden without KBN involvement and a serious risk of Kawasaki's being driven away.
c) Liquidation of Meriden with KBN involvement and handout to members, and a KBN operation for the North East.
12. All the options have serious presentational difficulties and a great deal more information is needed before any conclusion could be reached about which of them is best, or even whether they are valid, but I think that the minister should be aware of the implications if he is approached by Mr Brown on the Kawasaki proposition.

A. J. SUICH

A few days later Bob Cryer the junior minister at the Department of Industry responsible for encouraging the development of co-ops sent a blistering minute to the Minister of State, Alan Williams, complaining about an attempt to undermine the Co-op and about secret talks held with a competitor and the discussion of 'back-door' deals. He found Mr Suich's minute 'deeply disappointing' and called for positive support for Meriden. Alan Williams seemed upset by Bob Cryer's minute and in a further minute dated 20th October 1978 said that in Newcastle earlier in July he had discussed N.E.B. contacts with Kawasaki with a Mr David Brown and had talked about the possibility of sub-contract work to help Meriden. He ended up by saying, 'There is no deep laid plot to undermine the Co-operative'.

That seems to be true. But there does seem to have been a fairly straightforward plan to hand it over to a foreign company with an N.E.B. stake and then wind it up.

Battle No. 3

Civil servants are expected to exercise certain proprieties and observe certain conventions in the interests of good government. Whilst supporting their own ministers in their battles against their colleagues they should not seek to set one minister against another. They should support government policy and in their minutes at least hope that it works. They should use some discretion and sensitivity in the use of their language. Just how deeply and enthusiastically they should get involved in the political process by way of taking political initiatives is a matter for debate.

Some of these points can be illustrated from the events which both preceded and followed on the Government's decision announced in the House of Commons on 18th July 1977 to bring forward an order for the Drax 'B' power station and to allow the North-East firm Parsons to build the generator, since some of their workers were threatened with lay-offs. This decision was taken in the teeth of opposition by G.E.C. and attempts at the Department of Industry to play down Parsons' ability to carry out the contract and to get some sort of merger between G.E.C. and Parsons with G.E.C. having the controlling interest. On 26th April 1977 I learnt of one proposal which was that the N.E.B. should buy Parsons' shares and then sell them to G.E.C. over a five-year period. On 4th July 1977 I was fortunate enough to get hold of a draft paper for the Energy (Ministerial) Cabinet sub-committee (ENM) dealing with the Drax 'B' problem. At this time briefings putting the G.E.C. case were being given to the press by civil servants.

The paper, which had not been circulated at the time that I saw it, had been put up to the Secretary of State for Industry, Eric Varley, by a Deputy Secretary, Mr Richard Bullock. To my astonishment paragraph 10 referred to the 'lemming-like attitude of the Parsons' workforce'. It was hardly the language one expects from Cabinet papers and was a somewhat strange description to apply to some of Britain's most skilled men. I have no idea whether the phrase was Mr Bullock's or someone else's. It certainly smacked of top people sneering at workers. The fourth paragraph said that if the N.E.B. were given a majority stake in any merger, the new company would not command foreign confidence, a point which was queried at the same time by the chairman of the Electricity Council. The concluding paragraphs of the paper recommend that lay-offs should be allowed to take place at Parsons and should be used as a spur to bring recalcitrant Parsons workers to heel.

I passed the paper on to Tony Benn (who was then Secretary of State at the Department of Energy) only to be rung later in the day by his Private Office to say that they had an ENM Cabinet paper together with a note by someone to Tony Benn. The department, they said, had not officially received their copy. Was the note, they wondered, by me? I confirmed that it was (it was signed by me) and made it clear that I wanted the paper to go direct to Tony Benn and not to civil servants. The 'lemming' phrase disappeared from the paper which was eventually circulated to ministers.

That same day at a meeting that I attended, Eric Varley, Secretary of State for Industry, launched into a crude attack on Parsons, describing the management as being lousy and deriding their technical competence. He was challenged on these matters by Francis Tombs, the chairman of the Electricity Council, who argued that technically Parsons were every bit as good as G.E.C. When Varley was asked whether it was desirable for the C.E.G.B., a public body, to have to deal with a private monopoly supplier – G.E.C. – as he was proposing, all that he could do was to suggest a Planning Agreement.

Long after the Drax 'B' decision had been announced on 18th July the Department of Industry was still working hard to get some kind of merger in the power plant industry. A minute from Mr Bullock to Eric Varley dated 10th October could have been interpreted as seeking to divide ministers and as being unhelpful so far as Government policy was concerned. It wrote about individual members of the Cabinet as though they were representatives of competing foreign powers rather than colleagues. It even tried to divide them against each other. The flavour of the minute can be gleaned from the following quotations:

> My cynical view is that the Parsons workforce will not be likely to realise the perils of an independent future until the management's claim that more orders will be forthcoming in the wake of Drax 'B' is seen to be wearing thin . . .
>
> I should add that when I last discussed the situation with Sir Arnold Weinstock, he said that he had it in mind, when the dust of Drax 'B' had settled a little, to make an effort to start educating opinion in the north-east (he had in mind both Members of Parliament and the Parsons' union) about the real prospects for Parsons on their own. I am due to have a further discussion with him shortly and if this is still his intention it might be sensible to wait and see how far he gets first before exposing yourself again . . .
>
> . . . discussions with the unions on restructuring are of course entirely a matter for you and not Mr Benn: nor am I clear that Mr Booth has any part to play in them . . . if you feel that you need to take a more active line to avoid being up-staged by Mr Benn, then the letter at E4 would be appropriate.

The same day that I came across this document, 3rd November 1977, I put in a note which said:

> Tony,
>
> Is it not a bit unusual for a senior civil servant
>
> 1. to seek to divide ministers and
> 2. almost to wish the destruction of a large firm and the failure of Government policy
>
> It's a bit odd, too, isn't it, that the atmosphere exists in which he thinks he can get away with it.
>
> Brian

When the matter was brought to the attention of the head of the civil service, Sir Douglas Allen, he said that the minute should never have been sent nor should the Secretary of State for Industry have received it. The Secretary of State should have returned it as being unacceptable.

I think it is possible now to put the issue in better perspective and to offer two alternative explanations of the way in which Mr Bullock dealt with the problem facing him. The first is that he threw himself vigorously into the political affray on behalf of his minister and was glad that the minister had a powerful interested party, G.E.C., on his side. The other is that Mr Bullock was striving to re-assert the departmental line which had been dropped when the Cabinet sub-committee had taken its decision. Either way his actions do not fit in with the conventional theory of an objective, neutral and non-political civil service. Either way my note to Tony Benn missed the real point.

6 Lessons for Civil Servants

The advice that civil servants give to ministers is political and, in no sense of the meaning of the word, objective. Some of it, though not much, is overtly party political. Some of it is partial. Much of it closely reflects the values of producers and of industrial and commercial management. Little of it reflects the values of consumers or industrial workers. Much of it is now presented in a manner more befitting pressure groups than administrators dealing with the affairs of state. The evidence, some of it presented in this book, shows that this is the case. Governments may continue to argue and constitutional textbooks may continue to give sustenance to their arguments that the advice which civil servants tender is non-political, objective and confidential. None of these assertions will stand serious analysis. It may be the case, as it is put in 'Government's Observations on the Expenditure Committee's Report on the Civil Service', (Cmnd 7117, Paragraph 84), that 'by long established agreement between all political parties the civil service should be a non-political, permanent, career service'. The point is that whether ministers or civil servants are responsible for what has happened, the agreement does not correspond to reality.

Before asking what sort of civil servants we want we must be sure that we understand what sort of civil servants we have.

It is clear from the statistics there is a bias in the recruitment of higher civil servants towards 1. those who went to public schools 2. those who went to Oxford and Cambridge and 3. those with arts degrees.

Below I reprint, with the permission of the General Secretary of the Labour Party, Appendix 11 (Recruitment to the Civil Service) of their report on the civil service contained in their booklet *Statements to Annual Conference 1978*. The statistics in the tables were extracted from information provided by the Civil Service Department and the Department of Education to the Labour Party's Machinery of Government sub-committee of which I was a member.

The table set out below shows the number of external applicants for

Administration posts broken down according to the type of school they last attended; and compares the statistics for those applying with those successful. It also shows a comparison with proportions in the population as a whole.

Table 1. ADMINISTRATION TRAINEES – SCHOOL EDUCATION

School	1973				1974				1975			
	applicants		appointees		applicants		appointees		applicants		appointees	
	male	fem.	male	fem.	male	fem.	male	fem.	male	fem.	male	fem.
	%	%	%	%	%	%	%	%	%	%	%	%
(i) Public School	12.7	6.2	25.4	6.7	15.5	7.3	36.2	17.2	15.7	9.9	25.0	20.0
(ii) Direct Grant and other fee paying	18.8	23.6	20.3	24.4	13.6	20.2	25.5	37.9	18.7	22.7	22.9	36.0
(i) and (ii) combined	31.5	29.8	45.7	31.1	29.1	27.5	61.7	55.1	34.4	32.6	47.9	56.0
LEA	65.1	65.1	52.5	66.7	68.8	70.2	38.3	41.4	63.2	64.0	50.0	44.0

School population as a whole	
1975	%
Public School, Direct Grant and other fee paying	5.8
Local Authority Schools	94.2

Note: other categories have been excluded from the above table. Therefore figures do not necessarily total 100.

These statistics show clearly the bias in favour of those from an independent school background. Vastly disproportionate numbers of those appointed come from this section of the population as compared with their numbers in the population as a whole. Moreover, this distortion is further reinforced in the selection process as the proportions for the number of successful applicants shows.

When a similar analysis is made, according to the type of university attended, a further distortion becomes apparent. Table 2 shows the proportion of external applicants for Administration Trainee posts who attended Oxford and Cambridge Universities and likewise the proportions appointed who attended those establishments. Comparison is also made with proportions attending Oxbridge out of the total numbers at universities in this country.

Table 2 ADMINISTRATION TRAINEES – UNIVERSITY BACKGROUND

University attended	1973				1974				1975			
	applicants		appointees		applicants		appointees		applicants		appointees	
	male	fem.	male	fem.	male	fem.	male	fem.	male	fem.	male	fem.
	%	%	%	%	%	%	%	%	%	%	%	%
Oxford/ Cambridge	27.2	11.1	56.6	37.8	28.7	11.3	61.6	29.0	25.6	13.0	61.5	51.9
Other University/ Polytechnic	72.8	88.9	43.4	62.2	71.3	88.7	38.4	71.0	74.4	87.0	38.5	48.1

All University Students 1975	
Oxford and Cambridge	8 %
Other Universities	92 %

Again this provides ample evidence of bias. Not only are there a disproportionate number of applicants from Oxford and Cambridge, but once again this distortion is reinforced by the selection process. On average between 1971 and 1975 Oxford and Cambridge produced nearly a quarter of the total applicants for AT posts, and actually half of those appointed. Moreover, this phenomenon, far from decreasing, has actually shown a tendency to become more marked in recent years. This situation may in itself have an effect on potential recruits from other universities deterring them from applying.

It is interesting to compare the number of Oxbridge applicants for the high-flying AT post, with those for the lower Executive posts (*see Table 5 below*).

It is useful also to look at similar analysis for external Administration Trainee applicants, broken down according to degree subject.

These figures also bear out the statement that bias exists in favour of arts and humanity graduates, with applicants from these disciplines doing disproportionately well. It may be noted that science graduates make up only about one-fifth of the applicants. Perhaps they are deterred by knowing that the arts 'all rounder' is the sort of person the authorities are looking for.

Table 3. ADMINISTRATION TRAINEES – DEGREE SUBJECT

Degree Subject	1973				1974				1975			
	applicants		appointees		applicants		appointees		applicants		appointees	
	male	fem.	male	fem.	male	fem.	male	fem.	male	fem.	male	fem.
	%	%	%	%	%	%	%	%	%	%	%	%
Arts & Humanities	34.5	48.9	52.9	65.3	37.8	50.6	52.3	69.3	39.9	49.9	48.2	55.8
Social Sciences	34.4	33.2	26.5	24.0	39.9	34.6	33.9	19.4	40.9	33.6	34.1	23.1
Natural & Applied Sciences	25.6	14.0	18.3	8.0	20.7	12.5	12.3	11.3	17.4	14.0	17.1	21.1

ALL UNIVERSITY STUDENTS

Degree Subject	%
Arts & Humanities	24
Social Sciences	24
Natural & Applied Sciences	50

Note: other categories excluded. Figures do not necessarily total 100.

Table 4. ADMINISTRATION TRAINEES – SOCIAL BACKGROUND

Social Class	1975 applicants		1975 appointees		Population as a whole
	male	fem.	male	fem.	
	%	%	%	%	
I	19.6	21.9	25.9	23.1	
II	43.2	48.7	50.3	59.6	
Total I & II	62.8	70.6	76.2	82.7	39*
III – V	37.2	29.4	23.8	17.3	61*

**Note*: At the time of writing, exact corresponding figures were not available. These figures represent a maximum estimate for Classes I & II based on information from Social Trends. It may well be that the % of population in classes I & II is less, and that in III – V higher than stated, in which case this would further reinforce the evidence of class distortion.

The breakdown of external applicants and appointees to Administration Trainee posts according to parental social background and comparison with the population as a whole, also repays examination. This would seem to indicate that the bias already existing in the education system is being reinforced. Over three-quarters of those appointed are from middle/upper class backgrounds.

Interestingly, however, the biases shown in the case of applicants for Administration Trainee posts are not apparent in the case of applicants for the lower grade Executive posts and their equivalent.

Table 5. GRADUATE APPLICANTS FOR EXECUTIVE OFFICER AND EQUIVALENT

	1973				1974				1975			
	applicants		appointees		applicants		appointees		applicants		appointees	
	male	fem.	male	fem.	male	fem.	male	fem.	male	fem.	male	fem.
	%	%	%	%	%	%	%	%	%	%	%	%
Public School/ Direct Grant, etc.	17.3	15.8	18.3	13.4	17.4	15.4	19.2	13.7	19.3	16.5	20.5	17.7
LEA	77.1	79.5	76.9	82.9	76.6	81.1	74.1	83.9	73.9	78.2	73.3	77.9
Oxbridge	6.2	1.2	7.6	1.1	5.5	1.1	5.4	1.1	5.5	1.2	6.8	1.3
Other University/ Polytechnic	93.8	98.8	92.4	98.9	94.5	98.9	94.6	98.9	94.5	98.8	93.2	98.7
Degree												
Arts	27.0	46.0	29.5	48.6	25.6	45.4	29.6	48.2	28.5	47.1	30.5	49.4
Social Sciences	35.9	33.8	34.2	33.5	36.3	34.0	36.7	33.4	37.0	33.2	37.4	34.5
Nat & Applied Sciences	35.9	18.9	34.9	16.9	36.5	17.8	32.3	16.2	32.1	17.0	30.2	14.0

Here the number appointed from particular educational backgrounds are all roughly in proportion to those applying. This would seem to indicate that the bias applies only to those recruited to the upper echelons of the civil service.

These figures are further evidence that since C. P. Snow wrote about the 'small size, the tightness, the extreme homogeneity of the English official world' in *Science and Government* in 1960, nothing much has changed.

More than a decade ago the Fulton Committee reported on the superficiality of the gifted amateur who entered the civil service. The Committee contained many distinguished members including Lord Crowther-Hunt, who subsequently had ministerial experience to back up his academic judgments, and Robert Neild, a gifted Cambridge professor. Fulton wanted to create an administration that was less élitist, less amateurish and more professional. If the statistics are anything to go by the Fulton recommendations went largely unheeded. The Civil Service Commission still recruits in its own image and still shows a heavy preference for certain literary and oral skills helped in part by the method of selection and the high marks awarded at the Final Selection Board. Comparing the period 1966–68 with the period 1975–77 the number of Oxbridge graduates as a percentage of external recruits to the administrative grade rose fractionally (62 per cent to 63 per cent); whilst the number of arts graduates as a proportion of the total fell fractionally (59 per cent to 56 per cent). The number of specialists moving into the ranks of Under Secretary and above remained about constant at about 40 per cent throughout the period.

The establishment is unabashed by these statistics. First they argue that all that they show is a statistical bias. Then when challenged about that curious response, since any measurable bias is a statistical bias, they go on to say that the figures merely indicate an educational bias i.e. the people with the best brains who are most fitted to govern the country go to public schools and Oxford and Cambridge and there is nothing they can or should do about that. In short it is axiomatic to the establishment that the best people, as conventionally defined through certain types of degrees, are those best suited to govern the country. I do not find it axiomatic. If they are the best people and can adapt to anything, why must they be civil servants? Why should they not become plant managers in manufacturing industry upon whose ability Britain's future depends. And if it is axiomatic that they are the best people to govern the country, why is it that we are so badly governed by every test – economic management, economic success, social cohesion, social reform, international influence and so on.

The question of shared values is one that gives considerable cause for concern for the future. Governments through their budgets allocate millions of pounds between classes and institutions of people. Treasury officials have the responsibility of advising the Chancellor on whether money should be given or withheld to industrial workers or big corporations.

At a different level, Governments, through their sponsorship of the nationalised industries, award supply contracts worth many billions of pounds among private sector companies. Ministers with Cabinet approval are responsible for the awards of these immensely valuable contracts, public officials for advising them. In these circumstances the objective of industry and commerce is to seek to secure the goodwill and understanding of ministers and their senior officials. Big companies, merchant banks and city institutions regularly present themselves and their policies hospitably over excellent lunches and dinners. This is a traditional style of presentation which, together with the regular professional exchanges between senior officials and industries can be expected to lead to good working relations. In addition senior public officials may expect to be offered membership of exclusive clubs where they will meet leading figures from their professional world. Of late public officials at the highest levels have tended to be offered and to accept either before or immediately on retirement, lucrative jobs in industry or the big banks in spite of the fact that industrialists frequently complain that civil servants do not understand industry or its needs. Small and medium size companies and up and coming enterprises find it difficult, usually impossible, to compete with established, powerful corporations in this field, some of whom have whole departments dealing in government grants, loans and contracts and other relationships with government.

The advantages to industry in employing former senior civil servants are obvious. First the civil servants concerned are able to advise industry on the intricacies of how the government machine works and how best to lobby government departments and put pressure on ministers for help and assistance, financial and otherwise. Secondly it is clearly easier for industry to get its views across to government if this can be done through formèr civil servants who have friends and colleagues working in government who themselves might wish to enter industry on retirement. And thirdly the movement out of civil servants into industry and the City (there seems to be little permanent movement the other way) must be seen as part of an attempt to ensure that the Government reflects, sustains and reinforces the values of our financial and industrial establishment even if those values are antithetical to the aspirations of working people. Clearly for the Labour Party there are dangers in this approach.

At the very least impartiality in financial matters must be on the principle that any official should be above any suggestion of personal bias or gain. A relationship of the type described cannot protect senior officials from temptation or suggestion. It is perhaps fair to say that the sensitivity to political bias, indicated by regulations forbidding senior officials to take part in organised politics, is not paralleled by an equal sensitivity to financial bias.

Governments steadfastly refuse to change the rules on the movement of civil servants into industry or to legislate to prevent civil servants from moving into jobs on retirement where they formerly had or might have had an influence. Governments resolutely shut their eyes to the fact that the Permanent Secretaries who move into industry are those who effectively control so much of the departmental patronage and are responsible for handing out so many jobs to people outside government. The merry-go-round of patronage (i.e. top people looking after each other) may not yet be in full motion but there are signs that it is on the move. Even without a merry-go-round of patronage there is concern that advice to ministers by civil servants may be influenced by the growing idea that top officials ought as a matter of course to end their careers in industry. The influence may be direct, that is to say specific civil servants may gear their advice to the needs of specific companies which they might hope to join, or indirect in that civil servants may associate themselves with, for example, the needs of producers rather than consumers. Not for nothing has it been said that the Ministry of Agriculture is an organisation cloned from the National Farmers' Union. No one should be surprised if Permanent Secretaries from the ministry seek jobs on retirement at the N.F.U.

Even if there were no mismatch between the rules laid down by the Civil Service Department on the movement of their top people into industry and what happens in practice, the position is most unsatisfactory because the rules positively encourage the system of shared values. The rules say *inter alia*:

> *Acceptance of Outside Business Appointments by Crown Servants. The Rules*
> It is in the public interest that people with experience of public administration should be able to move into business and industry . . .
>
> The rules aim at avoiding any suspicion – however unjustified – that serving officers might be ready to bestow favours on firms in the hope of future benefit to come. They also seek to guard against the risk that a particular firm might be thought to be gaining an unfair advantage over its competitor by employing an officer who, during his service, had access to technical or other information which those competitors could legitimately regard as their own trade secrets.
>
> All officers of the rank of Under Secretary (or, in the Diplomatic Service, Counsellors) and above, and of the equivalent ranks in H.M. Forces, are required to obtain the assent of the Government before accepting within two years of resignation or retirement offers of employment in business and other bodies:
> (a) which are in contractual relationships with the Government;
> (b) which are in receipt of subsidies or their equivalent from the Government;
> (c) in which the Government is a shareholder;
> (d) which are in receipt from the Government of loans, guarantees or other forms of capital assistance; or
> (e) with which Services, or Departments or branches of Government are, as a matter of course, in a special relationship; and in semi-public organisations brought into being by the Government or Parliament.

Procedure

Assent to an application will take the form of approval by the Prime Minister in cases referred to an Advisory Committee, or by the minister in charge of the department in all other cases. It would however be open to a minister to approve arrangements under which defined categories of case would be dealt with at a specified level without reference to the Prime Minister.

Permanent Secretaries and Second Permanent Secretaries

All cases concerning Permanent Secretaries and Second Permanent Secretaries (and those of equivalent rank in H.M. Forces) must be referred to the head of the civil service and to the minister responsible for the department. Where the head of the civil service and the departmental minister are agreed that the proposed appointment is to a non-commercial body of such a nature that this procedure would be inappropriate (e.g. a University), the appointment may be approved without reference to the committee. All other cases will then be referred by the head of the Civil Service to the Prime Minister to be laid before the Advisory Committee . . .

Advisory Committee

The Advisory Committee will consist of three members having experience of relations between the Civil Service and the public or private sectors of industry. The members will on each occasion be drawn from a panel. Cases will be referred to the committee by the Prime Minister and it will report to him.

Any quick glance at some of the appointments of Permanent Secretaries in industry will show that the rules are liberally interpreted. It is also difficult to understand why it is so desirable for Permanent Secretaries who retire to go into the boardrooms of industry. It is even more puzzling why none of them have opted to work for trade unions on retirement, none of them take up full time employment in the cultural world, or in the world of charities and few of them go into academic life. Whether they join industry because of the money (to which has to be added a sizeable index-linked pension) or because they are unwilling to give up the exercise of power or for some other reason hardly matters. My own view is that the honour and integrity of public life requires that retiring Permanent Secretaries should not sit on boards of major companies most of which have substantial dealings with government. One member of the Fulton Committee suggested that Permanent Secretaries who do retire into boardrooms should be required to give up their knighthoods and their pensions.

From 1974 to 1977 27 Permanent Secretaries retired or resigned. Their movements, of immense interest and importance, can be charted thus:

MOVEMENT OF PERMANENT SECRETARIES ON RETIREMENT OR RESIGNATION 1974–77

	Department	Post retirement positions
	1974	
Sir W. Armstrong	Head of Civil Service	Chairman, Midland Bank The Banks Clearing House Ltd.
Sir M. Brown	Department of Trade and Industry	Electrical Research Assoc. Ltd. Ransome Hoffman Pollard Ltd. Schroder International Ltd. Deputy Chairman of Monopolies and Mergers Commission
Sir J. Dunnett	Ministry of Defence	Imperial Group Ltd. Chairman, Institute of Manpower Studies
	1975	
Sir G. Leitch	Ministry of Defence	Short Brothers & Harland Ltd.
Sir H. Ware	H.M. Procurator-General and Treasury Solicitor	No information
Sir J. Wilson	Ministry of Defence	Crown Housing Association Civil Service Appeal Board
Sir T. Brimelow	Foreign Office	Member, European Parliament 1977–79
Sir J. Jones	Department of Environment	School of Advanced Urban Studies, Bristol University
	1976	
Sir A. Part	Department of Industry	Orion Insurance Co. Ltd. Savoy Hotels Ltd. Metal Box Ltd. Lucas Industries Debenhams E.M.I. Life Association of Scotland
Sir D. Barnes	Manpower Services Commission	Chynwed Ltd. General Accident Fire & Assurance

MOVEMENT OF PERMANENT SECRETARIES ON RETIREMENT OR RESIGNATION 1974–77 *continued*

	Department	Post retirement positions
Sir R. King	Department of Overseas Development (special leave)	International Monetary Fund/ World Bank Development Committee
Sir D. Pitblado	Exchange & Audit	No information
Sir C. Heron	Department of Employment	No information
Sir A. Marre	Parliamentary Commissioner for Administration	No information
Sir N. Price	Inland Revenue	No information
Sir W. Geraghty	Ministry of Defence	Deceased
Sir A. Stainton	Parliamentary Counsel	No information
Sir L. Errington	Department of Health and Social Security	No information
	1977	
Sir A. Lord	Treasury (resigned)	Dunlop
Sir D. Dobson	Lord Chancellor's Office	Advisory Council on Public Records
Sir B. Hopkin	Treasury	University College, Cardiff
Sir D. Mitchell	Treasury (resigned)	Guinnes Mahon (merchant bankers)
Sir W. Skelhorn	Department of the Director of Public Prosecutors	A Recorder of the Crown Court
Sir P. Thornton	Department of Trade	Hill Samuel Courtaulds Rolls-Royce
Sir A. Peterson	Home Office	Chairman, Mersey Docks & Harbour Board
Sir R. Denman	Cabinet Office	European Commission, Director of External Affairs
Sir R. Radford	Customs & Excise	Secretary General, Customs Co-operation Council

Source: Who's Who and Directory of Directors 1976, 1977 and 1978.

The Secretary of State for Defence, Fred Mulley told the House of Commons on 8th March 1976 that five R.A.F. officers of the rank of Squadron Leader and above had applied for and been granted permission to join the G.E.C.-Marconi-Elliot group or its associated companies within two years of leaving the service. The movements took place in 1971, 1972, 1973 (two) and 1975. Sir Samuel Goldman, a Second Permanent Secretary at the Treasury who retired in 1972, joined Orion Bank Ltd. until he left in 1974 and then became Chairman of the Covent Garden Marketing Authority. In 1976 he became Chairman of Fraser Ansbacher Ltd. Sir Martin Flett, a Permanent Under Secretary at the Ministry of Defence, has since 1972 been a director of Decca Ltd. and Siebe Gorman Holdings Ltd. Sir Arnold France, who was Chairman of the Board of Inland Revenue, became after 1973 a non-executive director of Pilkington Brothers Ltd., a director of The Rank Organisation Ltd. and Tube Investments Ltd. and Chairman of the Central Board of Finance, Church of England. Sir William Cook, the Ministry of Defence's former chief adviser on Projects and Research, became in 1970 director of Buck & Hickman Ltd., from 1971 to 1975 Chairman, Marconi International Marine Co. Ltd., 1971–76 director of Rolls-Royce Ltd., and in 1972 director of G.E.C.-Marconi-Electronics Ltd. Sir Ronald Melville, who retired from the Civil Service Department in 1972 after being Permanent Secretary in the Ministry of Aviation from 1966–67, became a director of the Electronics Component Board and the Board of Westland Aircraft. Sir Frank Figgures, who retired as Chairman of the Pay Board in 1974 and who was a Second Permanent Secretary at the Treasury 1968–71 and Director General of N.E.D.O. from 1971 to 1973 and Chairman of Pay Board from 1973 to 1974, became a director of Julius Boer Investment Ltd. and Chairman of Central Wagon Co. Ltd. (All of the information concerning these former civil servants comes from *Who's Who 1978*).

I would stress that there is no suspicion of any financial impropriety in any of these cases, but the appointments to industrial and commercial boards create an uneasy feeling and simply ought not to have been allowed. I refuse to believe that they were or are essential to the survival of British industry.

The response of the Civil Service Department to these appointments is to create a trap of their own choosing; they point out that although a high proportion of Permanent Secretaries may take up appointments on resignation or retirement, the proportion is much smaller if the number of applicants for business appointments is assessed as a proportion of those who retired or resigned from the grades of Under Secretary and above. That is understandable. It is the Permanent Secretaries who exercise the real power and influence in Whitehall and naturally it will be their services which will be most valued. And there are only some 40 or so of them in Whitehall at any one time while there are some 800 civil servants of the rank of Under Secretary and above (of whom about 150 were Deputy Secretaries and about 600 were Under Secretaries in September 1979).

The figures provided by the Civil Service Department for the same years, 1974 to 1977, for the number of applicants for business appointments from the grade of Under Secretary and above are as follows:

APPLICATIONS FOR BUSINESS APPOINTMENTS
(1974–77 – Under Secretary and Above)

	Retired/Resigned	Applicants
1974	70	9
1975	73	6
1976	105	11
1977	34	6

Breakdown of Applicants 1974–77

Year of Application	Department	Level of Applicant	Number of appointments for which approval was sought	Field of prospective appointments
1974	Civil Service Department	P/S	1	Financial Institution
1974	Defence	U/S	1	Engineering Industry
1974	Defence	U/S	3	Engineering Industry
1974	Defence	D/S	1	Aircraft Industry
1974	Defence	P/S	3	Manufacturing Industry
1974	Environment	U/S	3	Engineering Industry
1974	Export Credit Guarantee	D/S	1	Financial Institution
1974	H.M. Stationery Office	D/S	2	Manufacturing Industry
1974	Trade & Industry	P/S	1	Financial Institution
1974	Trade & Industry	P/S	1	Electronics/Electrical
1974	Trade & Industry	P/S	1	Manufacturing Industry
1975	Agriculture & Fisheries	U/S	1	Manufacturing Industry
1975	Customs & Excise	U/S	1	Manufacturing Industry
1975	Dept. of the Environment	D/S	3	Engineering Industry

Breakdown of Applicants 1974–77 *continued*

Year of Application	Department	Level of Applicant	Number of appointments for which approval was sought	Field of prospective appointments
1975	General Communications Headquarters	U/S	1	Electronics/Electrical
1975	Office of Fair Trading	U/S	1	Manufacturing Industry
1975	Scottish Office	U/S	1	Engineering Industry
1976	Defence	U/S	1	Aircraft Industry
1976	Defence	U/S	1	Aircraft Industry
1976	Defence	P/S	1	Electronics/Electrical
1976	Employment	D/S	1	Engineering Industry
1976	Employment	P/S	2	Financial Institutions
1976	Health & Social Security	U/S	1	Medical Supply Industry
1976	Health & Social Security	U/S	3	Medical Supply Industry
1976	Industry	U/S	1	Financial Institution
1976	Industry	P/S	3	Manufacturing Industry
1976	H.M. Stationery Office	U/S	1	Manufacturing Industry
1976	Inland Revenue	P/S	1	Financial Institution
1977	Customs & Excise	D/S	1	Manufacturing Industry
1977	Defence	U/S	1	Aircraft Industry
1977	Industry/Trade/ Prices and Consumer Protection	U/S	1	Manufacturing Industry
1977	Industry/Trade/ Prices and Consumer Protection	P/S	1	Financial Institution
1977	Treasury	P/S	1	Manufacturing Industry
1977	Treasury	P/S	1	Financial Institution

Notes

1. Appointments include consultancies.
2. P/S – Permanent Secretary.
   D/S – Deputy Secretary.
   U/S – Under Secretary.
3. This table gives the number of applicants. There are no figures available to show how many were successful.

As I have said, patronage works in two directions. On the one hand civil servants are patronised on resignation or retirement: on the other they act as patrons themselves and very zealous they are in so acting.

In addition to politically sensitive appointments to Quangos and the appointment of chairmen and deputy chairmen of major public boards, which are subject to the Prime Minister's approval, there are various kinds of appointments in which civil servants themselves play a critical role.

Firstly, there are a number of part-time and often unpaid appointments and secondly there are a number of full-time executive posts to outside bodies and industries. Most of these latter appointments are by promotion within the organisation concerned. For example there were thirty such appointments concerning nationalised industry boards relating to the activities from the Departments of Trade and Industry from 1973 to 1976 and 90 per cent were filled by internal promotions.

Sometimes senior civil servants within departments make recommendations. Sometimes an advisory group of prominent industrialists, bankers and others under the guidance of the head of the civil service advise Permanent Secretaries, at their request, on appointments. Sometimes names are drawn from the list of the 'Great and Good' which has been compiled and vetted by civil servants in Whitehall. Michael Meacher, when a minister at the Department of Trade, put it like this in a paper he submitted to a Labour Party Study Group in June 1976 on 'Appointment to Public Bodies':

> Each year a trawl is made in the department, including the regions, for new names, and new finds are vetted at Deputy Secretary levels or sometimes by personnel selection consultants. The current DI-DT-DPCP [Departments of Trade, Industry, and Prices and Consumer Protection] list contains about 1,000 or so names. These departmental lists are then fed to the central Civil Service Department list, the Whitehall 'Great and Good', currently containing some 2,700 names. In addition a great deal of further information is held centrally on many more persons who have indicated a wish for appointment in the public sector.

Sometimes specialist 'headhunting' firms have been used. Mr John Methven's appointment as Director of the Office of Fair Trading and Mr Nigel Foulkes's appointment as Chairman of the Civil Aviation Authority came about in this way.

The democratic processes of advertising and selection or the involvement of employees in the industries concerned in the making of appointments has always been frowned upon by civil servants. Indeed a proposal in 1966 to set up a Central Appointments Bureau to advertise appointments was rejected although it was recognised that advertising was a more democratic method than was then currently used, and that it widened choice and brought out those with a genuine desire for appointment. Top people do not like the idea of responding to advertisements in a competitive environment. So ministers, often inadequately advised, make the appointments.

If advertising and selection conferences are not acceptable there is still an overwhelming case for involving more people in the trawl for the great and the good, including trade unions and employees, and there is an unanswerable case for a more systematic compilation of names of suitable persons by ministers themselves. Civil servants who are often personally opposed to the public sector of industry and who often recommend for such appointments people who have campaigned actively against the public sector are not the right people to perform this task.

At another level senior civil servants are recommending and vetting hundreds of appointments to consumer councils, user councils, NEDDY committees, safety councils, New Town Corporations, health boards, training boards, etc., etc., etc. . . At the regional and area level these people tend to reflect the values of those who are responsible for putting them there. Some people believe that it is a political system of appointments. This is a very small part of the truth. When I first joined the civil service the term 'politically suspect' was used about members of the Labour Party. Fifteen years later Labour ministers had hardly dented the system and it would be surprising if anything other than civil service influence was the reason.

This still leaves unanswered the question 'What sort of civil servants do we want for the future?' I would begin my answer by saying that the question is as much about how we want to organise and conduct the business of government in the future (about which this book makes many proposals) as it is about people of this or that particular type. It is as much about the relationship between institutions as it is about the individuals who run the institutions.

As regards these individuals I would say this. Firstly we need above everything else civil servants who respect the democratic process and in so doing are prepared to answer to their consciences. If, for example, civil servants knew that men and women who were being sent back to Russia from the United Kingdom just after the last war were going to meet their death, they should have spoken out. If civil servants knew that politicians were behaving improperly whether on the basis of some Watergate or lesser scandal, it would be their duty to expose the politicians. Doctrines of ministerial responsibility and accountability which I have strongly supported throughout this book cannot be a shield which allows politicians to act illegally or immorally. Therefore the accounting officer's minute referred to in Chapter 4, is useful if used properly and impartially. The proper use of such a minute might have spared the country the wasteful expenditure of hundreds of millions of pounds. In short a civil servant's overriding loyalty is to the democratic process.

Secondly, within the limits imposed by my first point, we need civil servants who are loyal to the ministers – loyal in advising them, loyal to their minister's ideas and decisions, and loyal to their ministers in their battles (which are part of the democratic process) with their colleagues. Such loyalty should not include deliberate attempts to cause friction between ministers or to vulgarise perfectly proper political debate between ministers. Discretion and integrity are needed in this field as in all others. This loyalty must override any loyalty which civil servants may feel that they have to their own colleagues in the service, to the service itself, or to the establishment or system or whatever. The Civil Service Department, the Think-Tank, and the Cabinet secretariat, for example, should not be regarded as institutions through which civil servants by-pass the views of their departmental ministers to achieve their own departmental ends.

Thirdly, we need at the very highest levels some civil servants – whether they be called political advisers or something else – who understand and are sympathetic to the political philosophy of the Government and the Party which are in power. When he took over at the Department in May 1979 Sir Keith Joseph, the present Secretary of State for Industry, told his senior civil servants, it is said, to read Adam Smith so that they would know what he was talking about. If the story is not apocryphal, Sir Keith was making a serious point. To look at it another way, I find impossible to accept the conventional wisdom that civil servants whose education, tastes, habits and background make them antithetical to certain political and philosophical views and values can advance those views and values in the advice which they tender to ministers. To ask civil servants to behave in such a manner is to ask them to behave as schizoids. In no other sphere in life does one ask advisers to behave like this. So why do we do it in government where it matters most? Hence part of the argument for establishing political offices inside Government departments. Sir Keith Joseph might have been better employed moving the Conservative Centre for Policy Studies into the Department of Industry rather than asking his civil servants to read Adam Smith.

Fourthly, we need civil servants who understand and respect the values of the majority of ordinary people. At the moment too many top civil servants together with others in the establishment spend too much of their time undermining the confidence of working people in themselves and encouraging others to lose confidence in the abilities of working people. The most devastating weapon, as this book shows, that civil servants (and others) use to make working people lose confidence in themselves is condescension and a refusal to tell them the truth in a crisis.

Fifthly, we need civil servants who can provide excellence and expertise. Not every civil servant can be a Keynes – urbane, civilised and genuinely expert – but too many civil servants at the highest level mask their real lack of expertise by their literary skills and political manoeuvring. Too much that passes for excellence is really fashion. Too many civil servants are propagating the latest European fashion, the latest economic fashion, the latest environmental fashion, the latest industrial fashion or the latest popular fashion.

Sixthly, we want civil servants who, because they play an important role in shaping our destiny, are prepared to accept legitimate criticisms. Occasionally Permanent Secretaries make very contentious public speeches. For example, Sir Peter Carey, Permanent Secretary at the Department of Industry, made a speech on 26th January 1978 to the Industrial Society with which I and many other M.P.s were profoundly in disagreement. The speech was cleared by the minister but the point is it was made by a civil servant in public. I do not object to senior civil servants making such speeches. The more the public hears them the more it will understand their values. What I do object to and what we should all object to is the kind of complaint that we got from Sir Ian Bancroft, the head of the civil service, at the Expenditure Committee hearing on 18th April 1978 (already referred to on page 16), when he said: 'I would not like to let it pass without deprecating the fact, the observations made by Mr Sedgemore about a serving Permanent Secretary, namely, Sir Peter Carey.'

Seventhly, we need civil servants who recognise that the strength of the bureaucratic power calls for countervailing political power. In particular, we need civil servants who will be able to work with departmental ministerial teams made up of industrialists, trade unionists, academics, M.P.s and others appointed by ministers and given executive functions. We need civil servants who will be prepared to work with powerful Select Committees in the House of Commons covering the work of each department. We need civil servants who will pay more than lip-service to open government. When the former head of the civil service, Sir Douglas Allen, instructed departments to make available to the public background papers on policy matters with which they were dealing (July 1977) few responded enthusiastically and some, for example the Treasury, simply ignored the instruction. At the moment civil servants regard any breach of closed government, save to damage a minister, rather as the army views cowardice in the field.

Civil servants should heed this constructive advice. The tide of informed public opinion is turning against them. Similar criticisms voiced in very different spheres from these I have discussed are to be found in *The Culture Gap – An Experience of Government and the Arts* by Hugh Jenkins, Minister for the Arts 1974–76, and by David Henke in *Colleges in Crisis*. A few at the top are making it more difficult for hundreds of thousands beneath them who serve their country well.

Looking back on these seven points, I do not think I am asking for a great deal, yet what I am asking could revolutionise British politics. Lord Rothschild once said that if only we were less suspicious of our civil servants and loved them more they would perform better. I would put it slightly differently. If only they performed better we would love them more. Democracy will always respect those who service their country well.

7 Parliament

The smooth running of Parliament depends for its survival on the existence of a large number of uninformed backbench members. M.P.s come very low down in the hierarchy of secrecy in our society, ranking behind ministers, civil servants, junior ministers, Parliamentary Private Secretaries, leaders of the corporatist institutions who deal direct with Government departments, and even favoured academics with access to Whitehall. Fortunately, frustration has given way to resentment in recent years and resentment has given way to the positive and in the main constructive proposals of the Procedure Committee of the House of Commons (First Report from the Select Committee on Procedure – Session 1977–78) and the Expenditure Committee (Eleventh Report from the Expenditure Committee, Session 1976–77, The Civil Service).

As a result of the Report of the Select Committee on Procedure important changes in the committee structure in Parliament are being made but they contain three stings in the tail. Parliament's reforming zeal has been sidetracked. The executive never yields power easily.

The House of Commons decided on 25th June 1979 to set up twelve committees as set out below 'to oversee every aspect of government business' and to 'examine the expenditure, administration and policy of the principal Government departments'. The committees have some nine to eleven members and are therefore about the same size as the sub-committees of the old Expenditure Committee. A further committee with eight members was established to oversee the work of the Parliamentary Commissioner for the Administration and of the Health Service Commissioners. The Public Accounts Committee was left much as it has always been.

I referred to three stings in the tail. The first sting comes from the refusal of the executive to allow the new committees to summon ministers to appear before them. Had such a power been granted, it would have been constitutionally significant for the future relationship between Parliament and the executive. It would have meant that Parliament was re-asserting, in a modern form, its constitutional

SELECT COMMITTEES OF PARLIAMENT – 1979

Name of Committee	Principal Government departments concerned	Maximum numbers of Members	Quorum
1. Agriculture	Ministry of Agriculture, Fisheries Food	9	3
2. Defence	Ministry of Defence	10	3
3. Education, Science and Arts	Department of Education and Science	9	3
4. Employment	Department of Employment	9	3
5. Energy	Department of Energy	10	3
6. Environment	Department of the Environment	10	3
7. Foreign Affairs	Foreign and Commonwealth Office	11	3
8. Home Affairs	Home Office	11	3
9. Industry and Trade	Department of Industry, Department of Trade	11	3
10. Social Services	Department of Health and Social Security	9	3
11. Transport	Department of Transport	10	3
12. Treasury and Civil Service	Treasury, Civil Service Department, Board of Inland Revenue, Board of Customs and Excise	11	3

Notes
1. The Foreign Affairs Committee, the Home Affairs Committee and the Treasury Committee have powers to appoint one sub-committee.
2. There may be a sub-committee, drawn from the membership of two or more of the Energy, Environment, Industry and Trade, Transport and Treasury Committees, set up from time to time to consider any matter affecting two or more nationalised industries.
3. The committees have powers to 'appoint persons with such technical knowledge either to supply information which is not readily available or to elucidate matters of complexity within the committee's order of reference'.
Source: Hansard 25th June 1979.

supremacy over the executive. Just as important, the granting or taking of such a power would have meant that ministers, or at any rate Cabinet ministers, would have appeared more regularly to give an account of their stewardship than will now be the case. The existence of such a power would have rendered ministers more responsive to the work and views of the members of those committees and hence to Parliament itself.The executive's answer to these arguments is that Parliament itself (as opposed to any of its committees) does have the right to summon witnesses. However this involves a cumbersome procedure rarely used and is basically related to Parliament's backstop role as the nation's highest Court.

When he was Prime Minister, Harold Wilson was criticised for refusing to let Harold Lever, then Chancellor of the Duchy of Lancaster, appear before the Expenditure Committee who were examining the Chrysler rescue operation of 1975. In his book *Final Term*, Harold Wilson writes that he told the chairmen of the principal Select Committees in Parliament through Edward DuCann, that:

> there would be no Downing Street interference with the attendance of any minister summoned to answer questions arising out of his departmental duties . . . There was a particular problem here in respect of ministers with no departmental portfolio, such as the Lord President, the Lord Privy Seal and the Chancellor of the Duchy of Lancaster, who from time immemorial have chaired Cabinet committees, or have been sent on missions by Prime Ministers. To call them would blur existing ministerial responsibilities, and impair collective Cabinet responsibility.

The second sting comes from the inability of the new committees 'to call for papers' from the Government. There are two types of papers that the committees must have access to if they are to do their work properly and which their own staffs, however well equipped, cannot supply. These are papers containing the advice which civil servants give to ministers, and papers containing information which is peculiarly within the knowledge of Government departments and which the committees want. In addition the committees need to know what facts and figures civil servants use as a basis for their advice to ministers and what their reasons are for selecting or preferring those facts and figures.

The third and final sting emerges from the refusal of the executive and back bench Members of Parliament to establish, staff and operate these committees in a manner which will enable them to function on a party political basis. It is a grave defect to which I return later in this chapter.

Under the guise of reform the executive has ceded very little. It has not even arranged for the committees to be properly serviced. As at present constituted there is no reason why civil servants and ministers should not be as disingenuous, tight-lipped and ashen-faced as ever in giving evidence. All the weird experiences described in this book can be repeated. And so it will continue to be until the 'right to know' (discussed in detail in the next chapter), at present as far away as ever, is granted through a proper Freedom of Information Bill. The 'right to know' should not be confused with the perennial Home Office desire to reform Section 2 of the Official Secrets Act 1911 so as to make it more effective and secure more convictions in the Courts. This regressive proposal is another that is presented to the public as though it were a radical reform.

When Margaret Thatcher and the Conservatives came to power in May 1979 the Civil Service Department along with all other departments was asked to volunteer cuts in public spending. They volunteered, successfully, cuts in limited funds which had been set aside by the previous Government to enable a very modest improvement to be made in the amount and quality of information that the public and Parliament receive. In short, the executive whilst claiming to be radical has once again triumphed over Parliament.

I must make two other points before leaving the subject. In setting out the proposals for the new committee system the Leader of the House, Norman St John-Stevas, after describing the change as one of the most important constitutional changes of the century went on to say that it had never been the function of Parliament to govern because that was the job of the executive. Coming even from a distinguished student of Bagehot that assertion is tormented constitutional nonsense. Parliament governs as much as the executive does. The idea that historically it has merely scrutinised the work of the executive is a constitutional fiction. The public would think it astonishing if they were told that when Parliament passes or refuses to pass legislation it is not governing. Moreover when the public talks casually to their Members of Parliament and refers to them, if they are in the governing party, as being part of the Government, they have perceived constitutional reality and the relationship of the Cabinet to Members of Parliament through the Whip system more accurately than Bagehot or the Leader of the House have perceived it. Parliament's role in government may only be a minor subordinate one (the thesis of this book, in effect) but it is a necessary one and one which will remain for as long as we want to be able to talk about Parliamentary democracy.

It has been suggested that Select Committees should not be content to exert influence on the executive through their investigatory role but that they should take control of the purse strings in two ways. The committee which scrutinises the work of the Treasury should have power to recommend to Parliament or even itself to set limits to the global amount that should be spent on public expenditure each year and should recommend or set budgets for each area of expenditure; and the other committees covering the work of each department should be responsible for or should make recommendations in respect of the allocation of the funds assigned to the work of that department amongst the various projects and fields for which that department is responsible. Thus the committee covering the work of the Department of Education might be allocated £10 billion by the committee covering the work of the Treasury. It would then be responsible for allocating or making recommendations on the disbursement of that £10 billion in the education sphere. It, for example, would say how much should be spent on university education as opposed to nursery education.

There is, of course, a world of difference in giving a committee the power to make recommendations on public expenditure within the sphere for which it is responsible and in giving it power to allocate the money or even block proposed Government allocations. These latter proposals would in effect destroy Cabinet government as we know it and signal a move to the complete separation of powers such as exist in America. My own view is that such moves would destroy the party political process in Britain and with it any semblance of democracy.

In a further development of these proposals and in a naive appreciation of the virtues of the American system Mr Geoffrey Smith in his booklet *Westminster Reform: Learning from Congress* has suggested that Select Committees in the British system should be given powers to amend Bills and in effect play a central role in the legislative process. The Select Committees might in other words take on, in addition to their role in scrutinising expenditure and other government activities, the task now assigned to Standing Committees who consider Bills. They would, under these proposals, become super Standing Committees with more wide-ranging powers. Again I see such proposals, which are certainly more radical (or is the word reactionary?) than anything I propose, as being a direct attack on Cabinet government and on party political debate. I see the proper role of Select Committees as being threefold: 1. that of expressing through detailed argument and analysis the clash of political ideas; 2. that of enhancing the quality of the public debate on issues through the release of information; 3. that of scrutinising government activity and bringing pressure to bear on Governments; and 4. that of calling to account the more important governing institutions that wield power in the corporate state and examining the relationship of these institutions to the executive. I do not see their role as that of weakening the effectiveness of what remains of Cabinet government.

In my view Parliamentary control of the executive can never succeed as long as Parliament chooses to believe in the liberal fallacy that the executive is expressing the will of the people through the operation of Cabinet government and a neutral administration. Unless Parliament is prepared to come to terms with the pivotal role of the executive in relation to the governing institutions of the corporate state then its control over that executive will be as ineffective and meaningless as it is at present.

The Select Committee system in Parliament was hopelessly haphazard until the new structure was introduced. Until then most activities of Governments were not subject to any scrutiny although the three most powerful Select Committees – the Public Accounts Committee (P.A.C.), the Expenditure Committee and the Nationalised Industries Committee – had in recent years extended their influence as well as the scope of their operations.

Even so the work done by these committees was not satisfactory and many lessons can be learned from the mistakes that were made. There is a clear need to strengthen the role of the P.A.C. and the system of state audit which works through the P.A.C. and the Exchequer and Audit Department headed by the Comptroller and Auditor General. A recent Labour Party paper, 'Reform of the House of Commons' made the following proposals with which I agree:

1. The expenditure to be audited should be redefined to cover all public expenditure, including the spending of state funds by private organisations.
2. The House of Commons, advised by the Public Accounts Committee, should appoint the Comptroller and Auditor General.
3. The House of Commons, advised by the Public Accounts Committee, should decide on the numbers, grading and qualifications of the audit staff.
4. The House of Commons, advised by the Public Accounts Committee, should decide on the information required in the accounts which are submitted.
5. The audit process should be extended to give the Public Accounts Committee the power to examine the management, the efficiency and the effectiveness of all spenders of state funds.

The work of the Expenditure Committee from 1974–79 of which I was a member showed up many fundamental weaknesses in the procedures. Some of these weaknesses are bound to remain even with the new committee system. The committee, with 49 members, which was charged to examine expenditure programmes by the Government and the policies that lay behind them, did its work through a number of sub-committees. I was a member of a nine-strong sub-committee called the General Sub-Committee whose primary function was to examine the Government's public expenditure plans and the annual Public Expenditure White Paper. In addition the sub-committee carried out a number of specific studies into related economic matters such as the European Monetary System, cash limits and financial accountability to Parliament. Through its works in these various spheres the committee was consciously seeking to turn itself, and not without success, into a general committee of economic affairs shadowing the work of the Treasury, although that was not its specific remit.

On the credit side the committee was generally thought by its colleagues in Parliament to produce reasonable and occasionally challenging reports. What other Members of Parliament think is always important to the status of a committee and therefore the way in which witnesses approach it. Relations between the Treasury civil servants who regularly give evidence to it were at arm's length but cordial. There was some concern expressed at one stage that relationships between one of the Clerks who serviced the committee and the Treasury were more than cordial in that information seemed to travel fast. Even so Treasury civil servants who gave evidence had no reason to feel themselves free from criticism. Indeed they and their political masters were occasionally given a rough ride by the standards which Parliament sets itself in these matters. Also on the credit side the questioning of witnesses usually drew out some clash of ideas between the two main political parties represented in the committee although this was rarely to be seen when its reports came to be published. The members were well informed in as far as the system allowed them to be. All this was to the good.

However a deeper analysis of the procedure shows up many defects in the work of the committee. The importance of these defects lies in the fact that they were symptomatic of defects in the work of other Select Committees in Parliament.

In the years 1974–79, with the concurrence and approval of the full Expenditure Committee which took responsibility for all its work, the General Sub-Committee produced the following reports:

WORK OF THE GENERAL SUB-COMMITTEE OF EXPENDITURE COMMITTEE 1974–79

Report	No. of public hearings	No. of witnesses called	No. of Memoranda Published	Total Time spent examining witnesses
Public Expenditure, Inflation and the Balance of Payments (Session 1974)	7	16	11	11½ hours
The White Paper 'Public Expenditure to 1978–79' (Cmnd 5879)	3	6	9	4 hours
The Public Expenditure Implications of the April 1975 Budget	2	5	4	3¾ hours
The Financing of Public Expenditure (Session 1975–76)	12	29	18	22½ hours

WORK OF THE GENERAL SUB-COMMITTEE OF EXPENDITURE COMMITTEE 1974–79 — *Continued*

Report	No. of public hearings	No. of witnesses called	No. of Memoranda Published	Total Time spent examining witnesses
The White Paper 'Public Expenditure to 1979–80' (Cmnd 6393)	3	5	2	5¾ hours
Planning and Control of Public Expenditure (Session 1975–76)	2	6	4	5¼ hours
White Paper on the Government's Expenditure Plans (Cmnd 6721)	1	4	2	1¾ hours
The Government's Expenditure Plans 1978–79 to 1981–82 (Cmnd 7049)	3	5	18	5 hours
The Government's Expenditure Plans 1979–80 to 1982–83 (Cmnd 7439)	1	4	17	2½ hours
Cash Limit Control of Public Expenditure (Session 1974–75)	1	3	1	2½ hours
Selected Public Expenditure Programmes – Stationery & Printing (Session 1976–77)	1	4	2	1¾ hours
The Civil Service – Session 1975–77	28	79*	91	55 hours
(Response to Government's Observations on Report)	3	9	5	4 hours
Supply Estimate and Cash Limits (Session 1977–78)	3	—	—	—
Financial Accountability & Parliament (Session 1977–78)	3	6	12	5 hours
Selected Public Expenditure Programmes – CO1	6	28	26	8 hours
The European Monetary System	2	9 (3 in private)	23	4 hours

* Plus informal talks in Paris and Washington.

Source: Reports of Committee Proceedings – House of Commons.

The most startling fact to emerge from a study of the work of the General Sub-Committee in these years, 1974 to 1979 is the narrowness of the enquiries in the sense of the very small number of witnesses questioned. Often the small number of people involved would consist of the same top Treasury civil servants followed later by the Chief Secretary of the Treasury. This was the usual format for consideration of the Public Expenditure White Papers. The Chancellor of the Exchequer rarely graced the committee with his presence (the enquiry into the European Monetary System was one of the exceptions) and usually sent along the Chief Secretary to the Treasury who admittedly was responsible to the Cabinet for the public expenditure plans. Even so, it is a sad state of affairs when it is not taken for granted that the Chancellor will appear annually before the House of Commons committee dealing with public expenditure and economic affairs. James Callaghan, who as Prime Minister was in charge of the civil service and responsible for the machinery of government and almost everything else, refused to appear before the committee although asked in writing when it made its very thorough study of the civil service. Instead the Lord Privy Seal, Lord Peart, who was not an elected Member of Parliament, was sent along as the minister in charge of the civil service and answerable in Cabinet for these matters. Generally it was a valid criticism of the work of the committee that too few experts (usually none at all) were questioned on the Government's public expenditure plans, although in the later years a number were invited to submit papers and this helped. In the studies which did not concern public expenditure plans, outside experts often gave oral evidence and submitted memoranda.

The brevity of the questioning of witnesses was both astonishing yet understandable to anyone who knows how the system works. By convention a hearing of the committee rarely lasted more than two hours and by convention the Public Expenditure White Papers which set out plans for the next four years – in theory an exercise much bigger than that of the Budget – were dealt with at two or three hearings. Also by convention the questions were shared out, with each member of the committee concentrating on one aspect of the questioning – not a bad thing in itself and one way of avoiding repetition. But by convention, and I was always very conscious of the fact that I was up against this convention, each member was expected not to take up more than some twenty minutes at the outside in his questioning. Of course each year's White Paper is in effect a rolling programme linking with earlier papers and the ones to come which limited the need for some questions. I accept too that sometimes the committee benefited from the truncated acuity of its members and the sharpness of their questions. Unfortunately the time factor meant also that the answers were often truncated, direct questions were often deflected with time-consuming and boring answers and many points were not pushed to their logical conclusion. And all this from one of the better House of Commons committees.

The committee was further impeded in its work by the refusal of Treasury witnesses to provide much of the information that members wanted. Treasury estimates of the level of imports for the coming year, projections on the level of unemployment, their expectations of price rises and the balance of payments position were all on the secret list. At times the Treasury hid behind suggestions that the markets might respond adversely if people knew what these estimates were, a suggestion that no economist could take very seriously. At times the Chief Secretary would say that as all forecasting was uncertain the public would only be misled by publication. At times it was said that publication of the information might create self-fulfilling prophecies. All the time the replies were given as though other people in the City, the C.B.I., the trade unions and the academic world were not making forecasts and as though expectations were not being created as a result of them. And all the answers were given as though the Treasury was not itself leaking information on some of these points. And they were given as though no country could manage without such secrecy when the committee itself knew from a visit to Washington how open the President's economic advisers were. This refusal to discuss sensibly even the basic parameters which affect the economy meant that the committee could not properly test the internal consistency of the Treasury arguments. In 1976 on one famous occasion, the committee were united in condemning the Treasury for forecasting an economic 'miracle' in its White Paper (see paragraph 9, The White Paper on 'Public Expenditure to 1979–80' Cmnd 6393) but they could never quite pin down the Treasury or understand (save possibly for crude political reasons) why it was misleading them. If policies are based on wrong premises then they should be changed or if there is some deeper and more alarming truth then it should be told. Almost inevitably events proved the committee right and the Treasury wrong.

Thus in 1976 whilst Sir Eric Roll, a former senior Treasury civil servant, a Director of the Bank of England and an independent member of the National Economic Development Council, was privately forecasting for the Government no more than a modest cyclical upturn in investment (I know this as I saw the papers) the Treasury were publicly projecting a massive upsurge. While rising unemployment was making a return to full employment, an impossibility in the foreseeable future on the then existing strategy, Treasury witnesses to the committee publicly suggested that there could be a return to full employment (unemployment down to 700,000) by 1979. And whilst imports were increasing at an alarming rate and exports were not, as one would have expected on past experience the Treasury witnesses thought up one reason after another as to why this was not happening. My point is that I am sure that they did not believe what they were saying. They were misleading Parliament and this made it impossible to make sensible criticisms of their strategy set out at the time in the Public Expenditure White Paper.

Some attempts to mislead the committee were absurd and I have already mentioned the Chancellor's behaviour over the European Monetary System (page 12). On an earlier occasion a senior Treasury civil servant, Mr J. Anson, went so far as to proclaim that he did not know what the chairman of the committee was talking about when he mentioned the Treasury's Medium Term Economic Assessment (The Government's Expenditure Plan 1978–79 to 1981–82, Second Report from the Expenditure Committee, Session 1977 – 30 January 1978, page 22 Q3, page 26 Q20 *et seq*) which is prepared every year, whereupon I produced a Bank of England document which discussed the Treasury's Medium Term Economic Assessment. The document showed that discussions had taken place on the Medium Term Assessment (MTA) between the Treasury, the Bank of England and Mr Wynne Godley from the Cambridge Economic Policy Group. I yield to no one in admiration for Mr Godley but can see no reason why Members of Parliament should be denied information to which he is privy. Moreover, and just as important, the Bank's document showed that the Treasury was working privately on assumptions widely different from those in the Public Expenditure White Papers which the committee was getting. The inescapable conclusion, there for every member of the committee to see because I distributed copies of part of the document to them, was that the Treasury were again seriously misleading Parliament and frustrating the work of one of its major committees.

The secrecy that the committee met has to be seen as part of a wider secrecy in economic affairs to which reference has already been made. I remember a Cabinet minister commenting when the Minimum Lending Rate went up on 14th February 1979, 'they never tell us about these things.' The Budget judgment, one of the most important decisions taken in government each year, is not a collective Cabinet judgment. The first that the Cabinet knows of the Budget judgment is when its members are given it on a take-it-or-leave-it basis on the Monday before the Tuesday when the Budget is presented to the public. For any self-respecting Cabinet minister it is a humiliating experience. On Sunday he does not know: on Tuesday at 5 p.m. he has to defend the decision he has not taken.

To be fair, James Callaghan, when he was Prime Minister, did widen the area of economic debate in the Cabinet. Overall strategy was discussed in the run-up to the second I.M.F. loan in November 1976. Moreover public expenditure priorities were (for the first time so far as Labour Governments were concerned) regularly discussed by the Cabinet in the run-up to the annual Public Expenditure White Paper. Yet the position, even for a Cabinet minister, is still most unsatisfactory.

To Members of Parliament on the committee, the Treasury were sometimes unhelpful in a very positive and forthright way. On a number of occasions the committee asked for help with economic projections using the Treasury model. Typical of the niggardly Treasury response is the following letter from the Chief Secretary of the Treasury, Joel Barnett, to the Chairman of the committee, Michael English, dated 8th February 1979:

> Dear Michael,
> I understand that during the hearing of the General Sub-Committee with Treasury officials on 31 January a request was made for calculations of the effects of alternative assumptions about the growth of public sector earnings in the current pay round. The alternative assumptions mentioned were 5 per cent, 10 per cent and 15 per cent. The request arose in the questioning by the sub-committee about the relative price effect and the public sector borrowing requirement.
>
> To produce an estimate of the relative price effect or of the PSBR, it is necessary to make assumptions and form judgments about the way in which a whole range of other elements in the economy would be affected. The Chancellor of the Exchequer gave, in the House of Commons debate on 25 January, what he described as a very rough and ready estimate of the problems which would ensue from a 15 per cent growth in average earnings in the current round, while making it clear that this was an assumption which he did not himself endorse. In particular he gave an indication of the increase in costs which would arise in the next fiscal year in various parts of the public sector from such an assumption. He also said that the effect on the public sector borrowing requirements would be considerably less – perhaps under half as much – but that a precise calculation would depend upon a whole range of other factors.
>
> The calculations requested at the hearing of the sub-committee would require a forecasting exercise covering all these other factors and involving a large number of judgments and assumptions. The Chancellor of the Exchequer explained to you in his letter of 10th November why he was reluctant to authorise the provision of such calculations – both because there would be a risk of appearing to

endorse such assumptions if a Government department were to carry out this work, and because it would divert those concerned from other work. I nevertheless hope you found the information given by the Chancellor to be of some help, and that you will understand why I cannot add to it at this stage. An up-to-date forecast of the prospects for the year ahead will of course be published in the usual way at the time of the Budget.

Yours
Joel Barnett

The fatuity of the claim about time and effort was shown by the fact that one of the advisers to the committee was able to get much of what the committee wanted by using the model of the Cambridge Economic Policy Group – although the committee would have preferred to have used the Treasury model. Ideally the committee should run its own model of the economy.

When drawing up its Report on the European Monetary System the committee was forced to comment in Paragraph 1 on 'the Government's reluctance to supply background papers because the Treasury failed to supply any written evidence at all preferring instead to let the Chancellor seek to dazzle the committee with science, something which he signally failed to do.'

Another related problem was the minimal amount of advice and facilities at the committee's disposal. In effect the committee had one full-time adviser (a former Deputy Secretary) and one part-time economic adviser. The Congressional Budget Office in America with its 160 professional economic advisers lurches to the other extreme but the contrast is clear. The committee had no modelling facilities of its own and only accidental access to the model of the Cambridge Economic Policy Group.

The committee suffered from one other defect too and that was the need, again by convention, to produce a consensus report which would satisfy all its members. Occasionally 'minority' reports remedied this defect. Those who oppose an extension or strengthening of the Select Committee system in Parliament, like the former Leader of the House, Michael Foot, latch on to this point about consensus politics. They say, rightly, that politics is about the clash of ideas and all-party Select Committees, with privileged access to information on specific subjects tying up MPs for days on end, and producing consensus reports, would destroy the essence of our party political democracy.

The work of the Expenditure Committee and all its sub-committees from 1974 to 1978 and the action which flowed from the work done, including some presentational changes in public expenditure, is summarised in the Third Report from the Expenditure Committee, Session 1978–79. The work of the General Sub-Committee for the period is described on pages 149–173 of that document. No criticisms of the work of the committee or its sub-committees are made.

Some of the criticisms that I have made would be overcome if these investigatory committees were staffed and advised on an overtly party political basis and were prepared, where it was appropriate, to produce reports on that basis as happens in America with the Joint Economic Committee of the Senate and the House of Representatives. It is essential for the party groups in any such system of committees to have adequate research and administrative support, including the ability to get the best possible advice from the universities, both sides of industry and elsewhere. There should also be a proper career structure for civil servants to encourage experts to work full-time on scrutinising and advising on legislation. The establishment of such committees would effectively disperse power in Parliament and out of it into the political parties, and to those groups and individuals who support political parties.

There are two different philosophies supporting the idea of strengthening and extending the system of investigatory committees in the House of Commons. Those on the right of the political spectrum see it as a way of frustrating strong government and limiting Cabinet government by a substantial move towards the separation of powers. They see the committees, operating as a consensus holding up government and slowing down the flood of legislation by substituting endless enquiries in place of decision-taking. On the left of the political spectrum are those who see the investigatory committees as a forum for the party political debate where outside opposition to the government's policies can be exposed as invalid. They see the committee system as strengthening the spine of weak Cabinets, and in the process strengthening Cabinet government by making it more responsible to the democratic process. Their proposals steer a middle course between those who see Parliament primarily as the servant of the executive and a place where the only function of backbench members is to support the leadership of their Parliamentary party, and those who believe that we should move firmly in the nineteenth century direction of the separation of powers and in the process take the management of the purse strings away from the executive, put policy firmly in the hands of backbench members, weaken the party political debate and with it the whole system of Cabinet government. Substantially the same mechanisms are being proposed to serve two entirely different political philosophies.

At present the procedures of the House of Commons do not allow for 'minority' reports from members of Select Committees. The only way a minority view can be expressed is by way of amendment to the main report. If an amendment is pressed then, although certain to be defeated, it will nevertheless be printed as part of the proceedings leading to the report. So if a member disagrees with the whole report he drafts an alternative report and then proposes that his report be read a second time in place of the draft report of the chairman of the committee.

Members of Parliament perform many functions, the most important of which are:

1. Helping their constituents, local industries and local organisations with particular problems. In the process Members of Parliament often find themselves acting as a kind of unofficial local ombudsman for the redress of grievances, plugging some of the gaps in Britain's haphazard system of administrative law.
2. Providing the debating forum of the nation on the floor of the House of Commons, and in the process seeking to express, interpret and translate into action the views of the people and also to inspire the people with the ideals that sustain the party political process.
3. Providing members who will make up the executive and carry out its work.
4. Scrutinising the work of the executive. This is often said to be the most important role of a backbench Member of Parliament. Certainly it is the traditional constitutional role of the M.P.
5. When their Party is in Government helping the executive push through its policies against the Parliamentary opposition, against outside vested interests and maybe against the opposition of the civil service. Clearly there may be tensions and conflicts for an M.P. performing both this role and that set out in 4. above. But, there is nothing inherently contradictory in an M.P. sustaining the executive in its power or helping it to overcome opposition at the same time as scrutinising the work of the executive in order both to improve it and to see that power is being exercised in a proper and legitimate fashion.
6. Legislating for social change that they consider either desirable or inevitable. Societies never stand still (they may by some definitions go forward or by others regress) and to pretend that they do so is to shut one's eyes to reality. It is said that we are over-governed, need less legislation or no legislation or a simplification of legislation but the legislative process will surely continue to occupy much of Parliament's time even with the most conservative of Governments.

Obviously the opposition M.P. and opposition parties in Parliament look at politics from a different angle. The primary role of the principal opposition party in British politics is to oppose the government, to expose what it is doing and to try to bring it down. In a country in which it is thought by politicians that Governments lose elections as opposed to oppositions winning them, this negative role has seemed in recent decades to predominate over the more positive role which oppositions have of explaining their philosophy and their policies. Indeed there seems to be a growing consensus amongst senior politicians of the two main political parties that it is dangerous to spell out too many detailed policies whilst in opposition for fear that they will prove impractical when in office. This idea sits uncomfortably by the side of the outlandish promises made and expectations created by most opposition parties during election campaigns.

There is also a growing feeling amongst politicians that the public in Britain do not like or are not interested in political ideology and therefore although it is easier for opposition parties to talk in ideological terms because they do not have to come to terms immediately with reality, they do not always do so. In this respect there was a marked contrast between the belief of most members of the Labour Shadow Cabinet after the May election of 1979 that the Party should be attacking the Conservative Government rather than engaging in internal debate on policies and the strong ideological stance of the Conservative Shadow Cabinet during their period of opposition from 1974 to 1979. The Labour Shadow Cabinet described it as a 'ridiculous constitutional wrangle'; others called it a debate on what kind of democracy the Labour Party should fight for.

Within well-defined limits it is accepted that almost any action is legitimate in the efforts of the opposition M.P. to obstruct the Government, including sustaining late night sittings designed to wear down the Government and its supporters, keeping Bills in Standing Committee for longer than is necessary to discuss them adequately, refusing to pair the sick and dying, and more generally using a host of procedural devices to upset the planning of Government business managers.

The well-defined limits within which opposition M.P.s are constrained stem in part from a recognition that the public will only go so far in tolerating the obstruction of Government business, especially if it has a clear majority in Parliament; in part from the knowledge that if it overplays its hand in opposing the Government it can expect similar treatment when it next forms an administration. Conservative M.P.s when in opposition can usually rely on the House of Lords and a majority of the press to support them in their attempts to undermine the government rather more than Labour M.P.s can when in opposition.

There are of course more orthodox devices by which oppositions can cause trouble for the Government, the main one being joining with government dissidents in the voting lobbies (or getting Government dissidents to join them) to defeat the Government. Some of these alliances can justly be described as unholy. Thus it was a combination of opposition Conservative M.P.s, *Tribune* M.P.s and Manifesto Group M.P.s on the Standing Committee of the Industry Bill, 1975, which was responsible for forcing the Government to accept an amendment by Jeremy Bray, the Labour M.P., obliging the Treasury to reveal some conditional and hitherto secret economic forecasting on an annual basis. On the other hand an examination of the voting records of that same Standing Committee will show that it was Conservative M.P.s who constantly bailed out Labour Ministers and enabled them to resist amendments from Labour backbenchers which would otherwise have been carried.

In the exercise of these functions M.P.s have different styles and some would say different degrees of commitment. Some live in their constituencies, others outside. Some hold 'surgeries' once a week to deal with their constituents' problems, some once a fortnight and a few once a month. Some regard being an M.P. as a full time job, some (hundreds) regard it as a part-time job and carry on in their businesses or professions. There are some startling consequences to the two job syndrome. Most committees in Parliament sit in the mornings but the Finance Committee which considers the proposals of the Budget never starts (unless it is sitting as a Committee of the whole House) until 4 p.m. Whatever the original reason the cause today seems to be the need for some members to fulfil their City obligations before coming down to Parliament. In consequence the Finance Committee frequently sits late into the night making a detailed line by line, word by word study of complex Bills. On four occasions when I sat on the Finance Committee which was considering the Finance Bill which introduced the capital transfer tax, the committee began at 4 p.m. and then sat through the night watching the darkness descend and the dawn burst out over the River Thames and finally rose at 8 a.m. to 9 a.m. the following morning. Some would say that admirable though this degree of commitment is (it killed one member), it is no way to run a country efficiently. Despite many pleas from anxious wives and some attempts, notably by Richard Crossman when he was Leader of the House, to get morning sittings Parliament has steadfastly refused to do what most legislatures in the world do – that is to sit at reasonable hours. The chamber of the House of Commons is more used to all-night sittings than even the Finance Committee. The executive is none too anxious for a change because the present system enables ministers to spend most of their day with their departments carrying on with the business of government away from the pressures of Parliament.

In the exercise of all his functions a Member of Parliament needs information both to be able himself to come to informed judgments and take rational decisions and to see if others inside and outside government are doing likewise. The prime and certainly the quickest source of purely factual information for an M.P. is the Parliamentary Question – written or oral. Providing that the factual information required is not classified, as a lot of important factual information undoubtedly is, the M.P. can and will get what he has asked for, accurately and in the form in which he asks for it, if it is available and none too great an expense to provide. Civil servants do take a lot of care over answering M.P.s' Questions, which are given a high priority. PQs are not, however, designed to give information on the way in which Governments are thinking still less on the advice they are receiving. Where questions are angled in this direction or where they seem to call for a mix of factual information and views, then the answers are often opaque. To this end civil servants have developed many skills and many standard unilluminating phrases. Yet perhaps because ministers and civil servants fear above all else Parliamentary rows (for they are public) as well as because of their desire to be helpful PQ answers are usually given straight. Hence the shock over a number of PQ answers already referred to on page 18 concerning sanctions-busting in Rhodesia which were inaccurate and which seriously misled Parliament. Hence the further shock when the House of Lords refused to join the House of Commons in setting up an enquiry into this matter.

By convention, and mainly by convention set arbitrarily by the Prime Minister and ministers, Parliamentary Questions cannot be asked on a whole host of important subjects. The Report of the Select Committee on Parliamentary Questions 1971–2 set out in Appendix 9 the matters upon which successive administrators had refused to answer Parliamentary Questions. The barred subjects, and they make up a formidable list, were:

Agriculture

Day to day matters of agricultural marketing boards.
Day to day matters of British Sugar Corporation.
Day to day matters of Meat and Livestock Commission.
Agricultural workers' wages.
Day to day matters of White Fish Authority.
Amount of strategic food reserves.
Forecasts of changes in food prices.

Attorney-General

Details of investigations by Director of Public Prosecutions.
Day to day administration of the Legal Aid Scheme.
Particulars of enquiries made by the Queen's Proctor.

Defence

Details of arms sales.
Operational matters.
Contract prices.
Costs of individual aircraft etc.
Details of research and development.
Numbers of foreign forces training in U.K.
Accident rates for aircraft.

Education

Curricular matters.
Discipline in schools.
Detailed expenditure within universities.
The Arts Council (no intervention on policy, or statistics of individual grants).
Instructions to research councils.

Employment

Strike statistics for individual firms.
Numbers employed in individual firms.
Forecasts of future levels of unemployment.
Forecasts of future trends in incomes.
Detailed matters of Industrial Training Boards.
Numbers of registered disabled persons employed by individual firms.
Day to day workings of the National Dock Labour Board.

Environment

Forecasts of housing starts.
Council house waiting lists.
Rents for Government offices.
Sports Council.

Exchequer

Economic and Budgetary forecasts.
Bank rate.
Exchange Equalisation Account.
Government borrowing.
Sterling balances.
Tax affairs of individuals or companies.
Day to day matters of the Bank of England.
Commercial activities of British Petroleum.
Administration of House of Lords attendance allowance.

Individual consignments of goods through Customs and Excise.
Regional figures for National Savings.

Foreign and Commonwealth

Proceedings of Commonwealth Sanctions Committee.
Supply of arms.
Terms of engagement of individual officers.
Future forecasts of overseas aid.
Elections in Security Council.
Ministerial meetings of W.E.U.; N.A.T.O. Council.
Attendance records at Council of Europe.
O.E.C.D. meetings.

Home

Telephone tapping.
Names of prohibited immigrants.
Regional seats of government.
Security source operations.
Operational matters for the police.

Lord President of the Council

Staff of the House of Commons.

Northern Ireland

Intelligence sources.

Post and Telecommunications

Programme content.

Prime Minister

Telephone tapping.
Cabinet Committees.
Cost of the 'hot line'.
Security arrangements at Chequers.
Detailed arrangements for the conduct of Government business.
List of future engagements.

Scotland

Commercial confidentiality of Ferry Services.
Enquiries by industrialists.
Proceedings of the Scottish Economic Planning Council.

Social Services

Purchasing contracts in the N.H.S.
Reasons for appointing individual members of hospital boards.
Names of holders of merit awards.
Day to day running of General Practice Finance Corporation.
Personal information gained from social security schemes.

Trade and Industry

Details of air-miss enquiries.
Commercial activities of the Overseas Marketing Corporation.
Trade statistics for Scotland.
Financial support for trade fairs in the U.K.
Details of export licences.
Relations between E.C.G.D. and individual exporters.
Reasons for refusal to refer mergers to Monopolies Commission.
Names of complainants about companies.
Individual transactions between National Film Finance Corporation and customers.
Day to day matters of English Tourist Board.
Details of defence research establishments.
Details of research contracts.
Forecasts of price movements.
Advice from Economic Planning Councils.
Details of financial assistance to individual companies.
Individual applicants or I.D.C.'s

Wales

Contracts of Forestry Commission.
Advice from Welsh Council.

Nationalised Industries

Day to day matters.
Statistics other than national.
Matters of commercial confidence.

Since then Jeff Rooker, the member for Perry Barr has asked each minister if he or she would list those topics on which it was his or her practice not to answer Parliamentary Questions, and if he or she would list any changes in practice since 1972, indicating in each case the date on which the change was made and the relevant reference in the Official Report. All the twenty-four questions were answered on 2nd May 1978. The answers which tell one as much about the ministers as about the information which they are prepared to release, are set out in Appendix 3.

Sometimes M.P.s manage to get Questions down on the Order Paper only to find ministers refusing to answer them. The sort of questions that ministers will not answer – all related to the work of one department, the Department of Health and Social Security – which were nevertheless accepted by the Table Office can be seen from the following unhelpful replies over the years.

Birmingham Regional Hospital Board (Membership)

Mr Leslie Huckfield

To ask the Secretary of State for Social Services on what grounds he has declined to renew the extension of Councillor Mrs Theresa Stewart's period of membership of the Birmingham Regional Hospital Board.

Sir Keith Joseph

Mrs Stewart's term of membership expires on 31st March 1971 in accordance with the Regulations governing the appointment of members. It is not the custom to state reasons for selection of individuals for membership.

(4th February 1971)

Abortions

Mr Ian Wrigglesworth

To ask the Secretary of State for Social Services, what was the total number of abortions carried out in the hospitals under the control of the Cleveland Area Health Authority during each year since 1970, and for the first six months of 1975.

Mr Tom Litterick

To ask the Secretary of State for Social Services, if she will publish in the Official Report figures showing the number of abortions carried out in National Health Service hospitals in each of the five health districts of Birmingham for therapeutic, social and other reasons during the latest 12 month period for which figures are available. . .

Dr David Owen

It is not the practice to publish figures for areas of treatment smaller than Regional Health Authorities in order to preserve confidentiality as required by Regulation 5 of the Abortion Regulations 1968.

(8th December 1975)

Invalid Tricycle – Current Type

Mr Arthur Jones

To ask the Secretary of State for Social Services, what was the cost of the current type of tricycle when last made available to a handicapped person and the comparative cost of a standard type vehicle adapted to provide similar facilities.

Mr Alfred Morris

It is not the custom to disclose contract prices. The cost of a tricycle varies according to the nature of the special features needed, as does that of an adapted standard car.

(18th October 1976)

Mr Walter Norval – Benefits

Mr Iain Sproat

To ask the Secretary of State for Social Services, what has been the income of Mr Walter Norval, sentenced in Glasgow High Court to 14 years for armed robbery, from social security benefits, in cash and in kind, unemployment benefit, any rent and rates rebates, &c., itemised by benefit including per average week over the last year; and whether his department allowed Mr Norval to draw or have drawn on his behalf, unemployment benefit for the period of his holiday in Tenerife in March 1977.

Mr Stanley Orme

Information of this kind about individual claims is regarded as confidential and it would be contrary to established policy to discuss it to the Hon. Member, without the individual's consent.

(30th November 1977)

Abortions – Greenwich and Bexley Health area

Mr John Cartwright

To ask the Secretary of State for Social Services, how many abortions have been performed at each of the hospitals in the Greenwich and Bexley Health area during each of the years for which records are available.

Mr Roland Moyle

For reasons of confidentiality it is not the department's policy to disclose by place of treatment information on abortions which is derived from notifications sent in confidence to the Chief Medical Officer.

(Tuesday 28th February 1978)

Consultant Merit Awards

Miss Jo Richardson

To ask the Secretary of State for Social Services, what is the total amount of public funds paid out in consultant merit awards; what is the distribution of the awards, both by region and to teaching as against non-teaching hospitals; what are the names of the recipients with their respective awards; and what are the criteria used in making the awards.

Mr Roland Moyle

Total expenditure on distinction awards in England and Wales is currently about £12 million a year. The detailed criteria used in making awards are a matter for the Advisory Committee on Distinction Awards, under the chairmanship of Sir Stanley Clayton, working within their general remit that awards are for professional distinction and, particularly at the lower levels of awards, outstanding service contributions to the N.H.S. The names of distinction award holders are not published at present, but I am discussing this and other aspects of the scheme with the representatives of the medical profession.

The tables below set out the distribution of distinction awards by N.H.S. Region and between teaching and non-teaching authorities at 31st December 1976, the latest date for which comprehensive information is available.

(3rd March 1978)

(Note: The tables were given but I have not printed them.)

Oral Question Time which takes place every day in the House of Commons is not purely or even primarily an exercise in the gathering of information. Indeed as a method of getting information out of the executive it is a farce. As a method of enabling Members of Parliament to check what the executive is doing, it fails almost wholly in its purpose. Yet Governments, as well as constitutional text-books, refer almost reverently to it as a means of close scrutiny by Parliament of the executive.

What takes place in fact is a kind of stylised minuet – Question asked by M.P., Question answered by minister whose civil servants have had a fortnight's notice of said Question, supplementary Question asked by M.P. who asked original Question and answered by minister whose civil servants have almost invariably anticipated said supplementary Question, one or two supplementary Questions, by other M.P.s also anticipated by civil servants. Even the weakest minister, providing always that he can read the supplementary answers prepared for him by his civil servants, finds it almost impossible to come unstuck. For the most part it is a ritual, a primitive expression of the clash of political ideas on the part of those who are playing a game called high politics.

The one valuable role that Question Time has lies outside scrutiny or the gathering of information. It lies in the ability of certain Members of Parliament to use the occasion to bring major current political issues into the debating chamber of the nation which would not otherwise happen on account of the procedures of the House of Commons which are not generally geared to discussing whatever is uppermost in the public's mind at any particular moment. Prime Minister's Question Time on Tuesdays and Thursdays from 3.15 p.m. to 3.30 p.m. invariably performs this useful role. From the point of view of bringing part of the political debate to the nation, Question Time has two further advantages. The first is the adversary nature of the process which makes for personal and political drama. The second, and it relates to the first, is that the journalists who report the proceedings of Parliament like this highly personalised, headline-catching format and are usually present at Question Time though absent from most of the rest of the formal proceedings of Parliament.

Closely linked to Question Time is the time given over to ministerial statements in the Commons on important matters of policy at the end of Question Time. Slightly more information can be extracted from ministers from the persistent questioning which follows these brief statements. The ministerial statement is valuable to M.P.s in that if an emergency arises (e.g. people are killed in a factory explosion or a mine disaster, or people are inconvenienced through an industrial dispute) they get the opportunity at least briefly to discuss it.

Ministers who are none too keen on being questioned about policy statements in the Chamber can successfully avoid any inquisition by arranging for a friendly M.P. to put down a planted Question on the Order Paper. The minister then makes his policy statement in a Written Answer, sometimes expanding on the answer at a press conference of lobby correspondents. In July 1979 a minor row broke out when it emerged that the Secretary of State for Industry, Sir Keith Joseph, was going to use the Written Answer rather than follow the ministerial statement procedure when announcing changes in regional grants. At the last moment, as a result of protests from M.P.s he was forced to abandon a press conference which was to have accompanied the Written Answer. If a Minister feels that even a Written Answer might embarrass him he can always hold over a statement until Parliament has risen and then just talk to the press. Akin to this process is the common tactic of making a statement on policy by way of Written Answer on the day that Parliament rises when no M.P.s are around. If no legislation is needed to make such policy statements effective (i.e. if administrative action will suffice) then Parliamentary control is lost altogether.

One important issue of policy which was never discussed in Parliament and which subsequently became the subject of public controversy concerned the Labour Government's attitude to the practice of jury vetting. On 25th March 1974 (Hansard Vol. 871, Cols. 10.11) I asked the Home Secretary if he would 'seek powers to require that, in respect of all police forces, intelligence services and others engaged in prosecuting criminal cases, no investigation should be made of the political background, allegiances or activities of those called for jury service with a view to objections being made to their acting as jurors in specific cases', and received the reply from Alex Lyon, a Home Office minister 'I am not aware that there is any such practice. If my Hon. Friend has evidence of it perhaps he will send it to me'.

I did so by letter on 26th March 1974 and when the Home Secretary and Attorney-General looked into the matter they discovered that jury vetting had been going on since 1945 and that it was being done on the authority of the Director of Public Prosecutions. Whether the DPP is responsible for his actions to the Attorney-General is a debatable point. Arthur Davidson M.P., who worked as a junior minister in the Attorney-General's office, kept me in touch with the nature of the discussions that were taking place between the Home Secretary and the Attorney-General. No one seemed interested when I raised the matter publicly on two occasions – one of them under a pseudonym in a magazine in 1972. The Home Secretary, Roy Jenkins, replied to my letter of 26th March 1974 on 30th May 1975 but I never received his reply and the first time I saw it was on 28th November 1978 when the Home Office, at my request, sent me a copy. So the public remained unaware of what was happening until 3rd October 1978, when the ABC trial, Regina v Berry, Campbell and Aubrey, opened at the Old Bailey and the fact that the jury had been vetted received widespread publicity. The Attorney-General then issued a statement on 10th October 1978 referring obliquely to my correspondence with the Home Office. In that statement he stated that Guidelines on the practice of jury vetting had been drawn up. Those Guidelines, as amended on 10th November 1978, were then made public. Subsequently complaints were made in Parliament and outside that the Attorney-General had never sought to get the approval of the legal professions or Parliament for the practice. On 10th October 1979 on a B.B.C.2 *Man Alive* programme, Sam Silkin Q.C. who had been the

Attorney-General concerned, said that as I had been told about what was happening it was quite wrong to say that the Government had proceeded by stealth over this matter. I find it odd that important statements of public policy should depend for their dissemination on the ability or willingness of individual backbench M.P.s to make public letters from ministers. I find it equally odd that there should have been no public debate about the matter.

In the Parliamentary rule-book under Standing Order No. 9 there is emergency procedure which allows Parliament to hold three-hour emergency debates on a specific issue if they are demanded, if the Speaker certifies that the emergency is important enough to take precedence over what Parliament would have discussed and if 40 M.P.s stand up to support the demand. The rules governing this procedure are strictly interpreted by the Speaker and Government business is rarely set aside. On 20th November 1978 Christopher Price, was refused an application under the Standing Order to discuss the implications for free speech of, 'the use by the Attorney-General of his discretion in allowing prosecutions in cases under the Official Secrets Act in the light of the verdicts and sentences in the case, Regina v Berry, Campbell and Aubrey which was settled on Friday' although if the applications had been granted no business would have been lost and all that would have happened would have been the shortening of a Second Reading debate on a Companies Bill from a full day to a half day. For the avoidance of doubt I would add too that I always found the Speaker, George Thomas, charming and helpful and, were it not for the taste of a glass of liqueur brandy he once gave me, would have no cause for complaint.

The Member of Parliament also exercises control over the executive and gets information through the legislative process and in particular through the Standing Committee stage of the legislative process which follows on a Bill's Second Reading. It has been suggested that the M.P. would be better informed if every Bill in Parliament were accompanied at its introduction by a document setting out the history of the proposal and the need for the Bill: a clause by clause analysis of the Bill stating why the particular means used in the clause had been adopted to achieve the ends desired: and appendices giving relevant statistical and background material.

It has been further suggested that the M.P. could be helped in his task if the Standing Committees which consider Bills in detail were replaced by new Legislation Committees which would have powers to call for persons and papers in the manner that Select Committees have, and which could take evidence regarding the contents of the Bill prior to the deliberating and voting on specific points. I see merit in these proposals. I see a serious threat to the democratic process in the existing procedure which encourages backbench M.P.s on the Government side to sit mute throughout Standing Committee consideration of Bills so that the Government can get its business through.

There can be no doubt that the combination of this legislative and investigatory committee reform backed by 'the right to know' would greatly strengthen the role of backbench Members of Parliament and make the Parliamentary process more responsive to the views and ideas of those outside Parliament.

In theory the remedy lies in Parliament's own hands for it controls its own procedures. In practice the executive largely controls the procedures of Parliament and the way in which it conducts its business. Parliament's legislative programme is largely controlled by the Legislation Committee, a Cabinet sub-committee which is set up to plan the Government's business and whose chairman is the Lord President of the Council and Leader of the House of Commons but which does not officially exist, which does not meet in Parliament and which has no Parliamentary standing, official or unofficial. Civil servants are instructed not to refer in public to the existence of the Legislation Committee and reference to it is hardly ever heard in Parliament.

The day to day business of Parliament is controlled through the 'business' or 'usual' channels which means communications between the Cabinet and the Shadow Cabinet. It is probably inevitable if Parliament is to manage its affairs in an orderly fashion. What is not necessary for the orderly conduct of business in Parliament are some of the squalid deals which take place between the 'usual' channels. These can range from agreements between the Leader of the House and his Shadow opposite number to curtail backbench debate for promises by the Chief Whip (also of course the Patronage Secretary) that he will ensure that private Bills, which are not the subject of 'whipping' and in which oppositions have an interest, will get through although opposed by members of the majority party. Such agreements which sometimes come unstuck are called 'gentlemen's agreements' though some would wonder how gentlemen could agree to act behind the backs of their colleagues.

All the evidence suggests that there are two distinct trends taking place in Parliament which are sometimes confused. Firstly there is the growing power of the executive, dealing more and more directly with outside interests and by-passing Parliament, which is rendering the backbench M.P.s more and more ineffective. Secondly, and to some extent working (largely unavailingly) in the other direction, is the breakdown of party discipline and the decline in the influence of the Whips. Younger Members of Parliament in particular are not prepared to defer to their elders. But notwithstanding the problems that their challenges to established party political authority creates, notwithstanding votes against the Government and notwithstanding Government defeats at the hands of its own members the power of the executive grows apace. On 10th March 1976 the Government was defeated in the Commons over its public expenditure plans. This vote made no difference to its public expenditure plans. The authority of the Whips re-asserted itself the following day when the Government put down a motion of confidence in itself.

The note in my diary records the scene in the Chamber of the House of Commons on 10th March 1976 as the vote was taking place:

> Thirty-five of us sat in our places as the vote was taking place, abstaining. It was inevitable that the Government would be defeated. Edward Short, the Leader of the House, came back into the Chamber after voting and snarled 'You're all a disgrace to the Labour Party.' His voice was but an echo from an earlier and decayed era. Denis Healey entered the Chamber, stood over Denis Canavan (a young Scottish M.P. with a nice turn of phrase who was sitting beside me), and swore at him.

Yet James Callaghan was one of those who argued that backbench M.P.s had never been more powerful – thus confusing power with indiscipline. What he was referring to was the ability of the determined backbench member to influence votes in a Parliament where there was a minority Government. That power is not new and to draw general constitutional lessons from the experience of a minority Government is a profound mistake. Mrs Audrey Wise and Mr Jeff Rooker did alter a Budget in the Finance Committee, legitimately and in pursuance of their committee duties: they were kept off subsequent Finance Committees by the Committee of Selection, itself a Select Committee, which is very much the creature of the Whips and ministers and usually rubber stamps 'lists' prepared by the executive and shadow executive.

Mr George Cunningham may have had a part in bringing down a Labour Government with his brilliantly argued amendment on Scottish Devolution which produced the 40 per cent rule in the referendum but to argue from these events that Parliamentary powers vis-à-vis the executive are increasing is to argue a case that will not stand analysis. While individual M.P.s may secure temporary victories the executive continues quietly to accumulate power. And so it will remain until Members of Parliament can make our society less secretive, élitist, oligarchic and bureaucratic.

If that is to happen the gentlemen's club that is Parliament needs a shake-up in its procedures. The club is ripe for reform but if the necessary reforms are to be made then some of the older gentlemen whose style is often more offensive than their policies will have to be thrust aside. Some of the older generation still believe that the essence of democracy is to be found in post-prandial late night oratory delivered to a half-empty, somnolent House. Some believe that it is all about trust – in them. As a generation they must bear the responsibility for breeding a terrible cynicism in and about politics. Their empty rhetoric is as out of accord with the ear of the younger generation as are their corrupt Whiggish attitudes. Let Browning be their epitaph: 'Hail glad confident morn never again.' Let Huxley be our inspiration: 'Knowledge is proportionate to being – you know in virtue what you are'.

8 The Right to Know and Be Heard

The right to know is perhaps one of the few rights that could usefully be enshrined in law in a democracy.

Outside government in Britain there is a measure of agreement on what needs to be done. 'Justice' (a distinguished national organisation concerned primarily with the law and civil liberties and whose Report on Freedom of Information in July 1978 found broad acceptance with the Labour Government), the Outer Circle Policy Group (a research group concerned with social policy and upon whose proposals Mr Clement Freud based his Official Information Bill from which the Labour Government were determined to delete 'the right to know' provision if it had looked as though it were going to reach the Statute Book), and the Labour Party have all produced detailed proposals. Tom Litterick, Ronald Atkins and Michael Meacher have all introduced Private Member's Bills in Parliament to change the law though none of them have been successful.

There is agreement amongst most of those concerned with reform:

1. that the right to know should be enshrined in law and that it should be based on the principle that information should be made available to the public unless the authorities can show that its release would damage the interests of the state. This is the principle which basically exists in America under the Freedom of Information Act 1967 as amended in 1974. It is the reverse of the principle enshrined in Section 2 of the Official Secrets Act 1911 which is that all information is secret unless its release is specifically authorised. 'Justice', it should be emphasised, preferred the establishment of a 'code of conduct' to the creation of a statutory 'right to know';
2. that the onus of proving that the release of any information would damage interests of the state should lie with the Government or the authorities concerned;
3. that there should be certain exceptions to cover defence and security matters concerning the criminal law, matters that are commercially confidential and matters that properly belong in the realm of personal privacy;

4. that the right to know should allow people to see and check files and computers which are kept on them, subject to the exceptions of defence and security and criminal matters;
5. that the right to know should include the right to know what advice civil servants are giving to ministers, and the contents of background papers given to ministers. Government departments should have their files put on microfilm and made available in the libraries which all departments have;
6. that the right to know would be ineffective unless the public knew what information was available and therefore there should be a Register or Record or Index of what information was available – nationally and locally;
7. that there should be some form of appeals procedure against the refusal of the government or the authorities concerned to supply any information;
8. that there should be a remedy available to the citizen in cases of non-compliance with the law.

The main differences that have emerged between those who support the concept of the right to know are:
1. Over the scope of the right to know. Some want to limit the disclosure of information, at least in the first instance, to the work of Government and Government departments. Others, in particular the Labour Party, want to extend the right to know, subject to the exceptions, to nationalised industries, local authorities and a hundred or so quasi-governmental bodies in addition to the institutions of central government (Statements to Annual Conference October 1978: Freedom of Information Bill).
2. Over the supervision of the disclosure of information. Some, including the Outer Circle, have suggested that the Ombudsman (who is often a former civil servant) is the right person to supervise the operation of any new laws on this subject. The Labour Government's response to this was that to allow the Ombudsman to control the operation would be to interfere with the concepts of collective Cabinet responsibility and ministerial responsibility. They stated that they would prefer Government departments to be the ultimate arbiters over what information should be released with the assurance that liberal guidelines would be adopted. Others have suggested that the Courts should act as arbiter in matters of dispute. There are two objections to this proposal. Firstly the Courts operate an adversary procedure in which the scales are usually weighted on the side of authority which can prepare its case expertly. They are weighted against the citizen who is often acting from a position of ignorance. Secondly the courts have traditionally sided with the executive on

matters outside their knowledge or experience. The Labour Party has put forward by far the most sensible proposal born of practical experience of the way in which government works; that the House of Commons should be responsible for the setting up of a Select Committee overseeing the work of an Official Information Panel to control the operation of any new laws in this field and to advise Parliament on its functioning. It is difficult to conceive of any better way of ensuring that the operation of any new Act is separated from executive control and yet remains fully accountable to the public. It has been suggested that the Panel would be a corporate body, though not an agent or servant of the Crown and its members, selected by the House of Commons Select Committee and would be drawn from those with experience in police, security, civil liberty, industrial and economic matters. The Panel would deal with appeals.

3. Over the disclosure of Cabinet and Cabinet sub-committee papers. Some have suggested that all Cabinet and Cabinet sub-committee papers should be secret for at least the life of one Government and that they should therefore be exempt from disclosure for a period of five years (at the moment the period is thirty years). The Labour Party has suggested a more limited two-year period of exemption for such papers with the qualification that the Prime Minister might in exceptional circumstances provide for a longer period for particular documents or clauses of documents. The two-year rule operates in Sweden for Cabinet papers.

4. The nature of any sanctions that might be taken as a result of the refusal of the Government or an authority to disclose information. It goes without saying that a citizen who had successfully appealed against a refusal to disclose information would be given the information for which he asked. The question is should he have recourse to the Courts for sanctions such as damages. The course suggested by the Labour Party is that (i) where any person is refused information he should commence an action in the High Court; (ii) the High Court would refer the issue of whether the information should be disclosed to the Panel; and (iii) the High Court would enforce the Panel's decision and have a power to order that damages be paid to the citizen who was initially refused the information. In seeking to determine what damages the Court would order it would have to have regard to the inconvenience caused to the citizen making the application as well as to any direct damages, and to the reasons given by the Government or the authorities for their failure to comply with the Act and release the information.

Almost the least powerful argument that the Government can produce against changes in the law so as to establish the right to know is that of cost. The cost is unlikely to be any higher, if indeed as high, as the existing cost of all the Government's information services which are designed to sift and filter information and to manipulate news and opinions. Democracy is not likely to prove any more expensive – although even if it were considerably more expensive the price would be worth paying – than the system which now operates based on principles which I have outlined.

Even more politically sensitive than the issue of the right to know is the issue of the right to be heard. In the first chapter of this book I spoke of 'the acceptance by that binds all modern Governments to the conventional establishment wisdom'. Press, radio and television all control and limit the right to be heard and play a large part in achieving this acceptance. Often, indeed most of the time, they operate in such a way as to deny to the public many alternative explanations of what is happening in society. They are owned and operated in such a way as to ensure that that is the case.

The ownership of the press is highly concentrated as the Report of the Royal Commission on the Press 1974–77 (Cmnd 6810) showed. The bare statistics in that Report do not tell the full story, as the Commission itself recognised. When the Commission reported in 1977, 220 separately controlled companies published newspapers compared with 490 in 1961 but of those 220 less than 10 groups were dominant by size and influence.

The Commission, which was not noticeable for its radicalism, concluded in Chapter 2:

> Our earlier analysis suggests that in the number and range of titles the press is very diverse especially when the ease of starting periodicals is taken into account. But if effective competition with large national and provincial newspapers is taken as the measure, diversity is markedly reduced even though it may be possible to launch daily papers for specialised readerships. The diversity created by small publishers is limited because their publications cannot be bought in many places.

My view is that the conclusion can be stated much more strongly. As the table below shows, one of the largest groups to own newspapers is S. Pearson & Son, Limited, best known for printing the *Financial Times*. S. Pearson & Son, Limited, is a company with activities in merchant banking, investment trusts, retail shops, industry and publishing, some of them in North America. But it is effectively owned by one person, Lord Cowdray, as an examination of the shareholders shows; 25.8 per cent of the issued voting shares are held by The Dickinson Trust Limited and The Cowdray Trust Limited. The business of these private companies is solely to act as trustees of trusts created by the first Viscount Cowdray and his descendants or their spouses. The shares of these two trusts are registered in the name of Broadminster Nominees Limited which as the Royal Commission tells us 'also holds shares as nominees for various individual descendants of the first Viscount Cowdray and their spouses, and for certain other trustees of trusts created by such descendants and spouses. The total shareholding of Broadminster Nominees Limited is 44.28 per cent of the issued voting shares of the company'.

No one should be surprised, given the theme of this book concerning the concentration of power in our society, to find that there is considerable inbreeding between national and provincial newspapers. No one should be further surprised to find that there is considerable cross-breeding between the owners of newspapers and the owners of radio and television. The *Daily Telegraph* has shares in London Weekend Television as does The *Observer* through The *Observer* (Holdings) Limited which also has shares in Capital Radio London. The *Daily Mail* group has many commercial television and radio holdings and the provincial Eastern Counties Newspaper Group has a stake in Anglia Television Limited. There are many other examples of a similar kind. One does not have to be cynical to see that such incestuous relationships could take some of the gloss off the assertion that we have a diverse press competing with an even more diverse media. Such relationships may impose restraints on the rights to know and be heard.

OWNERSHIP, CONTROL AND INTERESTS OF BRITISH PRESS – 1979
PRINCIPAL NATIONAL NEWSPAPERS

Ownership	Control and Accountability	Main interests of group
S. Pearson & Son Limited Financial Times Economist (50%) 64 provincial newspapers	Lord Cowdray[1]	Publishing, merchant banking, retail shops, industry, Madame Tussaud's
The Thomson Organisation The Times, Sunday Times 51 regional newspapers	Lord Thomson[2]	Oil, airlines, holiday and travel business, publishing
The Daily Telegraph Limited Daily Telegraph Sunday Telegraph	Lord Hartwell[3]	Newspapers
Atlantic Richfield[7] Observer	Directors of The Observer Ltd	Petrochemicals, coal, aluminium, metal products

OWNERSHIP, CONTROL AND INTERESTS OF BRITISH PRESS – 1979
PRINCIPAL NATIONAL NEWSPAPERS

Ownership	Countrol and Accountability	Main interests of group
The Scott Trust Guardian Manchester Evening News	The Scott Trust	Newspapers
The Daily Mail & General Trust Limited Daily Mail, Evening News, provincial papers	Lord Rothermere[4]	Magazines, taxis, transport theatres, North Sea Oil, entertainment
Reed International Daily Mirror Sunday Mirror Sunday People	Directors	Paper, packaging, magazines
Trafalgar House Daily Express, Daily Star, Sunday Express, Evening Standard	Mr Victor Matthews[5]	Construction, civil engineering, shipping, property development
News International Ltd. Sun News of the World	Mr Rupert Murdoch[6]	Publishing, paper, engineering, transport
Morning Star	Workers Co-operative	Newspaper

Notes
1. The parent company is controlled by Lord Cowdray through family trusts.
2. The parent company The Thomson Equitable Corporation is controlled by the Thomson family and by Thomson family trusts from Canada.
3. Lord Hartwell, the proprietor, holds shares as a trustee.
4. Lord Rothermere is the proprietor and principal shareholder of The Daily Mail General Trust Limited.
5. Mr Victor Matthews is Vice-Chairman of Trafalgar House.
6. Mr Rupert Murdoch is chairman of the Australian parent company News International Limited.
7. Atlantic Richfield is an American company.
Source: Company records and Royal Commission on the Press updated.

What motivates these men or these companies is not a subject on which there is much evidence save for the internal evidence of what is in the papers for which they are responsible. It is fortunate, therefore, that in

1979 Mr Nigel Broackes, the chairman of Trafalgar House, at the age of 44 published his autobiography, *A Growing Concern*, and in it told us something of the motives of Mr Victor Matthews, the Vice-Chairman of Trafalgar House who runs Express Newspapers. Mr Broackes said this:

> Let me revert to Victor and his state of mind at this time. He was morbid and morose . . . His horses . . . were not winning races . . . his wife was unwell.
>
> I had heard these problems before but this time I had to face the possibility that we might lose Victor altogether. I do not want to sound flippant, and there were several other good reasons to want to buy a newspaper group which, whatever its problems, sold more than twenty million papers per week, but I must admit that at the forefront of my mind was the desire to see Victor once again engrossed with a challenge – something that could gratify and occupy him, leaving free part of his time for the rest of Trafalgar House where we would have missed his wisdom, experience and judgment . . .

In a review of Mr Broackes' autobiography in the *Evening Standard* on 10th July 1979 Mr Matthews made this comment:

> Of course, buying companies, if you had enough cash, wasn't that difficult ten years ago. In fact, it seemed to be the name of the game and over a period of years I believe we had considered taking over almost every public company in this country . . . his [Broackes] account of how we bought Beaverbrook Newspapers . . . is incomplete. My own long-standing contacts with Beaverbrook Newspapers and Max Aitken over building matters had laid the seeds of such a move years before the company ran out of money.
>
> He described why he was anxious to acquire Beaverbrook, referring to my alleged moroseness and morbidity at that time. (Boredom would be a better word. I was chairing twenty-four subsidiary board meetings in twenty working days and found it almost impossible to take a day off for any purpose whatsoever.)
>
> I was not opposed to acquiring Beaverbrook but I had considerable doubt as to whether I wished to assume responsibility for it personally because to quote Nigel Broackes 'We can only do it if you'll do it, Victor'. Many times he had made the same observation in previous take-overs, including Bowater as mentioned in the book.

On 15th November 1979 on the B.B.C. TV programme 'Platform One' Mr Matthews made a significant comment on how he viewed the concept of the freedom of the press. He was asked whether it was true that he had once said that if his reporters uncovered a Watergate type scandal in Britain he would have difficulties in allowing them to print the story. He replied, 'I believe in Britain first . . . If it would harm Britain, I would suppress it.'

Some of these privileged and wealthy men admit that they are in the propaganda business. None of them seem to be associated, whether or not they interfere directly in the running of their papers, with publications whose views regularly challenge their own. They often appoint editors in their own image, nearly all of whom equate freedom of the press with their own freedom to print or not, to select, to slant or even distort the news as they think fit. Their power is immense and no book on the constitution dare ignore the way in which they exercise that power. Almost to a man they support the establishment on every major issue. Leaving aside the *Morning Star* they are all in favour of the philosophy of free-trade although one impeccably respectable school of economic thought in the U.K. argues that it is that philosophy which is destroying the economies of the Western world: except for *Express* Newspapers they were all agreed on the desirability of Britain's entry into the Common Market: they were all agreed in the economic crisis of 1976 that major public expenditure cuts were necessary though many economists took a contrary view and felt that such cuts were destabilising the economy: they all supported the cautious Mr Callaghan against the radical Mr Foot in the Labour Party leadership contest which was in effect electing the Prime Minister: they all crucify figures to the right or left of the political spectrum, be they Enoch Powell or Tony Benn, and they are all vulgar and vicious in so doing: and they are all capable of deceiving themselves about their concern for democracy. They do not mind whether Labour governs or the Conservatives govern so long as they govern in their interest. Indeed in Australia Rupert Murdoch, so Tony Benn and I were told over lunch with Larry Lamb the editor of the *Sun* on 9th March 1978, was responsible through his papers both for putting Mr Whitlam's Labour Party into power and for removing it from power. At the lunch in question he seemed upset at the suggestion that his editorials were the vulgar versions of the minutes of Whitehall's Permanent Secretaries and that the values behind them were the same.

In their defence the newspapers can point to the undoubted fact that they have developed from markedly different philosophical stables and that this comes through in what they say and the way in which they say it. One tries to retain a nineteenth-century individualistic ethic (*Guardian*); another by contrast to reflect the views of governing institutions in its reporting (*Financial Times*); yet another was for Empire and then crudely nationalistic in its approach when the sun began to set (*Daily Express*). Some give regular editorial support to the Conservative Party (*Daily Telegraph, Daily Mail, Daily Express*) and two of the parent companies S. Pearson & Son and Trafalgar

House gave financial donations to the Conservative Party in the fiscal year 1978–79 in the run up to the General Election of May 1979. One group, the *Mirror* Group, gives editorial support to the Labour Party and the *Daily Star* has decided to do the same; and so on. On the surface it seems quite diversified. Yet a closer analysis reveals a press where ideas do not compete seriously. If there are differences they are essentially differences in shadings, not in principles or philosophy. On specific and major policies there is often great uniformity which expresses the corporate attitudes and prescriptions of those few who determine the values of our society. The fact that most newspapers are now owned by giant industrial and commercial conglomerates (see table on page 201) and have to rely on advertising received from other conglomerates may make this sharing of values inevitable.

A second answer from those who control and work for the press is that they only reflect the prejudices of their readers but do not create them. In the sense that the press cannot, for example, change people's voting patterns save over long periods that is undoubtedly true. But over a period the press heavily reinforces the images that the establishment, of which they are part, projects to the public. In the end, and particularly on specific issues, the public starts reflecting those images back when pollsters and others ask them for their views. Of course the public is not entirely a victim of image creation. It can recognise its own self-interest when it sees it. But it never gets much of a choice save in terms of personalities presented to it by the press or the establishment.

Readers concerned to see the way in which television projects establishment values and pays scant attention to alternative views of society should study the work of the Glasgow Media Group and Greg Philo and Paul Walton as set out in their books *Bad News, More Bad News* and *Trade Unions and the Media*. Some of the video tape recordings which I have seen and upon which some of their accounts are based are quite startling. Their method of approaching these problems is still in its infancy and subject to some criticisms but the very fact that they seem to have caused such consternation in the B.B.C. suggests that they are close to the truth. The T.U.C. has also expressed concern, in its booklet, *A Cause for Concern – Media Coverage of Industrial Disputes, January & February 1979*.

There is an urgent need for detailed studies into such delicate matters as news presentation, the relationship between the Foreign Office and the external affairs service of the B.B.C., Treasury advice – or interference – into the presentation of economic matters on radio and television, etc., etc. Given the way our society works in other spheres it would be surprising if research into the relationship between Government and the media, and especially television, did not reveal other informal relationships of the kind that exist between editors and the Secretary of the 'D' Notice Committee in the realm of security, and more formal and sinister relationships of the kind that exists between the B.B.C. and the Metropolitan Police (which comes under the control of the Home Secretary) over the reporting and censorship of the reporting of police matters.

In his book to which I referred in Chapter 1, Keith Middlemas writing of the First World War and the period which followed it said thus:

> Governments, however, devoted themselves not simply to winning the lowest common measure of agreement, but to the management of opinion in an unending process, using the full educative and coercive power of the state. Propaganda agencies, techniques of persuasion were largely, though not entirely, the creation of the First World War emergency. During the Lloyd George Coalition Government they were not abandoned. Opinion management sometimes failed to work; large groups even refused to follow and Sinn Fein in Ireland repudiated both the state's authority and its right to coercion. But with this exception actual revolt was rare, short-lived and usually unsuccessful . . . Over the twenty-five years after 1921, the crude methods of the wartime Ministry of Propaganda developed into the informal (and highly immoral) methods used during the Coalition; in due course these were translated into an increasingly formal network of information-gathering and use essential to the functioning of an interventionist state authority, and grounded increasingly on the assumption that the process was actually neutral – a curious outcome, reinforced by the apparatus of control which ensured secrecy about what governments believed the public should not know.

We need to know much more about how the 'neutral' process of news management operates today not only in relation to the Government and the media but also in relation to corporate institutions, and especially companies, and the media.

Another book is needed if only because I often wonder just how the press, radio and television would respond to an open society given that private interests of most of those who own and control the media would be threatened by such a society. In America, a relatively open society, journalists and politicians have tended to close ranks, notwithstanding brilliant disclosures such as Watergate. David Halberstam in his book, *The Powers That Be*, suggests that this is in part because the media there are a branch of profitable and big business. He argues frighteningly. 'There is an unwritten law of American journalism that states that the greater and more powerful the platform, the more carefully it must be used and the more closely it must adhere to the norms of American society, particularly the norms of American government; the law says it is better to be a little wrong and a little too late than to be too right too quickly.'

If Halberstam is right and journalism in Britain follows the same path then it is clear that whilst an open society may be a necessary condition of a vigorous democracy it is not a sufficient condition for such a society.

9 Diary of a P.P.S.

A Parliamentary Private Secretary is a friend of the minister and is on hand to help when needed. His other duty, so it seemed to me, is to keep a diary so that he can tell others what it is like being a Parliamentary Private Secretary.

Tony Benn asked me to become his P.P.S. on 9th November 1976. The Prime Minister who might have been thought to have other more important things on his mind and whose 'approval' was required was not keen on the idea. He wondered why Tony Benn should have chosen me and thought that he should try to widen his political base by accepting someone with views nearer his (Callaghan's) own. He told Tony Benn that he wanted an assurance that I would not vote against the I.M.F. public expenditure cuts that were coming up in six weeks' time. It is interesting at this distance in time to note that the Prime Minister's decision on the cuts had been made weeks before the matter was ever discussed in Cabinet. Tony Benn's attitude was that he could not ask me for any such assurance because he himself did not know what cuts were going to be imposed and whether he himself would be able to support them. I was certainly not prepared to sign a blank cheque.

I could understand James Callaghan being edgy over the I.M.F. cuts. On 1st July 1976 shortly after he had become Prime Minister I had spoken to him, at my request, alone in his room in the House for an hour and had discussed the impending July public expenditure cuts and the economy. At that meeting I had stressed the importance of getting any package right and the terrible consequences that might flow if he came back later in the year with another package. In a wider discussion at that meeting he had been very scornful about 'soft Liberals' and had quoted Lenin, and I had remarked that he was always quoting Lenin and Marx. The one other person he revered was the French President – Giscard D'Estaing. 'Giscard is going to balance his budget you know' he had said almost in awe. I wrote at the time 'It confirmed my belief that we are all monetarists now'.

The further package of cuts that I had warned him about in July came in December. One Cabinet minister at the time, not Tony Benn, summed up the Prime Minister on 16th December as 'a bad tempered, cantankerous old man who has to have rest periods and cannot deal with more than one subject at a time'. He confirmed that Left-wing Cabinet ministers (he wasn't one) had fought off social benefit cuts, an end to the indexing of public service pensions and prescription charges.

Correspondence took place between the Prime Minister and Tony Benn (copies of which I have) in which the Prime Minister asked for written assurances about my future behaviour. Tony Benn pointed out that as Cabinet ministers were not asked to give such assurances, he could not ask them of a prospective P.P.S. It was one thing for a P.P.S. to accept the consequences of his actions, (i.e. he would have to resign if he voted against the Government), quite another to ask for assurances in advance about hypothetical situations.

On 17th January 1977 Tony Benn and I all but agreed that he should look for someone else. I had just voted for a Tribune group amendment in support of cuts in defence expenditure. Tony said he would give it one last try and that he would tell Callaghan that I would resign if I decided to vote against the Government but I would sign nothing. Believing that there is nothing like a public row to bring issues to a climax I told the press about the argument between Callaghan and Tony on an 'unattributable basis'. The following day, 18th January, it was on the front page of the *Guardian* and *Telegraph* and in most of the other papers. Frances Morrell rang me up to say that Tony had telephoned from Brussels saying that Jim had agreed to the appointment. Civil servants at the Department of Energy blamed Downing Street for the leak to the press and Downing Street blamed the Department of Energy. My dismissal was to be a much more exciting affair.

It was ridiculous, but at Tony Benn's suggestion I turned up at the department at 8 a.m. the following morning only to find that there was no one there. My predecessor, Joe Ashton had deliberately not involved himself in departmental issues. He had been a brilliant publicist for his minister. His predecessor when Tony Benn was at the Department of Industry, Frank McElhone who became a junior minister was present with the minister at the department and on visits far more than I was to be. I only went along to what I considered to be the more important meetings. Even when I was at the department I spent a lot of time, entertainingly and valuably, with Tony's two political advisers.

The subject of patronage kept cropping up. On 2nd February 1977, at a meeting of nationalised industries Tony Benn suggested that vacancies for chairmen of nationalised industries should be advertised and selection procedures set up with a final oversee by a Select Committee in Parliament. It was the only time that I remember the blood draining from the face of Sir Jack Rampton, the Permanent Secretary. The note in my diary records his response thus:

> 'Well, Secretary of State, like you I think the patronage system needs changing. But other ministers would like it . . . Eh . . . you see . . . as civil servants we have little say in what goes on . . . it's ministerial patronage really . . . as for a Parliamentary committee, no committee that I know would be competent to judge . . . we do want efficiency'. Talk about who are the masters now.

The issue of patronage came up again in May 1977 when civil servants from the Civil Service Department blocked a recommendation of Alex Eadie's (who was the minister responsible for the coal industry) for the Scientific Adviser to the Coal Board. Inevitably the suspicion arose that the department's civil servants had been responsible.

Finally the issue of patronage broke out in a more dramatic form and at the highest level. Sir Douglas Allen the head of the civil service, was due to retire as a civil servant and had to be found a job. When he did resign, jobless, he was reported in an article in *The Times* as saying that he did not want a job. That is not quite my documented recollection. The plan was for Sir Douglas to become deputy chairman of the British National Oil Corporation. On 14th November 1977 I argued strongly that Tony should not allow the appointment to go ahead. I pointed out that the appointment would mean that Britain's top civil servant would have to break the two-year rule which he was supposed to enforce on other civil servants. The fact that the job was a plum public appointment only made the situation worse and potentially more explosive. I said that it would suggest to the public too cosy a relationship between the minister and civil servants. Somehow the advice that Frances Morrell and I were giving got mixed up with a discussion on what should happen to Sir Jack Rampton and whether Sir Douglas Allen might help to get rid of him.

On 17th November Tony Benn got Sir Douglas to agree, with some irony, to advertise the B.N.O.C. job but told him that he could reply to his own advertisement if he so wished. Sir Douglas kept cool, did advertise the post but did not apply. Top civil servants cannot be expected to apply for jobs and he was the top civil servant. In the end no one of sufficient quality applied for the job and Sir Douglas did join the board of B.N.O.C. He also became an adviser to the Bank of England.

It will come as no surprise that working for Tony Benn brought forward a number of examples of the exercise of Prime Ministerial authority and the lengths to which it could go. Sometimes these illustrated the tensions that could occur when the doctrine of collective Cabinet responsibility was too rigidly interpreted. This was inevitably the case over E.E.C. matters where the doctrine had in any event been set aside by Harold Wilson the Prime Minister, during the Referendum Campaign of 1975. One such incident occurred on 3rd June 1977. Parliament was not sitting. The note in my diary records it thus:

> A day of high drama and much alarm. On Monday I had noticed that Tony had agreed to speak at a press conference organised by the Common Market Safeguards Campaign, an organisation of which he was a member. I realised then that Callaghan might cause difficulties so I drove into London early this morning to see if I could help.
>
> When I arrived at the Department of Energy, Downing Street were querying what was happening. Tony showed me a copy of his speech. It was the second draft, about 600 words long, drawn up by Frances and apparently much milder than the first draft. All the adjectives had been excised. Despite its elegant language it was an uncompromising attack on the Common Market. Four options, one of which referred to withdrawal, were put in such a way as though the Government might be considering one or other or all of them.
>
> I told Tony that in my view the document was inconsistent with collective Cabinet responsibility and membership of the Cabinet; that it would provoke a furore and that Jim would not like it. He asked me if in the event of Jim forbidding him to deliver it I would go to the press conference, give his apologies and make the statement on his behalf. I said that I would but the consequences might be the same. Frances was worried and thought that a caveat or two might make the thing more balanced. As always she expressed herself somewhat more forcefully than I did.
>
> Then Jim rang from Chequers and Tony spoke to him on the telephone from his Private Secretary's room. Jim said that Tony would damage the party by appearing at the press conference (a silly suggestion) to which Tony replied that the press might try to damage the party but all he wanted to do was to present facts and options.
>
> Jim said he would not instruct him not to appear but he should make the Government's position clear. Tony commented dryly, afterwards, that it was one of the few occasions that Jim had not threatened to sack him.
>
> We then set off in the official car for the Cabinet Office where Tony had a meeting on industrial democracy at a Cabinet subcommittee. He was late. Time 11.45 a.m. In the car I suggested that having spoken to Jim on the telephone, he should now let me take the text to Downing Street so that they could ring it through to Jim. He was not at first keen on the idea but I pointed out that if he was

confident that his telephone conversation with Jim accurately reflected what he was going to do, then simple courtesy suggested that he should show Jim the text. There was everything to gain now from openness.

So Tony went to the Cabinet Office and I was driven to 10 Downing Street. I handed the text together with a handwritten letter drawn up by Tony in the car to one of Jim's Private Secretaries, commenting 'Jim and Tony have spoken on the telephone and Tony thought it would be an act of courtesy to show Jim this.' I telephoned Frances over the car radio to tell her what had happened. Tony's Private Office then confirmed with Downing Street that the text had been read over to Jim.

Ron, Tony's driver, asked rhetorically 'is it all up this time? It used to be like this every day in the Department of Industry'.

Ron picked up Frances from the Department of Energy and we drove back to the Cabinet Office. Tony appeared and read out eight suggested alterations which he had drawn up in the Cabinet Office at the sub-committee meeting which he had left early. These alterations balanced the text considerably and made it much more difficult for Jim to object. Frances still wanted a different approach.

On the way to the Waldorf where the press conference was to be held I suggested that Downing Street should be informed of the alterations immediately as the press might ring them up for comments and Downing Street might give them on the basis of the unaltered text.

Since the text had been altered the copies of the original could not be distributed because the changes would have been obvious and led to immense speculation. The basic changes made were:

1. a clearer statement of Government policy was inserted and a greater distinction made between Government policy and the options which the Government were discussing;
2. a sharper commitment by Tony personally to accepting the verdict of the Referendum;
3. a statement that in his period as Chairman of the E.E.C. Energy Council of Ministers he had worked hard for success;
4. a statement that our troubles could not be put down to the E.E.C. – there was for example the world slump;
5. the removal of any conceivable inference that the Government could be discussing the options, including possible withdrawal;
6. a statement that he would not talk about direct elections – a subject on which the Prime Minister was super-sensitive.

Tony rattled through his statement thus making it virtually impossible for journalists to follow (who could not understand why there was no press release) but I noticed that Ian Aitken from the *Guar-*

dian was out Benning Benn with a tape recorder. Tony had a tape recorder on the table.

He avoided answering all the questions from the journalist . . .

Outside the Waldorf Hilary Benn came over and Tony said 'That may be it, Hilary', but Hilary seemed in good spirits.

Back at the Department of Energy, Downing Street had been telephoned about the changes straight away and Audrey, one of the secretaries, immediately transcribed the tape. Tony underlined all the changes for the Prime Minister including his opening remark which had not been in the original: 'Welcome to the meeting', or something similar.

Throughout this incident there was the fear that Jim Callaghan's apparent forbearance was designed to tempt Tony Benn into breaching collective Cabinet responsibility and then use this as a reason for sacking him.

In the event Jim Callaghan and Tony Benn did not part company until Labour lost the election and Tony Benn did not take up a place in the Shadow Cabinet.

On the whole the Prime Minister seemed remarkably reluctant to let his Cabinet ministers talk to anyone about anything. In February 1978 he asked Tony Benn not to discuss his Nuffield seminar, already referred to, on the conflicting accountability of a Cabinet minister. The idea had been that he should discuss the issue with Robert McKenzie on TV.

Then just over a year later on 8th March 1979 the Prime Minister used a Cabinet meeting to instruct Tony Benn not to address four hundred *Times* workers at a meeting specially organised so that he could do so. The reason given was that the Secretary of State for Employment was pushing through a new initiative that very day to get *The Times* re-opened. But Albert Booth had no objection to Tony Benn addressing the journalists and others as he himself confirmed to me a few days later on 12th March when I spoke to him about it. The *Sun* story about his objections he said was 'untrue'. In the event, although I had ceased to be Tony Benn's P.P.S. by then, I stood in for him – making virtually his speech after a long talk with him in the House of Commons tea-room.

One of the roles of a P.P.S. is that of the stand-in and earlier I had stood in for him to speak to the Labour Parliamentary Association (2nd March 1977) and to lecture to Workers Educational Association students (6th April 1977). One of the worries for a P.P.S. stemming from this stand-in role is that everything he does and says will be taken as the actions and sayings of the minister for whom he works although everyone knows that the rules of appointment of a P.P.S. clearly state that he should not pass himself off as the minister or even a minister. Yet sometimes it can be for the convenience of the minister that his P.P.S. should make a speech setting out views which the minister holds but which he could not himself express because of the limitations of the doctrine of collective Cabinet responsibility. Thus on 24th June 1977, the evening before a Chequers meeting at which the Cabinet were to discuss the economy, I delivered a speech to my General Management Committee and told the press that the speech represented the views of the minister. In fact we had spent two hard days drafting it at the department. So on one occasion at least the headlines in the *Guardian* and *Financial Times* about Benn's aide were true.

Government Press Officers are paid large sums of money. The P.P.S. is a voluntary worker. Yet the P.P.S. was expected to provide back-up facilities in this somewhat distasteful sphere too. I remember one such occasion when the Liberal leader, David Steel, issued an advanced press release of a speech containing a strong attack on Tony Benn. Ostensibly the attack concerned the contents of a proposed Bill to reorganise the electricity supply industry but the real force of the speech was an indictment of Tony Benn for not responding more enthusiastically to the Lib-Lab pact. Neither Tony Benn nor the department were pleased. The electricity division in the department issued me with an 'unattributable' brief for the press before Mr Steel's speech went out. It was delivered by hand to my home in Luton by Tony Benn's Private Office. A copy appears below. In as far as it was an explanation of the contents of the Bill it was admirable. As an answer to the political point that Mr Steel was making it was useless. It was certain that the press would not use it. So I wrote out a few words of my own, telephoned a number of journalists from the responsible press, gave them the gist of the departmental brief and dictated my own words, telling the press that they had the official stamp of approval. Inevitably the press used quotes from this statement which accurately reflected the view of ministers and ignored the departmental brief. The Bill, it must be understood, to which this briefing referred was itself a secret. It had not been published or presented to Parliament. Liberal Members of Parliament had seen it through the existence of the Lib-Lab pact but Labour Members of Parliament had not. They, not surprisingly, resented this. The 'unattributable' departmental brief and my statement were as follows:

ELECTRICITY AND NUCLEAR MATERIAL BILL

Unattributable factual brief for Mr Sedgemore

The organisation

1. Plowden Report concluded that the 'basic weakness of the industry's structure is slow and cumbersome central policy making

caused by divided responsibilities and a rigid statutory framework'.
2. The Secretary of State made a statement to the House on 19th July 1977 agreeing with Plowden on the need for a structure fostering strategic control but which did not bring with it the dangers of over-centralisation.
3. The Bill will unify the industry transforming the Electricity Council into a new Electricity Corporation; the existing C.E.G.B. and Area Boards would be dissolved and their functions transferred to the Corporation.
4. The Secretary of State would have the power to specify the structure by Order and to change it by Order from time to time subject to Parliamentary approval. This gives flexibility and scope for organisational evolution in future.
5. The first Order envisages a Central Board with generation and distribution devolved to subordinate boards (similar to the present generating and area boards).
Safeguards against over-centralisation
6a. The Secretary of State would appoint members of the Corporation and of the subordinate boards thus retaining contact at all levels and safeguarding against over-centralisation.
6b. Future organisation changes would be made following a report by the Corporation; Orders would be subject to the Parliamentary process.
7. The Corporation will devolve managerial responsibility to the maximum extent again as a safeguard against over-centralisation.
8. Consumer Representation will be strong: the Electricity Consumer Council will be a statutory body with membership of the Corporation and will have a regional structure.
9. *Innovations*
i. *Wider duties*

The Bill will be innovative; setting out a new approach to nationalised industry. In addition to the more usual duty to break-even financially the new Electricity Corporation will be expected:
(a) to have regard to national energy policies;
(b) to have regard to the needs of consumers;
(c) to provide more information about its activities and to publish Codes of Practice.
(d) to promote industrial democracy.

ii. *New Powers*

There will be powers for the Secretary of State to issue specific directions in the national interest for which compensation will be paid where appropriate.

iii. The Corporation will have new powers to manufacture electrical plant and fittings, to explore for minerals and to pro-

mote combined heat and power in the interest of energy conservation.
Electricity Division
3rd March 1978

Unattributable brief by B. Sedgemore
Senior government ministers believe that Mr David Steel, the Leader of the Liberal Party, is very concerned at the many criticisms of the Liberal's handling of the discussions on the Electricity Bill. His concern is thought to stem from the fact that the spokesman dealing with the Bill, Mr David Penhaligon, is not up to the job. Ministers have found it difficult and sometimes impossible to deal with him on a sensible basis. On no occasion has he been specific about his objections to the Bill. On one occasion he refused to discuss the Bill because he deemed it more important to show his child around London. Trade unionists in the industry have made it clear that they will inform everyone of their 175,000 members that the Liberals are prepared to wreck their industry. There is concern that the Liberals have no policy themselves for the industry.

It was a terrible statement to make, particularly the silly (though true) reference to Mr Penhaligon's child which was of course precisely one of the references that the press picked up.

The terrifying lesson though to be drawn from these examples, and it does not reflect well on myself, is how everyone gets sucked into and then consumed by the system. Try though one might to stand apart from it one finds oneself, to a greater or lesser extent, accepting its corrupting values.

Perhaps the most useful task that a P.P.S. performs, apart from being around, is that of discreetly feeding information to Members of Parliament interested in the subjects which come within the department's purview whose constituents are likely to be affected by matters with which the department is dealing. Over the Drax 'B' power plant issue I was able to keep M.P.s informed of what was happening and which ministers were taking which decisions and keep the minister informed of M.P.s' views. I am sure this helped the Government to come to a sensible conclusion. Another associated P.P.S. function was to arrange meetings between the minister and backbench M.P.s, either on an individual basis or in groups. These were always worth attending. For there was a real seriousness of purpose at the meetings which the humour, the excitement and the emotions of success and failure could not hide.

I could multiply activities and examples indefinitely but the publication of the diaries of a P.P.S. is a big task and must await another book.

It would be wrong though not to end this one where I began it – with the subject of secrecy.

Inevitably there are rules governing the role and status of a P.P.S. to which he is expected to adhere. He is not, however, allowed to see the rules. These are for the eyes of the minister only. Fortunately I had seen a version of the rules when I was a civil servant so I knew how I was expected to behave. But there were problems with papers and discussions. Whilst a P.P.S. can see documents classified 'confidential' and below he is not allowed to see (in theory) documents classified 'secret' and above. However, he constantly attends meetings where such documents are discussed, thus rendering the position absurd and at such meetings courteous civil servants show him the documents. Moreover the P.P.S. himself might make proposals or suggestions for points to go into Cabinet papers which he then could not be shown, thus rendering the position even more complicated.

As an example I remember Tony Benn hesitate to show me a Treasury paper concerning Budget proposals to put up Petroleum Revenue Tax which was marked 'secret'. Yet at the ensuing meeting on 12th December 1977 all the secrets were revealed including figures for the after-tax B.P. profits on the Forties field and the after-tax Occidental profits on the Piper field which were multiples of anything that I had seen in public guesses. When the history of the U.K. in the last quarter of the twentieth century comes to be written, the publication of these figures will show just how much the oil companies ripped-off the British Exchequer. The Treasury were slow to move and when they did act, they did far too little to secure Britain's interests. In retrospect it will be seen as a public scandal.

I always seemed to be having difficulties with the Treasury and their papers. On one occasion at a Tribune group meeting I criticised the Chancellor for misleading the group over investment prospects and referred to a paper by Sir Eric Roll on the subject. The Chancellor accused me of indulging in 'title-tattle' whereupon I told him I had the relevant document downstairs (we were in a committee room). On another occasion (3rd May 1977) in the Chancellor's room at the Treasury he accused me of writing something in *Tribune* that was wrong concerning a visit of the Expenditure Committee to Washington and discussions with U.S. officials. Fortunately, John Garrett M.P. who had been on the trip was in the room at the time and he was able to inform the Chancellor that what I had written was correct. On yet another occasion (10th November 1977) when Tony Benn and his advisers went to discuss the use to which North Sea Oil revenues could be put with the Chancellor in his room in the Commons, Denis Healey point-blank refused to have the P.P.S.s present although I had already seen all the papers. An argument between the ministers ensued until I left to stop it developing, commenting quietly 'I want you to know that I regard this as a most unfriendly act . . .'

Perhaps therefore it was appropriate that my sacking should have concerned a Treasury paper. The events that took place between the hearing of the Expenditure Committee on Friday 3rd November 1978 when I disclosed some of the contents of a Treasury document on the European Monetary System during questioning of the Chancellor of the Exchequer and my sacking onWednesday 8th November 1978 are so bizarre, yet in keeping with the main thread of the arguments in this book, that they must be told. They provide a fitting end to the story of our hidden constitution.

For the record the note which I have retained setting out the Treasury's view on the consequences for the U.K. joining the European Monetary System is set out below. It should be noted that economists, in another department to whose work I also had access, felt that the Treasury were being too pessimistic though even these economists could see no good coming from our joining the EMS.

EUROPEAN MONETARY SYSTEM

Summary of Note by Chancellor of Exchequer to Cabinet Colleagues Implications for the United Kingdom of More Fixed Exchange Rates – GEN 136 (78) 14

1. *Scenario 1 (1979–82)*

Assumptions

(i) U.K. joins European fixed exchange rate system in 1979.

(ii) Domestic monetary and fiscal policies unchanged (including unchanged public expenditure and continued tax indexation).

Effects after 4 years (1979–82)

(i) exchange rate up 23%

(ii) lost competitiveness 19%

(iii) Gross Domestic Product (GDP) down 5%

(iv) unemployment up by 1½% and more later

(v) wages/prices reduced by 6%

2. *Scenario 2*

Assumptions

(i) U.K. deflates by raising personal taxes so that Balance of Payments and current account unchanged. i.e. increase in taxes £1.7 billion in 1979. Goes on deflating

Effects after 4 years (1979–82)

(i) exchange rate up 23%

(ii) tax rise stimulates higher wage demands so the reduction in inflation in Scenario 1 much reduced

(iii) GDP falls by 9½%

(iv) loss of competitiveness 21%

(v) unemployment up 2.7%
3. *Scenario 3*
Assumptions
(i) from base of lower earnings forecast, higher initial exchange rates, lower interest rates and lower money supply
Effects after 4 years (1979–82)
(i) exchange rate up 13%
(ii) loss of competitiveness 12%
(iii) fall in GDP 3%
(iv) unemployment up 1%
4. *Scenario 4*
Assumptions
(i) 5% devaluation after 1 year in 1980
Effects after four years (1979–82)
(i) exchange rate up 17%
(ii) loss of competitiveness 15%
(iii) GDP falls 3½%
(iv) Retail Price Index and earnings fall 3½–4%
(v) unemployment up 1%
Source: H.M. Treasury

The clash between the Chancellor and myself aroused little interest in the press on Saturday 4th November save in *The Times* where there was a far more detailed account of the relevant Treasury document than I had given to the committee. One member of the Expenditure Committee, Ian Stewart, jealous of the fact that he was unable to perform his Parliamentary duties properly and arm himself with the information necessary to make mature judgments had, however, written on the day before to the Prime Minister in the following terms:

3rd November 1978

Dear Prime Minister,
The Chancellor of the Exchequer appeared this morning before the General Sub-Committee of the Expenditure Committee of the House of Commons to give evidence about the proposed European Monetary System. The proceedings of the sub-committee were open to the public and I understand that a recording of them was made with a view to the possibility of broadcasting. At this meeting Mr Brian Sedgemore, M.P. quoted certain figures from an apparently confidential Treasury document which had come into his possession. Neither I nor other members of the sub-committee had been provided with copies of this document and from Mr Healey's reaction there appeared to be considerable doubt whether it was proper for Mr Sedgemore to have access to it.

I believe from notes taken during the meeting that the document concerned is entitled 'Implications for the U.K. of More Fixed Exchange Rates', reference GEN 136 (78)14, by the Chancellor of the Exchequer.

In this situation I must ask you to consider whether this case constitutes a prima facie breach of the Official Secrets Act, and if so to initiate a full enquiry into the means whereby this document was made available to Mr Sedgemore, and in particular as to whether any member or members of your Government may have been involved. If not, I hope you will agree that relevant documents of this kind should be supplied to all members of the sub-committee or to none. A copy of this letter is being released to the press.

Yours sincerely,
Ian Stewart, M.P.

The Prime Minister used this letter as an excuse to get agitated, as I was to discover on Monday 6th November 1978 when Michael Cocks, the Government Chief Whip and Patronage Secretary, summoned me to a series of meetings.

The first meeting began just before 4.45 p.m. My note of the meeting is as follows:

Just before 4.45 p.m. on Monday 6th November Michael Cocks, whom I saw outside the Whip's Office in Parliament, asked if he could see me in private at No. 12 Downing Street immediately. As we walked around the back of the Foreign Office he apologised for 'the cloak and dagger stuff'. We could have gone into the Whip's Office unseen but Michael insisted on going to No. 12 and going round the back of the Foreign Office and not up Whitehall. At No. 12 Downing Street in his office I gave him a list of young Labour M.P.s whom I thought would be fit for office. He had asked me for the list last Thursday evening. He stressed the importance of secrecy. He said I'd let him down over 'the other business' i.e. the suggestion made by him of a job in the Government.

He then said he wanted to speak to me 'informally' about last Friday's events before putting some 'formal questions'. 'I don't understand these things', he said, and added that the Prime Minister was 'old fashioned about these things'. In 1974 he had been away most of the time at the Foreign Office and so he did not understand the attitudes of the new younger intake. He did not understand my attitude. He believed in party discipline. The Chief Whip repeated and stressed this point and I took it as something of a threat. The P.M. lost his temper over some issues and this was one. He had got up out of his chair shouting when he heard what had happened.

I then warned the Chief Whip that the P.M. could walk into a trap and find himself embroiled in a serious constitutional argument about the rights of backbenchers. He should be careful about his next move.

The Chief Whip then formally put three questions to me and I append these together with my answers. As he asked the questions he was standing by the desk that Gladstone had used, in front of which was Disraeli's writing bureau and beside which was the chair on which Churchill had sat in his bunker.

The questions and answers were:

Regarding GEN 136(78)14 – were you shown it by a minister, civil servant or third party?

As a member of a Select Committee where this issue arose I deem this question to be improper and an attempt by the executive to impede a backbench Member of Parliament in carrying out his constitutional duty.

Who was it?

I give the same answer as I did to Q.1.

Will you co-operate with an enquiry?

I give the same answer as before.

I then told the Chief Whip that I might raise the issue in Parliament as a matter of privilege and contempt on the part of the Prime Minister. I repeated that I thought that a serious constitutional issue was involved. I asked him what Jim was up to. He replied 'I don't know'. He asked me not to raise it as an issue of contempt and privilege because that would cause trouble. After further discussion I told him, indeed I gave him my personal assurance, that I would not raise the issue in the Commons tomorrow but would reserve the right to do so if Jim raised the matter again. I told him that if he was concerned about leaks the P.M.'s Press and Political Offices might be a good place to start.

On leaving, Michael said that I had embarrassed him over the issue of a job in the Government. I hope we meet again under more auspicious circumstances. Quite what the Government Chief Whip was doing in conducting part of a 'leaks' enquiry I do not know.

At 8 p.m. on the same day I met the Chief Whip in the Central Lobby beside the Whips' offices. I suppose it would have been too simple a matter to have gone unseen into his own office. Instead he took me on a tour of the House of Lords, down corridors I had never before seen until we ended up in an empty room I know not where. For the first time in my life I realised that I was important. First Gladstone, Disraeli and Churchill and now this. This was the stuff of which history is made. We sat down.

At this meeting Michael told me that politics was a 'filthy business'. I concurred. He then hit me below the belt with a reference to how it had caused him personal suffering. I felt a tear welling up. He reiterated that I had let him down over 'the other business'. Then he called for my resignation saying that that course was in the interests of the party and the government. There was no other solution to the problem. I told him that I would of course put the interests of the party and the Government first but the only problem that existed was that of the Prime Minister's temperament. As long as that was clear I would resign but before any statement was made I would have to clear it with Tony Benn.

I then went to Tony Benn's room and wrote the following letter:

6th November

Dear Tony,

This is just a line to tell you that I have resigned as your P.P.S. I would like to add that I have found working for you these past years a delight.

Best wishes,
Brian

I then telephoned Tony Benn at his home in Holland Park and read out the letter. He refused to accept my resignation. So I went round to see him. There he argued that I had done no wrong and that it would be a breach of privilege for him to sack me. We both spoke to Frances Morrell on the telephone. I telephoned Michael Cocks to say that as the matter was, as he had put it, so important for the party and the Government, I would like to sleep on it.

The same day I had written to Michael English, the Chairman of the General Sub-Committee of the Expenditure Committee, in the following terms:

6th November 1978

Dear Michael,

I am writing to you in your capacity as Chairman of the General Sub-Committee of the Expenditure Committee of the House of Commons to express my concern as a member of that Committee at the events which took place during Friday's meeting.

As you know the Treasury failed to provide the Committee with either a written brief or working documents despite a formal request to do so. When I asked the Chancellor at Friday's hearing if he would supply us with a copy of the background papers he had submitted to the Cabinet sub-committee which was considering the subject he replied at first that he did not know what I was talking about. When I questioned him on the contents of one of the papers concerned he answered in terms which could not have enlightened the committee.

This is not the first time these difficulties have arisen on our committee and we are in danger of reaching a situation where it is regarded as accepted practice for Treasury and Bank of England witnesses to deny the existence of documentation and facts to Parliament which are clearly in circulation within Government. You will remember for example the occasion on our committee when I distributed to the Committee a Bank of England document discussing the Treasury's Medium Term Assessment of the U.K. economy after a witness had denied the existence of any such assessment.

The task of a Select Committee is to advise and make recommendations to the House on an informed basis. Part of the task of the House is to examine openly that advice and those recommendations in pursuance of its varying roles including that of checking the executive.

Conduct of the kind that I have outlined above makes it impossible for Select Committees and the House to perform their roles properly. Indeed such conduct, sometimes contemptuous, sometimes offensive and always irksome detracts from the authority and respect of Parliament itself. It also reveals the hollowness of the words of paragraph 47 of the Government's White Paper, Cmnd 7285.

'In order to achieve the reasonable objectives of open government in the British context, where policies and decisions of the executive are under constant and vigilant scrutiny by Parliament and ministers are directly answerable in Parliament, it may be neither necessary nor desirable to proceed to legislation of a kind which may be justifiable in other and often very different contexts – for instance, that of the United States'.

The question of whether or not Britain should join the European Monetary System raises profound constitutional and economic issues upon which Parliament must decide. A Treasury paper setting out some of the possible consequences of entry has been denied to the House and its existence at first virtually denied to one of its Select Committees. Yet if the committee is to perform its constitutional task this is precisely the document which it must have before it. We should in my view now order that the paper be provided.

This is an issue of principle. In view of the fact that another member of the committee has written to the Prime Minister on this subject and copied his letter to the press, I am making copies of this letter generally available.

Yours ever,
Brian

The view that the sub-committee subsequently took was that I ought to have distributed copies of the document to them when I was questioning the Chancellor on it.

On Tuesday 7th November Tony Benn made it clear to the Chief Whip that he was not accepting my resignation and that an issue of principle was involved. I wrote to the Chief Whip as follows:

7th November 1978

Dear Michael,

This is just to tell you that after talking to Tony and giving the matter careful consideration I think it would be in the best interests of the party and Parliament if I did *not* resign as Tony's P.P.S.

Best wishes,
Yours,
Brian

I was then summoned to see the Chief Whip and this time we did meet in his office. He told me that I was sacked. I told him that only Tony Benn or the Prime Minister could sack me and there was no question of my being sacked until either of them informed me. He asked if it would help if the P.M. minuted Tony. I said there was no other way out. I added that I was fed up with talking to him about the matter in weird circumstances.

I constantly read in the history books that great men do strange things under stress. I am sure it is best to laugh at them afterwards.

At this point in the conversation the Chief Whip rose from his chair and surveyed the room. There were three doors off it – one into the large Whips' Office, one into the office of one of his advisers, and one into the corridor to get out. He then secured all three doors. Looking around I could see that my only means of escape was to throw myself out of the window behind his chair into the courtyard below.

'You are playing with dynamite. You'll have to watch it' he said gravely.

'Oh yes, and who will detonate the dynamite, me or you, Michael,' I replied and then left, unlocking one of the doors.

Later that day 'Downing Street guidance' informed journalists that I was resigning/sacked. Reporters relayed the news to me at my Putney flat and foot-in-door journalists turned up in numbers.

When I saw Tony Benn on Wednesday, 8th November 1978 he

showed me the Prime Minister's minute withdrawing his 'approval' to my being his P.P.S. He then wrote to me as follows:

Secretary of State for Energy
8.11.78

Dear Brian,
As you will have seen in this morning's newspapers the Prime Minister has dismissed you as my P.P.S.

I deeply regret this and would like to thank you for your outstanding services to the party during your tenure of that position.

It has been a privilege to work with you over the period.

Yours ever,
Tony

I issued a statement which said.

1. I have today written to Mr Speaker about interference by the executive in the right of backbench Members of Parliament who sit on Select Committees, arising out of questions which I put to the Chancellor of the Exchequer at last Friday's meeting of the General Sub-Committee of the Expenditure Committee.
2. I should make it clear that the information I received and used in my questions to the Chancellor on Friday at the Expenditure Committee did not come from the Secretary of State for Energy nor any ministers, officials or others from the department, nor did I consult or inform any of these people in the department before I put my questions. Indeed it is a matter of record that the Treasury paper to which I referred was only circulated to a small group of ministers who were appointed to examine the EMS and neither the Secretary of State for Energy nor officials nor others in his department received these documents. None of my questions were therefore in any way related to my position as P.P.S. to Rt. Hon. Tony Benn M.P., Secretary of State for Energy.
3. Working for Tony Benn these past two years has been a delight. I have greatly valued the confidence and trust he has placed in me.

I then wrote to the Speaker (and to the Prime Minister and Chief Whip to tell them that I was writing to the Speaker) in the following terms.

8th November 1978

Dear Mr Speaker,

The Privileges Of Parliament And Pressure From The Executive

On Friday, 3rd November, the General Sub-Committee of the Expenditure Committee questioned the Chancellor of the Exchequer on the proposed European Monetary System. As a member of that Committee, I put a number of questions to the Chancellor over certain documents and their contents.

Subsequent to that hearing, I was summoned to see the Government Chief Whip, told that I had behaved improperly in questioning the Chancellor, warned as to party discipline, and asked certain formal questions as part of an enquiry set up by the Prime Minister. Subsequently I was told that I should resign as P.P.S. to Tony Benn and then, when I refused to do so, was dismissed by the Prime Minister.

My concern in this case is whether it is in accordance with the privilege of this House that the executive should seek to bring pressure to bear on a Member of Parliament for carrying out his constitutional duties as a member of a Select Committee. In my judgment a grave constitutional issue has been raised. If the executive can succeed in this case, without comment by Parliament, what is to stop it further diminishing the rights of members of the House and its committees?

The purpose of this letter is to ask for your advice and guidance on this matter of privilege. In so asking, could I refer you respectfully to the Sandy case, the Report of the Committee of Privileges 1939 (Report on Privileges 1924/1940) and the Parliamentary Debate which followed on 23rd November 1939 (Commons Vol. 353, 1938/40).

This is the first opportunity I have had of raising this issue since my dismissal by the Prime Minister today. I will raise the issue on the floor of the House today if you deem this course appropriate.

I should make it clear that the information I received and used in my questions to the Chancellor on Friday at the Expenditure Committee did not come from the Secretary of State for Energy nor any ministers, officials or others from that Department, nor did I consult any of these people in the department before I put my questions. Indeed it is a matter of record that the Treasury paper to which I referred was only circulated to a small group of ministers who were appointed to examine the EMS and neither the Secretary of State for Energy nor officials nor others in his department received these documents. None of my questions were therefore in any way related to my position as P.P.S. to Rt. Hon. Tony Benn M.P., Secretary of State for Energy.

Yours sincerely,
Brian Sedgemore

The Speaker replied:

9th November, 1978

Dear Brian,

Thank you for your letter of 8th November about your dismissal as a Parliamentary Private Secretary and its implications in respect of privilege. As you know, the procedure adopted by the House on 6th February requires me to consider applications made to me by letter by Honourable Members who wish to raise matters of privilege in the House. I am then required to form my opinion as to whether the matter merits priority over the orders of the day. In doing so, I am to have regard to the various recommendations contained in the Third Report of the Committee of Privileges in Session 1976–77.

I have considered your letter with the greatest of care but have come to the conclusion that I cannot give the complaint precedence over the orders of the day as a matter of privilege.

It is, of course, open to you to put down a Motion on the matter; but this would not of course have precedence as a matter of privilege.

Yours ever,
George Thomas
Speaker

Michael Foot, the Leader of the House, asked me to withdraw my letter to the Speaker but I could see no reason to do so.

On Thursday 9th November the issue was raised at a meeting of the Parliamentary Labour Party by Neil Kinnock and the Prime Minister replied saying that he had 'enlarged my freedom'. I could now say things that I could not otherwise have said. This book is an expression of that freedom granted to me by the Prime Minister.

I thank the Prime Minister for that and end with a quote from the Report of the House of Commons Committee on Privileges 1939 (Report on Privileges 1924/1940).

Your committee would emphasise a point mentioned in the report which they made to the House in the last session of Parliament, namely, that the privilege of freedom of speech enjoyed by Members of Parliament is in truth the privilege of their constituents. It is secured to members not for their personal benefit, but to enable them to discharge the functions of their office without fear of prosecutions civil or criminal. The Commons in their famous protestation of 1621 declared the privileges of Parliament to be the birthright and inheritance of the subject. There are, no doubt, dangers even in the limited immunity from prosecution under the Official Secrets Act secured to members by Parliamentary privilege. But they are dangers which must be run if members are to continue to exercise their traditional right and duty of criticising the executive. 'Parliaments without Parliamentary liberties,' said Pym, 'are but a fair and plausible way into bondage,' and it remains as true today as it was in 1610 that 'freedom of debate being once foreclosed, the essence of the liberty of Parliament is withal dissolved.'

Appendix 1

Report on the Civil Service
Eleventh Report from the Expenditure Committee
(Session 1976–77) Proceedings 28th July 1977 (pg. lxxviii)

Motion moved in name of Mr Sedgemore to leave out Chapter 1 and insert new Chapter 1 as follows:

Introduction

1. Politicians exist to improve society by facilitating social change. That they are not very successful at this is in part due to the structure of power in our society which is undemocratic and hence unresponsive to changing needs and circumstances. Civil servants exist to serve elected politicians. That they do not do so well as they should is too well established to merit long and hard debate. It is the experience of all of us whether as Members of Parliament with access to ministers and civil servants, as Parliamentary Private Secretaries, or as former ministers and civil servants. As such our experience conflicts sharply with the evidence given to the committee by the previous Prime Minister, Sir Harold Wilson, and by the present Secretary to the Cabinet, Sir John Hunt, in as far as that evidence related to the relationship between ministers and civil servants. We did not feel that these eminent witnesses, who could have helped the committee so much had they been frank with it, treated the committee with the openness that we would have liked or that Parliament and the public would have expected.

2. We regard the resolution of the struggle for power between the executive, by which we basically mean the Cabinet, and the bureaucracy, by which we mean those top civil servants who claim to be policy advisers in favour of political power and authority and against bureaucratic power and authority as a central need of our age. It is part of the struggle for democracy itself. As such it should be seen as one of a series of parallel struggles for the democratic control and extension of power in our society, taking place between the elected House of

Commons and the unelected House of Lords, the executive and the bureaucracy, Parliament and the executive, party political supporters and party representatives, shop stewards and combine committees on the one hand and trade union officials on the other, and finally workers and managers as against shareholders. Although our study of the civil service leads us into only two of these struggles – that between the executive and the bureaucracy and that between Parliament and the executive – we believe that if democarcy is to flourish in the United Kingdom we will have the solution of all these problems our first priority in the decade to come. We hope that this report is a partial contribution to that end.

3. From the point of view of politicians most of the problems of the civil service stem from the fact that top civil servants misconceive their role in our society. They come to the civil service, as we show in a later chapter, with what Balliol men used to refer to as the unconscious realisation of effortless superiority – though judging by the evidence we received from Sir Douglas Allen their superiority is becoming less unconscious. Their self-anointed superiority brings them almost immediately up against their obvious and almost complete lack of experience, the lack of which does not improve as much as it might with their work, experience or training. In short, there is a conflict between their superior intellect and the little that they have to offer in a practical way. There is, as should be, no role in our society for people with little to offer in a practical way but civil servants have got round this stumbling block by inventing a role for themselves. The role that they have invented for themselves is that of governing the country. They see themselves, to the detriment of democracy, as politicians writ large. And of course as politicians writ large they seek to govern the country according to their own narrow, well-defined interests, tastes, education and background, none of which fit them on the whole to govern a modern technological, industrialised, pluralist and urbanised society. They justify this role to themselves and to others by reference to their superior intellect and by the difficulties, real or imagined, of ministers deciding or being told about the very large number of important decisions that have to be taken. They can and do relegate ministers to the second division (appropriately enough they call their own union the First Division) through a variety of devices. These include delay, which is a potent one when Governments are in a minority situation or coming to the end of their political life; foreclosing options through official committees which parallel both cabinet sub-committees and a host of other ministerial committees; interpreting minutes and policy decisions in ways not wholly intended; slanting statistics; giving ministers insufficient time to take decisions; taking advantage of

Cabinet splits and politically divided ministerial teams; and even going behind ministers' backs to other ministries and other ministers, including the Prime Minister. In doing all these things they act in what they conceive to be the public good. Some would say they perceive that good in the interest of their own class: others that they see it in terms of the tenets and taboos of their caste. In doing all these things there is an esprit de corps which can be frighteningly intense as between ministers' Private Offices and as between Permanent Secretaries. Fifteen years ago the complaint was often heard that civil servants in one ministry regarded their colleagues in another ministry as though they were representatives of foreign powers. Today the complaint is more that they are tempted to regard ministers as representatives of foreign powers wanting to pursue policies different and apart from their own. Morale is high and not unexpectedly growing as civil service power itself grows. But this is hardly the point. In doing all these things civil servants are frustrating democracy. They are arrogating to themselves power that properly belongs to the people and their representatives.

4. There are plenty of examples of course in history where bureaucracies have risen above their station and taken over the role of government. Some bureaucracies, unlike our own, have actually governed effectively and efficiently. Whereas the French bureaucracy has sometimes proved itself undemocratic and effective the British bureaucracy has proven to be undemocratic and ineffective in the post-war years. Our own bureaucracy is more dangerous than some other bureaucracies because it is an intelligent and hard working bureaucracy. It is this fact taken together with the empirical observation that few individuals or groups ever give up power voluntarily that makes reform more difficult. Being intelligent enough to realise some of their own limitations in governing our complex society some of the ablest of our civil servants have seen that their future, if not our future, lies in the development of corporatism rather than in the development of democratic institutions. They are the power-élite of our ageing democracy, providing us with government by bureaucracy but, like everyone else who seeks to govern Britain, they can only do so by consent. They see corporatism as one way of achieving this consent. It is against the whole development of corporatism that the major political parties need to guard and many of our suggested reforms are intended to help them in stopping further moves in that direction.

5. It would be as wrong to accuse top civil servants of overt party political bias as it would be foolish not to recognise that Labour Governments seeking to alter society in a socialist direction have more difficulty with civil servants (who are seeking in conjunction with other establishment figures from the City, the Bank of England, industry,

the established Church and the monarchy to maintain the status quo) than do Conservative Governments who wish to leave things roughly as they are. By their very nature bureaucracies become conservative however radical their intake. Conservative Governments who come unstuck in the same manner as Labour Governments are those who want to change society in a radical direction. Seen in this light the nineteen seventies has been a good decade for the civil service and a bad decade for the politicians. For it is a matter of record and observation that civil servants obstructed the radical Selsdon-man policies of the last Conservative Government as much as they have frustrated the more socialist policies of this Labour Government. Sir Bryan Hopkin, the Chief Economic Adviser to the Treasury, commented on his impending retirement that the politicians had 'messed up capitalism'. It might be truer to say that he and others at the Treasury had messed up everything over the past 25 years.

6. It is not difficult to find illustrations of these points though our aim must be to concentrate on reform rather than to complain about the past. As a Committee dealing with the policies which have lain behind the Government's public expenditure cuts we have been embarrassed by civil servants arguing the impossible even to the extent of producing mutually exclusive theories. Civil servants at the Department of Industry have been culpable in frustrating the interventionist industrial policies of the current Government. In this case political bias may have played a part. The result is that instead of an industrial strategy we have a series of industrial problems. The Department of Trade contains civil servants who are steeped in nineteenth century Board of Trade attitudes, totally out of sympathy with any ideas of a positive trade policy, and gullible in the extreme when it comes to understanding and taking appropriate counter action over the way in which other countries take the United Kingdom for a ride over trading rules and practices. Civil servants at the Department of Trade are also known to be hostile to any meaningful form of industrial democracy although it is Labour Party policy. Glib statements to the effect that multinational corporations will not invest in the U.K. if Bullock is implemented are a substitute for proper analysis and argument. The Home Office, the graveyard of free-thinking since the days of Lord Sidmouth early in the nineteenth century, is stuffed with reactionaries ruthlessly pursuing their own reactionary policies, which is not so bad when reactionary governments are in power but less good otherwise. So far as the B.B.C. is concerned officials have on more than one occasion badly advised ministers and some Foreign Office officials interpret being a good European as being synonymous with selling out British interests. The Vichy mentality which undoubtedly exists in some parts

of our Foreign Office establishment does not to the best of our knowledge and belief reflect the views of Her Majesty's ministers. And so we could go on.

7. We recognise that our nation is not very good at facing up to problems such as those we have outlined and develop further in this report but we believe that it is urgent that steps be taken to re-establish, or possibly establish for the first time, political power and authority in the land. This will necessitate more than fundamental changes in the recruitment, training and organisation of the civil service even if changes in these spheres are desperately needed. It will call for a conscious effort to build up countervailing political power. It will require a more open society, an end to Section 2 of the Official Secrets Act, and more public scrutiny of the processes by which we are governed and the information upon which decisions are taken. It will require that ministers and the Cabinet be given weapons to take on the civil service. Whether through the appointment of powerful ministerial back-up teams or 'cabinets', chosen by ministers and including Members of Parliament if ministers so desire and to whom civil servants at Deputy Secretary and Under Secretary level would report and be accountable, or through developing the role of political advisers, or through political appointments of top civil servants at Under Secretary level and above, or through other devices ministers must inject more party political clout into the upper echelons of the administration. It will require that Parliament and backbench M.P.s be given weapons first to help the Cabinet in combating the power of the bureaucracy and second to help check what the executive itself is doing. The establishment of powerful investigatory committees on a systematic basis covering the work of each department by the House of Commons is one overdue weapon in this field. A more powerful and professional system of audit and efficiency answerable to Parliament is another long overdue weapon. The latter proposal might be linked to the former.

8. Arising out of the work of our General Sub-Committee on Public Expenditure we see the need, for example, to set up Select Committees on Economic Affairs which should, through statutory backing, be given a new and important investigative and advisory role in economic affairs. The new committee should have its own specialist staff. Indeed the major political parties represented on the committee should have their own specialist advisers paid for through government funds. These might work along the same lines as the advisers to the Joint Economic Committee of Congress in the United States. The committee would do its own forecasting and develop its own model. The Treasury would be compelled by statute to provide the committee with revenue data,

revenue forecasting and other factual data and economic projections. Legislation would provide for the Chancellor personally and his civil servants to give evidence to the committee both before the Budget and public expenditure processes begin and after they have been presented each year. That legislation would compel the Chancellor and the Treasury to take account of the views of the committee before policy decisions were taken. The Chancellor and the Treasury would be expected to answer the arguments put forward by the committee before decisions were taken. In practice all this would mean that Chancellors and their civil servants would be encouraged to take heed of the views of the majority of the committee which hopefully and normally would mean the views of the backbench members of the governing party. This new process would open up and revolutionise economic debate in the U.K. Cabinet ministers could find themselves strengthened against the power of Treasury civil servants. Similar developments must take place to cover the activities of other government departments.

9. We recognise that the changes which we propose would alter the balance of power within the constitution. But they would steer a middle course between those who see Parliament merely as the servant of the executive and a place where the only function of backbench Members of Parliament is to get the Government's business through: and those who believe that we should move firmly in the direction of the separation of powers and in the process take the purse strings away from the executive and give them back to Parliament. Indeed under our proposals it is clear that backbench Members of Parliament would be playing a dual role – helping the executive in its struggle with its own bureaucracy on the one hand and challenging the executive itself on the other hand. The main effects of our proposals would be to place far more power than at present in the hands of backbench Members of Parliament in general and in the hands of backbench Members of Parliament of the majority party in particular. They would get round the objection voiced by the present Leader of the House, the Rt. Hon. Michael Foot, M.P. that if the emphasis in Parliament moved from the floor of the House and into a new and powerful committee structure then we would get consensus government by all-party committees. Effectively our proposals would lead to the dispersal of power in Parliament and down through and into political parties and those groups which support political parties. This we believe is the right way for democracy to develop and for the House of Commons to play a much more important role in the development of that democracy than at present.

10. We are conscious that in a country where democracy has gone to

sleep there will be profound resistance – not least by the bureaucrats – to the necessary changes which we put forward in this report but who better than a group of elected politicians to begin the process. We believe that our proposals will contribute to four major objectives:

(i) a more relevant and efficient civil service;

(ii) a bureaucracy which is properly accountable to the executive for which it works;

(iii) an executive, which together with its bureaucracy is properly accountable to Parliament; and

(iv) an executive and a Parliament which accept the reality of the party political struggle as being the essence of democracy in Britain today.

11. Nothing in this report is intended to be construed as in any way criticising the loyalty, dedication and hard work of the majority of our civil servants. They serve their country well and are not over-rewarded for that service. As a committee we certainly deplore the now fashionable sniping at them, and regret that amongst the snipers are a number of ill-informed politicians whose primary aim is not to sustain and improve our public services or the administration of the country but rather to make our public servants, including civil servants, a scapegoat for economic ills which cannot properly be laid at their door. We salute civil servants at large and pay just tribute to them. – (Mr *Sedgemore.*)

Question put, That the proposed new Chapter I be read a second time.

The Committee divided:

Ayes 11	Noes 15
Mr Bernard Conlan	Sir Frederic Bennett
Mr Robin Corbett	Mr W Benyon
Mr Bryan Davies	Mr Michael English
Mr John Garrett	Mr Geoffrey Finsberg
Mr Ted Garrett	Miss Janet Fookes
Mr Peter Hardy	Col Sir Harwood Harrison
Mr Ron Lewis	Mr Robert Rhodes James
Mr Alexander Lyon	Mr John Loveridge
Mr Max Madden	Mr John MacGregor
Mr Sedgemore	Mr Robin Maxwell-Hyslop
Mr Julius Silverman	Sir Anthony Meyer
	Mr Nicholas Ridley
	Sir John Rodgers
	Mr Fred Silvester
	Mr John Wakeham

Appendix 2

Response to the Government's Observations on the Committee's Report on the Civil Service Expenditure Committee Hearing 18th April 1978

Examination of witnesses by Mr Sedgemore

(The witnesses were: The Rt. Hon. Lord Peart, Sir Ian Bancroft K.C.B., Mr R. W. L. Wilding, Sir Anthony Rawlinson K.C.B., and Mr J. Anson.)

Mr Sedgemore

46. I would like to ask a number of questions about your reply. In paragraph 3 you say: 'Throughout, they have considered the recommendations against the background of their belief that the interests of the country will continue to be best served by a non-political, permanent civil service working under the close policy supervision of the Government of the day.' In paragraph 84 you say: 'By long-established agreement between all political parties that the civil service should be a non-political, permanent, career service, ministers delegate to their Permanent Secretaries the managing and career development of departmental staff.' Going back to paragraph 3, you say: 'The Government do not therefore favour developments which would detract from the principle that the advice tendered to ministers by civil servants should be confidential and objective . . .' I want to ask you some questions about the words 'non-political', 'objective' and 'confidential', and my questions are designed to suggest that the Government or civil service, or both, have misled the committee and the public. I want to illustrate that by referring to an interview given by Sir William Armstrong, who was head of the civil service from 1968 to 1974, and in the process of my questions I will be referring to a transcript of a Thames Television programme called 'Miners – State of Emergency' transmitted on the 15th March 1978. That transcript I have checked against the video tape which Thames supplied to me upstairs. I will also be referring to an interview between Brian Connell and Sir William

Armstrong in the *Observer* on 13th November, 1976. Could we take first the word 'non-political'. In both the interview which the former head of the civil service had with Brian Connell and the transcript of the television programme Sir William Armstrong made it clear that he gave advice to the then Conservative Prime Minister, Edward Heath, about the date of the election. Can you, Lord Privy Seal, conceive of anything more political than that the head of the civil service should give advice to a Conservative Prime Minister about the date of an election when the Government is in conflict with the miners who are being supported by the Labour Party? – (*Lord Peart.*) I did not hear that programme. I think we should discuss this because it is an important matter – whether we call civil servants non-political people or whether they are really non-party. Neither term is perfect, but let us get the meaning clear. I do not know about this case. I would like to see it or hear it. You can give it to me and I will have a look at it. First of all, in advising ministers civil servants must be thorough and dispassionate. We want them to be that. Whether they are I do not know. There are occasions when they may fall down. They must not select or weigh the arguments according to their own preferences for society, or how the country should be run. Secondly, in carrying out ministers' decisions, their plain and simple task is to carry them out, so they cannot at any one time be impartial about those policies or which policies they will carry out. Of course, at any one time one party is in Government and that is the Government they serve. Thirdly, they must carry out with equal loyalty the policies of different parties and Governments at different times. Most people would understand that package to be non-political, but perhaps the choice of words matters less than whether there is some aspect of these three requirements on which we disagree. As to giving advice about a date for an election, I do not know. It may well be that he talked to the Prime Minister. You say it is a breach of discipline or it is wrong. I am not so sure.

47. You may not be so sure, but Sir William Armstrong said this himself: 'Now, the question of an election or not is a highly political matter – something which no civil servant would dream of having an opinion on, and yet it seemed to me it was a move in the chess game that I had been having with the Prime Minister, and I could not refrain from giving him my opinion.' Are we to understand that Sir Ian Bancroft would be playing chess or ludo and giving advice to the Prime Minister on the date of the next election? – I would think that the people who would give advice to the Prime Minister on the date of an election would be the members of the Cabinet.

Chairman

48. My own view is that I am glad Sir William Armstrong, as he then

was, gave the wrong advice? – (*Sir Ian Bancroft.*) Can I answer the question about whether I am playing ludo or chess and giving advice about the date of the next general election? The answer, categorically, is that I would not be playing ludo or chess or giving any such advice.

Mr Sedgemore
49. Can I develop this question, because the interviewer, Llew Gardner, said right at the end of the programme: 'The lessons of Heath's fall have been well learned by the Labour Government. But by now how far did he fall?' and then the former head of the civil service replied: 'The astonishing thing in many ways is that we got as far as we did, and as near as we did. I don't think that excuses anybody who puts their foot wrong at different times, or takes away from the tragedy of it.' Is it appropriate for the head of the civil service to refer to the fall of a Conservative Government as a tragedy, bearing in mind that he served both the Labour Government in 1968 and the Conservative Government in 1974? – (*Lord Peart.*) I do not want to get involved in the views of Sir William Armstrong. If he said that I must say I am rather surprised. I still think that what I have argued today is the right approach. As to Sir William Armstrong, I cannot follow it up because I have not read the transcript. If I had to repeat what a lot of people said to me, even ministers, we would get nowhere. I am not defending it at all.

(*Mr Sedgemore.*) This is the ex-head of the civil service. Is it not the fact that Permanent Secretaries take their tone from the head of the civil service, and might that not explain the actions of Sir Antony Part and Sir Peter Carey? Is it not the fact that other civil servants take their tone from the head – the tone of Sir William Armstrong which was overtly party political.

(*Chairman.*) If I may supplement that, there is a difference. The former Sir William Armstrong, now Lord Armstrong, is now chairman of Midland Bank, and the former Sir Douglas Allen, now Lord Croham, is an adviser to the Bank of England, a public corporation. In my view there is clearly a difference between those two things, and I think that is relevant to the point where you agreed to take back to the Government your disagreement with our fourteenth recommendation.

Mr Sedgemore
50. I will not let it go there. As you read through the transcript, of which I will give you a copy, Sir William Armstrong continually uses the expression 'We did this' or 'We did that'. Incidentally, Edward Heath would not appear in the programme. For example, Sir William Armstrong said: 'We would have done better to withdraw the White

Paper and start again.' It is not for the head of the civil service to withdraw White Papers; it is a matter for ministers, is it not? – Mr Sedgemore, you have made your point. I will look at the transcript carefully.

51. As to the 'we' used by Sir William Armstrong, naive people might think he was talking of Sir William and Edward Heath, but I am sure Sir Ian can tell us (he was in the civil service at that time) that the royal 'we' used throughout this interview – for example, 'We did this', 'We did that' 'We were worried about the miners' and, 'We thought Joe Gormley was doing this' – was a reference to the Permanent Secretaries; it was a reference to the civil service rule. Was that not what he was talking about? – (*Sir Ian Bancroft.*) I do not think I could answer that question because I am not in the mind of Lord Armstrong, but, commenting on one of the points you made about Permanent Secretaries generally taking their tone from the head of the civil service, that is at least a debatable point in my experience, but I would not like to let pass without deprecating the fact, the observations made by Mr Sedgemore about a serving Permanent Secretary, namely, Sir Peter Carey.

52. If you really want me to ask you questions about Sir Peter's political views I am quite prepared to go into them at length? – (*Lord Peart.*) I think you are going a bit too far, Mr Sedgemore.

53. You keep saying that, but the point of a report like this is to educate the public in the way in which we govern, not to mislead the public into some fantasy about how they might be governed in a perfect world? – Nobody wants to mislead the public; I certainly do not.

(*Chairman.*) I have a feeling that in some respects, as you yourself pointed out, by implication the language of the reply is accidentally designed to mislead. Quite frankly, in my view a Permanent Secretary who is non-political is not worth paying. We should not be paying him for doing the job, because he is supposed to be running a department of a political organisation. We said we believed that the executive control of a minister and a Permanent Secretary over a department should remain. It is a different matter that he should be non-party in the sense of supporting whichever party happens to be in power, which is a very difficult thing to do in all cases, and I imagine that like most human beings not all Permanent Secretaries are the same in that respect.

(*Mr Sedgemore.*) I have not come here to ask the Chairman questions or listen to his statements. Sir William Armstrong had an interview in the *Observer* after we published our report on 18th

September 1977. As you know, in our report there was a chapter signed by most of the Labour Members present at the time, including Mr Bernard Conlan, Mr Robin Corbett, Mr Bryan Davies, Mr John Garrett, Mr Ted Garrett, Mr Peter Hardy, Mr Ron Lewis, Mr Alexander Lyon, Mr Max Madden, Mr Sedgemore and Mr Julius Silverman.

(*Chairman.*) It was not signed.

Mr Sedgemore

54. If the chairman, would allow me to put the question, Sir William Armstrong in an interview in the *Observer* said, in relation to some of the recommendations the subject of that view of those Labour Members: 'Under the cover of an attack on civil servants that he thinks will be popular, he wants proposals that will give the Tribune Group a grip on the Government. If the left became a majority in the Labour Party, they would not dream of letting right wing backbenchers into their departments to screw them back.' In all honesty, given that most of these people are not in the Tribune Group and given the strange and vulgar language which Sir William Armstrong used, can you conceivably suggest that here we are talking about a non-political civil servant? – Sir William Armstrong is no longer in the civil service.

55. Are you saying that once he left the civil service he became a totally different person from the man who advised Mr Edward Heath and Harold Wilson? – I do not want Sir William Armstrong to cloud our discussions today.

56. I will move on to the word "confidential". In fact we are told – and I am using this for illustrative purposes – that Ted Heath invited Joe Gormley, President of the N.U.M. for an afternoon talk in the garden of No 10 Downing Street. The meeting was kept secret from the union's executive and from Mr Heath's Cabinet colleagues. My question is this: is it not the truth that in both finance and the world of foreign affairs they are a lot of small cabals selected by Prime Ministers of all political parties which in fact keep the Cabinet in the dark? – I do not accept that. I think this conspiracy theory is wrong, and I am surprised you fall for it.

57. You say it is a conspiracy theory, but I did not say that. Sir William Armstrong said that? – Then Sir William Armstrong is wrong if he said that.

58. Do you think he was actually telling a lie when he said there was a meeting about which his Cabinet colleagues had not heard? – I do not know.

59. I can give you an up-to-date example. Let us go back to late last year when the Government decided to let the pound appreciate – a

major economic decision. I understand there was a meeting between the Prime Minister, the Chancellor of the Exchequer, Harold Lever, the Governor of the Bank of England and Sir Douglas Wass, but no member of the Cabinet was told of the meeting. It was at that meeting that the decision was taken to let the pound appreciate. I am not saying it is a good or a bad thing, but is that not an example of a cabal of which the Cabinet is not informed? Are you saying that that did not happen? – I cannot comment on that. I am a member of the Cabinet.

60. Here we have Sir William Armstrong talking about secret meetings and about advice given to the Prime Minister. We know that Cabinet ministers are subject to a 15-year rule. Are civil servants subject to that rule, or can Sir William Armstrong break confidences and the Official Secrets Act? – I make no comment.

61. You talked about the Government moving towards a system of open government. It is not right that the Government have just taken the decision not to tell the public how the Cabinet sub-committee works, and how does that square with the Government's desire to move towards a more open system of government? – I cannot comment on that.

62. Can you tell us something about the Cabinet sub-committee which considered this report? – No, I cannot, and you know I cannot. How can you expect me to answer that?

63. I am asking the questions, Lord Peart, if you do not mind. I am here to help the public understand how we are governed. Do you not think it is right that the public should be told about the basic principles of the British constitution? – The basic principles of the British constitution are well known to many people outside Government circles. We are not arguing about that. You are asking me about matters which you say are secret and were discussed by Cabinet committees. I cannot reveal that. It would be very wrong of me to do so. There are some people who would like to have it open, but I think it would be crazy.

64. Could the Prime Minister reveal it if he came along and gave us some answers? – I cannot comment on that.

Appendix 3

Parliamentary Questions which Government departments will not answer

(See Chapter 7, page 187, 'Jeff Rooker, the member for Perry Barr has asked each minister if he or she would list those topics on which it was his or her practice not to answer Parliamentary Questions: and if he or she would list any changes in practice since 1972, indicating in each case the date on which the change was made and the relevant reference in the Official Report.')

Answers to Jeff Rooker – 2nd May 1978

Agriculture (Mr John Silkin)

It is not possible to provide a definitive and exhaustive list of Questions which I might decline to answer. It is my practice to consider each Question on its merits including cost of preparing the reply.

However, the topics listed in Appendix 9 to the Report from the Select Committee on Parliamentary Questions – Session 1971–72 reflect the broad approach which my predecessors and I have followed over recent years. I do not of course answer Questions which, since 1972, have become the responsibility of other ministers.

Attorney-General (Mr Sam Silkin)

It is not possible to provide a definite and exhaustive list of Questions which might exceptionally decline to answer on grounds other than cost. Each Question will continue to be answered on its merits, but examples which would fall into this category would be Questions about:

1. the propriety of decisions given in individual cases by courts of law, administrative tribunals and similar bodies, such as legal aid committees;
2. advice given to and by the Lord Chancellor about judicial and other appointments;

3. confidential exchanges between the Lord Chancellor and the judiciary;
4. details of investigations by or on behalf of departments for which I am responsible, in connection with prosecutions or civil actions and confidential information relating to such proceedings or possible proceedings; and
5. legal advice given to or by the Law Officers and their department.

Civil Service (Mr Charles R. Morris)

It is my practice to be as helpful as possible, consistent with the need to protect personal and commercial confidentiality, and security. It is not possible to provide a definitive and exhaustive list of Questions which I would exceptionally decline to answer other than on grounds of cost. But by way of example, details of the information used in evaluating tenders for computer projects, and information supplied on a confidential basis by outside organisations to the Civil Service Pay Research Unit would fall into this category.

Defence (Mr Fred Mulley)

The topics on which it is not the practice to provide information are as follows:

> Details of arms sales, operational matters, contract prices, costs of individual aircraft etc, details of research and development, the numbers of foreign forces training in the U.K. and accident rates for aircraft.

Duchy of Lancaster (Mr Harold Lever)

I answer all Questions that fall within my current area of ministerial responsibility, but not those relating to details of future engagements. There has been no change in this practice since 1972.

Education and Science (Mrs Shirley Williams)

My practice is to answer Parliamentary Questions about all subjects within my ministerial responsibility except where the answer would:

- infringe the proper exercise by other persons or bodies of responsibility vested in them.
- touch upon matters which are at the time sub judice or subject to arbitration.
- involve a breach of confidence of security.
- involve a disproportionate cost to secure the information requested.

I am not aware that this represents any change in the practice of my predecessors.

Employment (Mr Albert Booth)

It is not possible to provide a definitive and exhaustive list of Questions which I might exceptionally decline to answer on grounds other than cost. As in 1972, each Question will continue to be considered on its merits but, by way of example, the following would continue to fall into the category:

questions seeking information regarding employment, wages and salaries at individual firms or concerning individuals which has been supplied to the department for statistical purposes subject to statutory or other confidentiality safeguards and other information relating to individual firms or persons given in confidence to officers of my department in the course of discharging their functions.

Energy (Mr Anthony Wedgwood Benn)

It is my normal practice to attempt a definitive answer to all Questions tabled, save where confidential, commercial or security information arises, or exceptionally, on the grounds that assembling the information requested could be unduly costly. Where matters of management arise which do not involve policy questions I would normally refer the Member to the Board concerned.

Environment (Mr Peter Shore)

It is my practice to answer all questions on topics falling within my responsibilities, subject only to generally recognised restrictions relating to certain types of information, notably:

(i) information which is commercially confidential (for example details of the leases of individual Government office buildings);
(ii) some aspects of the management of my department and the formulation of policy (for example personal information relating to the appointment or employment of individuals, and details of the advice given by individual officials);
(iii) information which is classified for security reasons;
(iv) information which can only be obtained at disproportionate cost.

I am, however, unable to provide information on topics which fall outside my ministerial responsibilities, such as:

(v) Matters which are entirely within the responsibilities of individual local authorities (for example, a council's decisions in respect of people on its waiting list for housing; the staff matters of individual authorities);
(vi) matters relating to the day-to-day management of nationalised industries, government agencies and fringe bodies (for ex-

ample the water authorities and the Nature Conservancy Council).

No list of 'prohibited topics' is maintained by my department. Each question is dealt with as it arises. I am therefore unable to provide the information requested in the latter part of the Hon. Member's Question, except to say that there has been no change in general practice since 1972. (The responsibilities of the Department of the Environment changed when the Department of Transport was formed in 1976).

Foreign Office (Dr David Owen)

It is my policy that positive answers should be given, as far as possible, to all Questions put down to me, but it is not possible to provide a definitive and exhaustive list of Questions which I might exceptionally decline to answer on grounds other than cost. I can assure my Hon. Friend that each Question will continue to be considered on its merits but, by way of example, the following topics would fall into this category.

(a) details of individual arms sales (cf. my Hon. Friend's written reply of 25th April to my Hon. Friend the Member for Harlow).

(b) confidential exchanges between Governments (cf. my Hon. Friend's written reply of 27th April to my Hon. Friend the Member for Derby North).

Home Office (Mr Merlyn Rees)

It would not be possible to give a definitive and exhaustive list of the topics on which I might judge it right not to give information in reply to a particular Question; the prevention and detection of crime, the security of the State, and privacy and commercial confidence are among the relevant considerations. There have been no changes in practice since March 1974.

Industry (Mr Leslie Huckfield junior minister to Eric Varley)

It is not possible to provide a definitive and exhaustive list of Questions which my Rt. Hon. Friend might exceptionally decline to answer on grounds other than cost. Each Question will continue to be considered on its merits but, by way of example, the following questions would fall into this category:

Details of financial assistance to individual companies except to confirm details of regional development grant and selective assistance published in 'Trade and Industry';

Matters of commercial confidence including, for example, statistical information about individual businesses;

Individual applicants for Industrial Development Certificates;
Matters which are the responsibility of public bodies, i.e. day to day matters, including statistics other than national;
Confidential details of research contracts:

On N.E.B. matters I would refer my Hon. Friend to the statement to the House by the noble Lord, the then Lord President, on 18th December 1975. (O.R. Vol. 902 cols. 1656–62).

Lord Advocate's Office (Mr Ronald King-Murray)

There is no topic within my ministerial responsibility on which as a matter of practice I am not prepared to answer Parliamentary Questions. However, in answering Questions there are certain limitations on the information which I would be prepared to give – for example, with respect to legal advice which I have given to a Government department or information in relation to a case considered for prosecution.

There has been no change in practice since 1972.

Lord President of the Council (Mr Michael Foot)

It is not possible to provide a definitive and exhaustive list of Questions which I might exceptionally decline to answer on grounds other than cost. Each Question will continue to be considered on its merits, but by way of example, Questions on relations between the political parties, the pay and conditions of individual members of the staff of this House, and the pay, allowances and pensions of individual Members or former Members, would fall into this category.

Northern Ireland (Mr Roy Mason)

It is not possible to provide a definitive and exhaustive list of Questions which I might exceptionally decline to answer on grounds other than cost. Each Question will continue to be considered on its merits but in some cases information is withheld for security reasons –see for example, the reply given on 6th February to the Hon. Member for Londonderry.

Overseas Department (Mrs Judith Hart)

It has never been the practice of my ministry to give detailed future forecasts of overseas aid, and I do not think it possible to change this practice for a number of good reasons. But the annual Public Expenditure White Paper provides a four-year forecast of aid within the public expenditure programme.

Prices and Consumer Protection (Mr Roy Hattersley)

It is not possible to provide a definitive and exhaustive list of subjects within my responsibilities on which I might exceptionally decline to answer Questions on grounds other than cost and commercial confidence. Each Question tabled to me will continue to be considered on its merits.

Prime Minister (Mr James Callaghan)

The matters on which I follow the practice of my predecessors in declining to answer Questions include security matters, telephone interception, Cabinet committees and detailed arrangements for the conduct of Government business and lists of past and future engagements. I am not aware of any changes in practice since 1972. It is not possible to give a definitive and exhaustive list of Questions relating to my responsibilities which I might decline to answer on grounds other than cost, but generally speaking, Questions that relate to the responsibilities of individual ministers are transferred to them for answer.

Scotland (Mr Bruce Millan)

It is not possible to provide a definitive and exhaustive list of Questions which I might exceptionally decline to answer on grounds other than cost. Where this issue arises I consider each Question separately and with particular care, but I can instance the following subjects as being among those which would fall into this category:

> matters within the statutorily prescribed or delegated authority of nationalised industries or other public bodies; matters of commercial confidence or national security; personal clinical details of individual patients; personal or private information in connection with the granting of distinction awards or appointment of individuals to public office; private information about individuals employed in departments for which I am responsible.

Social Services (Mr David Ennals)

It is not possible to provide a definitive and exhaustive list of Questions which I might exceptionally decline to answer, other than on grounds of cost. Each Question is, and will continue to be, considered on its merits but, by way of example I (or my predecessors) have in the past declined to disclose:

> Personal information about individual beneficiaries or patients obtained in the course of administering the social security schemes or through other departmental channels, e.g. my right Hon. Friend's reply to the Hon. Member for Aberdeen South on

30th November 1977 (Vol. 940 c.276–7). The reasons for appointing individual members of health authorities, e.g. the right Hon. Member, for Leeds North East's to my Hon. Friend the Member for Nuneaton on 4th February 1971 (Vol. 810 c.448).

Figures relating to abortions by place of treatment or for areas smaller than Regional Health Authorities, e.g. my Hon. Friend's reply to my Hon. Friend the Member for Greenwich, Woolwich East, on 28th February 1978 (Vol. 945 c. 191); and my Right Hon. Friend's reply to my Hon. Friends the Members for Teesside, Thornaby and Birmingham Selly Oak on 8th December 1975 (Vol. 901 c.81–2).

Information relating to the day to day running of the General Practice Finance Corporation, e.g. the reply to my Hon. Friend the Member for Nuneaton on 24th March 1979 (Vol. 780 c.206).

Commercially confidential information relating, for example, to Government contracts in the National Health Service, e.g. my Hon. Friend's reply to the Hon. Member for Daventry on 18th October 1976 (Vol. 917 c.282).

In addition, the names of holders of consultant distinction awards are not published at present, but as my Hon. Friend said in his reply to my Hon. Friend the Member for Barking on 3rd March 1978 (Vol. 945 c.415–6) we are discussing confidentiality along with other aspects of the distinction awards scheme with the representatives of the medical profession.

Trade (Mr Edmund Dell)

It is not possible to provide a definitive and exhaustive list of Questions which I might exceptionally decline to answer on grounds other than cost. Each Question will continue to be answered on its merits, but the principal examples of subjects on which I do not answer Questions are as follows:

Details of air-miss enquiries

Reasons for investigation or non-investigation of aircraft accidents

Details of aviation security measures

Commercial activities of the Overseas Marketing Corporation

Details of Export Licences

Relations between E.C.G.D. [Export Credit Guarantee Department] and individual exporters

Matters of commercial confidence including e.g. statistical information about individual businesses

Names of complainants about companies

Names of companies being investigated under the provisions of Section 109 of the Companies Act 1967

Names of private companies being investigated under the provisions of the Companies Acts
Reasons for exercising investigatory powers under the Companies Acts
Individual transactions between National Film Finance Corporation and customers and between National Film Development Fund and applicants
Day to day matters for English Tourist Board
Financial support to individual organisers of Trade Fairs in Britain
Nationalised Industries and other Statutory Corporations
Day to day matters other than those which raise questions of urgent public importance
Statistics other than national
Matters of commercial confidence

Transport (Mr William Rodgers)

I have had no 'practice' of this kind since my department was set up in 1976 but obviously I answer only those Questions for which I have ministerial responsibility.

Treasury (Mr Robert Sheldon junior minister to Denis Healey)

It is not possible to provide a definitive and exhaustive list of Questions which my Rt. Hon. Friend might exceptionally decline to answer on grounds other than cost. Each Question will continue to be answered on its merits, but by way of example Questions would not be answered on the tax affairs, etc of individual persons and companies; details of firms subject to discretionary action in support of pay policy who have not consented to publication, or Questions on the immediate prospects in the domestic and external financial markets which would prejudice the operations of the authorities in those markets.

Wales (Mr John Morris)

No such list is maintained in my department. Each case is considered individually. The main criterion which I apply, except where considerations of normal confidentiality are relevant, is whether a matter does in fact lie within my direct field of responsibility. I would, for example, not be prepared to give commercial information which had been provided to my department on the understanding that it would be treated as confidential; nor would I be prepared to give a substantial answer to a Question about the activities of a local authority on a matter wholly within its discretion.

Index